# Marginal to Mainstream

*Alternative Medicine in America*

Millions of Americans are using complementary and alternative medicine and spending billions of dollars, out of pocket, for it. Why? Do the therapies work? Are they safe? Are any covered by insurance? How is the medical profession responding to the growing use of therapies that were only recently thought of as quackery? These are some of the many questions asked and answered in this book. It describes a transformation in the status of alternative medicine within health care. Paving the way toward legitimacy is research currently underway and funded by the National Institutes of Health. This research is proving the safety and efficacy of certain therapies and the harm or inefficacy of others. Although some therapies will remain alternative to conventional medicine, others are becoming complementary, and still others are busting the boundaries and contributing to a new approach to health and healing called integrative medicine.

Mary Ruggie, former Professor and Chair of the Sociology Department at Columbia University, is on the faculty of the Kennedy School of Government, Harvard University. She is the author of *The State and Working Women: A Comparative Study of Britain and Sweden* (Princeton, 1984) and *Realignments in the Welfare State: Health Policy in the United States, Britain, and Canada* (Columbia, 1996).

# Marginal to Mainstream

*Alternative Medicine in America*

*by*

**MARY RUGGIE**
*Harvard University*

PUBLISHED BY THE PRESS SYNDICATE OF THE UNIVERSITY OF CAMBRIDGE
The Pitt Building, Trumpington Street, Cambridge, United Kingdom

CAMBRIDGE UNIVERSITY PRESS
The Edinburgh Building, Cambridge CB2 2RU, UK
40 West 20th Street, New York, NY 10011-4211, USA
477 Williamstown Road, Port Melbourne, VIC 3207, Australia
Ruiz de Alarcón 13, 28014 Madrid, Spain
Dock House, The Waterfront, Cape Town 8001, South Africa

http://www.cambridge.org

First published 2004

Printed in the United States of America

*Typeface* Sabon 10/13.5 pt.   *System* LATEX 2$_\varepsilon$   [TB]

*A catalog record for this book is available from the British Library.*

*Library of Congress Cataloging-in-Publication Data*
Ruggie, Mary, 1945-
    Alternative medicine in America : from quackery to commonplace / Mary Ruggie.
        p.   cm.
    Includes bibliographical references and index.
    ISBN 0-521-83429-5 (hbk.) – ISBN 0-521-54222-7 (pbk.)
        1. Alternative medicine.    2. Self-care, Health.    I. Title.
    R733.R84 2004
        615.5 – dc21                                    2003053292

*For John and Andreas, who give my life a special meaning*

# Contents

# Tables

# Acronyms

| | |
|---|---|
| AMA | American Medical Association |
| CAM | Complementary and alternative medicine |
| FDA | Food and Drug Administration |
| HMO | Health maintenance organization |
| MCO | Managed care organization |
| NCCAM | National Center for Complementary and Alternative Medicine |
| NIH | National Institutes of Health |
| OAM | Office of Alternative Medicine |
| RCT | Randomized controlled trial |
| RFA | Request for applications |

# Preface

A social transformation is taking place in American health care. It started as more and more people (now millions) began to spend out-of-pocket dollars (now billions) on what has come to be called complementary and alternative medicine (CAM). Policymakers in both government and health care began to take notice of this groundswell of interest. Some of them are simply watching and waiting to see what happens next, whereas others are actively supporting change. Most interestingly, growing numbers of physicians have begun to take courses on therapies that stood outside the norms of medicine throughout the 20th century, even though some had been used for millenia. These physicians want to learn more about what their patients are trying to convey to them – how healing is as important to health care as curing. Insurance companies are also hearing the sounds of consumer interest and slowly responding to market demand. For its part, government has done more than listen to people who are using alternative medicine. Congress, the National Institutes of Health, and the White House have each recognized that the government must respond to impending changes in health care by, in this instance, fulfilling its obligation to assess the safety and efficacy of products that heretofore have existed in a totally unregulated private market. Millions of dollars are being devoted to scientific research that is paving the way for further consideration of regulatory measures.

This book is full of questions – what is CAM; why are so many people using it; do they know what they are doing; do the therapies work; are they safe; are they just placebo; how are physicians, insurers, and government responding to the growth of CAM; and what does all this mean for the future of health care? These are the questions that sparked my interest in pursing this project and that guided my research.

Although I have been interested in such practices as yoga and meditation for many years, the idea of writing a book on CAM did not occur to me until 1997. My personal interest deepened when I was given access to the many resources available to breast cancer patients – support groups, movement classes, relaxation techniques, information on nutrition and personal care, and much more. My professional interest was piqued when later that same year I attended a faculty seminar at Columbia University, where I was then teaching. Presenting the topic of discussion were two representatives: one from a clinic offering selected alternative therapies to cardiac patients, and another from an insurance company offering (limited) coverage for alternative therapy services and practitioners. Attendance at the seminar was unusually high, and so was the temperature of some of the participants. Amazed and baffled by the hostility expressed by the biomedical scientists in particular, I sat back and put on my sociologist's hat. Before me the basis for a research project was unfolding.

As I learned more about the growth of CAM and the debates about the relationship between CAM and science and medicine and health care, this book took shape. At its core is the transformation that is occurring in the status of alternative medicine – from a broad and amorphous set of practices that were once thought of as quackery (not too long ago, as the seminar at Columbia indicated) to a specialized and specified set of practices that are beginning to enjoy qualified legitimacy in the field of health and healing. The role of the different actors – users, physicians, researchers, insurers, and government – involved in this process of transformation structures the chapters in this book.

Along the way, I have met many remarkable people. It's been fascinating to watch the work of some (and on occasion experience it) and hear about the endeavors of others. I cannot thank them all by name because I promised confidentiality. However, I am grateful and deeply indebted to the researchers who took time out of their overfilled days to talk with me. I hope this book makes a small contribution to acknowledge and perhaps further their efforts.

There are others whom I can name, however. When I was still a novice in the world of CAM, Janet Mindes opened her file cabinets and out flowed a wealth of information, contacts, and inspiration. David Eisenberg welcomed me into the fold, invited me to conferences, and introduced me to professionals I could never have met on my own. Michael Cohen became a dear colleague and friend, and in both capacities read an early draft of this book. Pat Oden also read a draft; he and Madeline Oden became my "intelligent laypersons." Larry Brown read the final manuscript with enormous care and insight; he's a marvel to everyone who knows him. An anonymous reviewer for Cambridge University Press offered very helpful comments. This time Andreas, my son, contributed his ideas on my ideas – what a joy! And, of course, where would I be without my husband, John, without his support, encouragement, patience, and love? As always, this book is dedicated to John and Andreas.

# Introducing CAM ... and the Many Questions It Raises

In 1971, *New York Times* reporter James Reston was stricken with acute appendicitis while in China to cover the Secretary of State's visit. He had surgery in a Beijing hospital. His article, describing how his postoperative pain was relieved by acupuncture, stimulated interest in the United States. Today Americans make more than 5 million visits per year to acupuncturists (Eisenberg et al. 1998).

In 1975, Herbert Benson, a cardiologist at Harvard Medical School, published a pathbreaking book, *The Relaxation Response*, which showed how cardiac disease could be slowed, even reversed, through meditation. New knowledge about nutrition also began to help heart patients. Dietary guidelines, revised in the 1980s, warned against eating red meat and other animal fats and encouraged heart patients to increase their intake of fiber.

In the early 1990s, cancer clinics across the United States introduced patients to stress reduction, visualization, music therapy, and aromatherapy, to name a few novel treatments, to help them through the traumas of chemotherapy and survive the trials of their illnesses. Palliative care clinics also expanded and are now a gratifying source of solace for dying patients and their families.

In the late 1990s, reports that sham surgery – that is, placebo – worked as well as real surgery for patients with Parkinson's disease and for people with arthritis of the knee stunned the medical community and put some surgeons in a precarious position. This after earlier reports that, in clinical trials, placebo worked just as well as a number of standard medical treatments (glomectomy for bronchial asthma, levamisole for herpes infection, gastric freezing for duodenal ulcer). That "placebo works" is no longer news.

On July 9, 2002, millions of women were shocked to learn that the hormone replacement therapy they had been taking to relieve symptoms of menopause may cause cancer. Within two weeks, *The Wall Street Journal* published an article detailing the rush by manufacturers of herbal products to fill the hormone void. One problem, however, is that herbs are not regulated by the Food and Drug Administration (FDA) and the safety and efficacy of the more commonly used herbal remedies for menopausal symptoms have not yet been fully tested.

The problem of readily available yet untested herbal preparations was vividly brought to public attention on February 17, 2003, when Steve Bechler, a 29-year-old baseball player, died of multiple organ failure as a result of heat stroke during spring training in Florida. He had been using ephedra for weight control. The extent to which ephedra was a contributing factor in his death was widely debated in light of his other risk factors for heat stroke. Nevertheless, several months before this high-profile case, the Secretary for Health and Human Services had asked the FDA "to evaluate the best scientific evidence available and recommend the strongest possible mandatory warning label possible for ephedra products" (*FDA News*, October 8, 2002, 1).

Interest in complementary and alternative medicine (CAM) is sweeping the United States. CAM has become one of the fastest-growing fields in health care. Millions of people are spending billions of dollars, out of pocket, on therapies that until just recently physicians considered to be quackery. Although segments of the medical community remain skeptical, even dismissive, of the disparate set of practices and modalities that constitute CAM, some physicians are responding positively to their patients' interests, to recent developments in research, and to the new courses on alternative, complementary, integrative, and holistic medicine being offered by medical schools. Government has also turned its attention to the growth of CAM and, in fact, is contributing to it by spending millions of dollars to fund research on the safety and efficacy of certain therapies.

Along with the broadening interest a growing number of questions are being raised. What is CAM, why are so many people using it, do they know what they are doing, do the therapies work, are they safe, are they just placebo, how are they going to affect health care? These are among the many questions I address in this book. I investigate several dimensions of the growth of CAM, explore a number of explanations for the surge in its popularity, and look both inside the phenomenon to understand the processes and dynamics behind its recent gains, as well as outside it to understand its relationship to broader institutions and changes in American health care and American society. This chapter offers a brief overview of the main issues that are shaping how we understand CAM and how we are assessing its impact on American health care.

WHAT IS CAM?

Complementary and alternative medicine is an umbrella term given to a collection of disparate healing practices.[1] Some of the therapies are well known and fairly widely used in the United States (herbs, acupuncture); others are more obscure (qigong, reflexology). Naming specific therapies is one way to answer the question, what is CAM – but just barely. Table 1.1 does a little more. It lists those therapies identified by participants at the first conference (known as the chantilly conference) on alternative medicine sponsored by the National Institutes of Health (NIH) in 1992 (known as the Chantilly Conference) and, in keeping with decisions made at the conference, it organizes these therapies into a system of types based on fields of practice.[2]

---

[1] As we will see, some of these practices are so different that one risks committing a fundamental error by lumping them all under the rubric of CAM. I best acknowledge up front that I am at fault in this book. I ask the reader to bear in mind that my use of the acronym "CAM" is for convenience only. We will also see that neither the acronym CAM nor the three words that comprise it are altogether correct as descriptions of the current state of affairs. The word "integrative" has replaced the word "alternative" in some arenas. Although certain practitioners think of their work as medicine, others say their practices are therapies. For the sake of readability, I vary my use of the acronym CAM with the word "alternative" to describe practices and practitioners.

[2] In this book I discuss only a few CAM therapies – those that are the subject of the research elaborated in Chapter 6. Because of the research, these therapies are developing a new and special relationship with medicine. Certain herbs, certain mind–body therapies, certain movement therapies, certain manual therapies, and certain holistic systems are coming to be accepted by some physicians. They are undergoing a process of mainstreaming. Whether other therapies, those that are not the subject of research, will also be mainstreamed is too hard to predict at this point in time.

TABLE I.I. *CAM Therapies*

**Mind–Body Interventions**
Psychotherapy (psychodynamic, behavior, cognitive, systems, supportive,
    body-oriented therapies)
Support groups
Meditation (transcendental meditation, relaxation response)
Imagery
Hypnosis
Biofeedback
Yoga
Dance therapy
Music therapy
Art therapy
Prayer and mental healing

**Bioelectromagnetics**

**Alternative Systems of Medical Practice**
Professionalized health systems
    Traditional oriental medicine (acupuncture, moxibustion, acupressure,
        remedial massage, cupping, qigong, herbal medicine, nutrition, dietetics)
    Ayurvedic medicine (individualized dietary, eating, sleeping, and exercise
        programs, including yoga, breathing exercises, and meditation)
Homeopathic medicine
Anthroposophically extended medicine (practices that seek "to match the
    key dynamic forces in plants, animals, and minerals with disease
    processes in humans to stimulate healing" [xvii])
Naturopathic medicine
Environmental medicine (the science of assessing the impact of environmental
    factors on health)
Community-based health care
    Native American Indian (Lakota, Dineh, or Navajo practices, such as
        sweating and purging, herbal remedies, shamanic healing, singing)
    Latin American rural (Curanderismo includes a humoral model for
        classifying activity, food, and drugs, and a series of folk illnesses, such
        as "evil eye," "fright," "blockage." Santeria is a Cuban-American
        variant.)
Urban community-based systems (Alcoholics Anonymous)
Popular health care (from informal sources)

**Manual Healing Methods**
Physical healing methods
    Osteopathic medicine
    Chiropractic
    Massage therapy (Swedish, deep tissue, sports, neuromuscular, manual
        lymph drainage)

      Pressure point therapies (reflexology; traditional Chinese massage;
         acupressure systems, such as shiatsu, tsubo, jin shin jyutsu)
      Postural reeducation therapies (Alexander technique, Feldenkrais method,
         Trager psychosocial integration)
      Structural integration (Rolfing)
      Bioenergetic systems
   Biofield therapeutics
      Healing science
      Healing touch
      Huna (traditional Hawaiian)
      Mari-el
      Natural healing
      Qigong
      Reiki
      Specific Human Energy Nexus (SHEN®) therapy
      Therapeutic touch
   Combined physical and biofield methods
      Applied kinesiology
      Network chiropractic spinal analysis
      Polarity therapy
      Qigong longevity exercises
      Craniosacral therapy
   Physical therapy

**Pharmacological and Biological Treatments**
Antineoplastons
Cartilage products
Ethylene diamine tetraacetic acid (EDTA) chelation therapy
Ozone
Immunoaugmentative therapy
714-X
Hoxsey method (herbs such as pokeweed, burdock root, buckthorn)
Essiac (herbs such as sheep sorrel, burdock, slippery elm inner bark, rhubarb)
Coley's toxins
MTH-68
Neural therapy
Apitherapy
Iscadore/misletoe
Revici's guided chemotherapy

**Herbal Medicine** (ingested, inhaled, salves, poultices)

**Diet and Nutrition in the Prevention and Treatment of Chronic Disease**

*Source:* Adapted from Workshop on Alternative Medicine. 1995. *Alternative Medicine: Expanding Medical Horizons. A Report to the National Institute of Health on Alternative Systems and Practices in the United States.* Washington, DC: U.S. Government Printing office.

From the table we can see that yoga, for instance, is a type of mind–body intervention as well as a component of Ayurvedic medicine. Although the typologies represent a major first step toward getting an analytical handle on the therapies, they also present some puzzles. To suggest a couple: why are reiki and other biofield energetics not considered mind–body interventions, and what is prayer doing on the list, let alone why is it combined with mental healing?

The conference participants confronted some of the many issues raised by the very topic of CAM in a major publication that resulted from the conference (Workshop on Alternative Medicine 1995). They described most of the therapies named in the list and suggested how some therapies are similar and therefore collected into a typology and how some differ even though they are listed under one typology (such as the different kinds of massage). When one examines specific therapies to learn more about them, one quickly appreciates that this theme of similarities and differences is an important and useful organizing tool. But one is also struck by its limitations for grasping the complexity of the therapies.

Consider the list of mind–body interventions. Although these various therapies aim to achieve a similar outcome, relaxation, their techniques for doing so are very different – so different, in fact, that one begins to wonder how they can all be classified under the same category. Some of the mind–body therapies require a significant measure of intervention by a practitioner (imagery, hypnosis); others require only minimal intervention or none at all (support groups, meditation, prayer). Some of the practitioners require considerable training (psychotherapy), others less so (art therapy). In some of the therapies the recipient is active (yoga, dance therapy); in others less so (meditation, hypnosis). The therapies also differ in origin (time and place), theoretical framework,[3] "technologies" (the body, music), and even use of modern technology.[4] If this degree of difference exists among

---

[3] Transcendental meditation and yoga are based on the principles of Ayurvedic medicine, which require that they be part of a holistic regimen that includes diet. Hypnosis is based on the assumption of a deep state of consciousness similar to a trance, in which individuals are guided by a practitioner to concentrate their thoughts on a desired outcome.

[4] Biofeedback uses sophisticated instruments that monitor voluntary and involuntary bodily activities and functions. Some computerized music therapy goes far beyond ancient drumming and chanting.

therapies within one category, what might the differences be across categories?

Consider next herbs and acupuncture, two very different therapies in terms of technique and theory – that is, what practitioners and recipients do, what their mechanisms of action are in the body, and so on. Yet, herbs and acupuncture are closely related within the holistic health system of traditional oriental medicine. Notice, though, that Table 1.1 also lists qigong and tai chi (two forms of body movement coordinated with breathing) and reflexology (a type of acupressure applied to the feet and, sometimes, hands) as components of traditional oriental medicine. Yet, these various therapies are not always combined in practice. Anyone who has traveled to Shanghai and Beijing, for instance, knows that reflexology is used more in Shanghai than in Beijing. Also, not all acupuncturists in either city recommend either tai chi or qigong and those who do may prefer one over the other. At the same time, not everyone who practices tai chi or qigong also sees an acupuncturist, herbalist, or massage therapist. In Hong Kong, practitioners of traditional Chinese medicine prescribe herbs but generally do not perform acupuncture. In New York, acupuncture and herbal medicine can be so distinct that practitioners and users of either one may be remarkably unfamiliar with the other. So, where does this information leave us? How are we supposed to understand herbs and acupuncture, whether alone or linked with each other or with other therapies? If we must understand each as unique, on what basis are they linked within traditional oriental medicine? Why is acupuncture not listed under manual healing method when it is theoretically closer to acupressure and reflexology than to herbs?[5] The list of questions based on a few facts easily expands.[6]

---

[5] According to the principles of traditional oriental medicine, acupuncture, acupressure, and reflexology act on a theoretical system of meridians, which are pathways of energy that run throughout the body. A particular form of acupuncture, electroacupuncture, is also a type of bioelectromagnetic therapy.

[6] There are several other analytical problems with the category "alternative systems of medical practice" because it is difficult to grasp what is common among these very different practices. Some of them clearly involve "folk principles" that can be distinguished from other types of CAM by their "very close [alliance] to specific ethnic [groups; they] are largely derived from the groups' culture of origin or ancestry" (O'Connor 1995, 1). Folk medicine is different from, say, herbal medicine because, even though many ethnic groups use herbs, they do so in accordance with a larger belief system. So, we would want to distinguish among ethnic groups because, regardless

## WHAT IS THE RELATIONSHIP BETWEEN CAM AND MEDICINE?

As a means of grasping the significance of some of these questions and perhaps formulating some preliminary answers, we can turn to the field of medicine. Medicine also consists of a number of different practices and products: diagnosis, treatments such as chemotherapy and surgery, and prognoses on how long one might still live. The practice of medicine also has a number of specialized branches (cardiology, dermatology, pediatrics), each of which uses specialized products,[7] focuses on a different part of the body, and approaches body dynamics differently. We do not ask how these specialized branches, practices, products, and approaches can be lumped together because we know that medicine is unified by a common epistemology – science. However, we should be more attuned to epistemological differences within medicine; indeed, some of us have been made all too aware of the fact that science alone does not always unify medicine. One oncologist, for instance, tells a breast cancer patient that she needs a lumpectomy, radiation, and chemotherapy, whereas another says that a mastectomy and radiation are necessary. Both oncologists were trained in the same school, read the same journals, and have the same information about the patient. So, why the difference? Some possible answers: perhaps they are interpreting the data differently, perhaps they have different clinical experiences with the treatments, or perhaps they are in different

of whether they use similar herbs for similar disorders, their belief systems and values differ. However, we do not yet know the significance of these various similarities and differences. The committee named only the 4 most common ethnic-based practices in the United States, and made some unusual ties and separations. For instance, it decided to unite traditional oriental medicine and Ayurveda with environmental medicine and anthroposophically extended medicine, which combines naturopathy and homeopathy, under the subheading "professionalized health care systems." It also distinguished these from Native American Indian and Latin American modalities, designating the latter, together with Alcoholics Anonymous, as community-based practices. To be sure, these terms all reflect certain real-world characteristics of the health care systems. We can see, however, that groupings and labels may also have unintentional consequences, in this case an unfortunate devaluation of, for example, curanderismo as not professional and more linked with Alcoholics Anonymous (even though the latter is urban and not community based) than with Ayurveda. The endeavor demonstrates how difficult it is to make language scientifically precise without connoting some social relationships.

[7] Although pharmaceuticals are pervasive, they are highly specialized; for instance, drugs that control or reduce cholesterol in heart patients may differ from those prescribed for obese children.

hospitals that have developed different cultures of practice. These answers speak less to science than to other factors that inform the practice of medicine and that create disunity within the medical community.[8]

Applying these ideas to CAM, we might suggest that the different kinds of therapies resemble the disciplinary fields of conventional medicine. Each therapy has its own practices and products, practitioners make recommendations based on the particular approach to healing found in their field of practice, and practitioners within the same field may differ in their interpretation of the information they have about any one patient. The analogy is not entirely satisfying, however, because it begs the question of a unifying epistemology that does for CAM what science does for medicine. If the various therapies, even those classified within one "field of practice," are based on different techniques and different theories, how can they (let alone all of CAM) cohere epistemologically?

Alternatively, we have seen that some of the therapies do cohere, both within and across categories. Is there enough of a commonality among certain therapies to allow us to say that they are unified in a way that is similar to what we find among the disciplines in medicine? To investigate this possibility means that we would have to set aside the typology developed by the first Workshop on Alternative Medicine, decide on another framework for sorting the therapies, throw them back up into the air, and see where they land.

This is what is happening now. It is a process I call mainstreaming. Once again the NIH, specifically the National Center for Complementary and Alternative Medicine (NCCAM) at the NIH, has gathered researchers and practitioners from both the medical and CAM communities. This time, however, the NCCAM has decided on the framework – science. It is asking the researchers to investigate specific alternative therapies, those that are more widely used in the United States and for which there is some preliminary evidence of efficacy, and to discover whether these therapies can be understood scientifically. The

---

[8] My references to the "the medical community" and "the CAM community" require the same qualification as my use of the acronym CAM – these are for convenience only. As we will continue to see, there are deep divisions within both "communities," as well as between them, so the reader should bear in mind that the reference is always to "some" within the category.

NCCAM is generously supporting this research. The story of how and why mainstreaming is occurring and what we can expect from it will unfold in the course of this book. We will see that, ultimately, what mainstreaming is all about is the effort (1) to identify some of the similarities between CAM and conventional medicine, and (2) to strengthen the links between these two approaches to health care. Mainstreaming can also be thought of as a process of understanding CAM – a relatively new field of health care – in terms that are more familiar to us, pertaining to the field of medicine.

The role of science is becoming a critical factor in how we understand CAM, and it is demonstrating some interesting and important linkages between CAM and conventional medicine. For instance, science is offering a new approach to herbal medicine. Research underway on certain botanicals closely resembles research on pharmaceuticals. Chapter 5 explains the methodology of randomized controlled trials (RCTs) and the debates about the appropriateness of this method for investigating alternative therapies. These debates aside, we are learning how certain herbs work in and of themselves – that is, their organic mechanisms of action – as well as how effective they are in treating certain ailments. We are also learning more about how acupuncture works and for what conditions acupuncture might be more appropriate than, say, surgery. Research on acupuncture is aiming to address other issues as well, some of which are difficult to answer scientifically. For instance, acupuncture and surgery are both used to treat lower back pain. If they are shown to be equally effective, might it not be better to use acupuncture because it is less invasive than surgery? Although RCTs can help evaluate these forms of treatment, determining which is better, for what and for whom, and introducing concerns about invasiveness require a different kind of discourse, one that draws on interpretations and preferences. Physicians are beginning to learn, if they do not already know, that these tasks are as much a part of medicine as scientific investigations of various treatments. As CAM enters the field of health care, issues of interpretation and preference are coming more to the forefront of decision making about treatment options, whether these issues are raised by patients or result from research findings that can answer only certain questions.

In other words, scientific investigations are not only influencing how we understand CAM. They are also affecting the role of alternative therapies in health care. CAM is still a type of health care that people undertake themselves – by visiting alternative practitioners, buying herbal supplements, taking yoga classes, meditating, and so on. It is widely assumed that these practices and therapies are health promoting and perhaps even preventive. New research is aiming to understand whether certain therapies can, indeed, keep certain illnesses at bay and, if so, how and why. To the extent that this research is fruitful, a very significant link will be forged between CAM and medicine. However, along with the link will come the question of the relationship between CAM and medicine. If certain kinds of alternative medicine help to prevent certain illnesses, will these particular treatments be considered complementary or primary? If the latter, should primary care physicians become trained in their use? If so, how will this affect their approach to medicine? After all, despite their many commonalities, CAM and conventional medicine are fundamentally different approaches to health care. CAM embodies a more holistic approach to its primary goal of healing; medicine relies on scientific validation of its more technological approaches to curing. Will these two approaches stand beside each other under the common umbrella of health care? Will they stare or glare at each other, or will they join hands?

Whether these issues will be resolved and benefit health care as a whole depends very much, I argue in this book, on how the medical community responds to the research on alternative medicine that is currently underway. I predict that some of this research will satisfy physicians – above all, research that is based on RCTs, is methodologically sound, and has clear findings that can be replicated. Some of the studies discussed in Chapter 6 will fill the bill. A great deal of sorting out among the various therapies will be occurring in the foreseeable future, and scientific research will ground the selection of some and rejection of others. All this research will prove the safety and efficacy of specific therapies, and the specific nature of potential harm and/or lack of efficacy in others. Research will also clarify for which specific health and illness conditions these therapies are best suited. Eventually, some of the research will explain mechanisms of action – that is, how the therapies work. The research will not, however, answer the questions raised here about the relationship between CAM and medicine and the role of alternative therapies in primary care or in health care in general. These issues will require much introspection within the CAM and medical communities, as well as consideration of varying interpretations and preferences.

Answers will also involve politics. If by politics we mean the struggle for power and status, we will see that it has been a significant factor in the relationship between CAM and medicine. The medical profession as a whole has a long history of hostility toward CAM. The American Medical Association (AMA) was formed as an organization of "regular" (that is, scientifically trained) physicians, who sought to distinguish their practice from that of "irregulars," many of whom were quacks, some of whom were what we now call CAM practitioners (as well as midwives and others). As late as 1990, the AMA was still attempting to appeal a court ruling that held it in contempt of antitrust laws for its prohibitions against chiropractors. As recently as 1998, a leading medical journal published an editorial condemning alternative medicine as nonsense (Angell and Kassirer 1998). Those in the medical community who are still skeptical and, perhaps, hostile toward CAM justify their position by claiming that the most fundamental difference between conventional and alternative medicine is that the former is based on science and the latter is not. What this generally means is that CAM is "unproven," meaning that its efficacy has not yet been tested. But there is more to it. Saying that CAM is not scientific means that the therapies are grounded in belief, that what makes a therapy effective is the user's and, sometimes, the practitioner's willingness to suspend rational understanding and simply believe that the therapy will work. Or, to put it differently, it is a way of dismissing CAM as "all in the mind." This conjecture also implies that users and practitioners of alternative medicine may not fully understand the therapy, or at least, they do not understand it in the same way that they or we understand medicine – scientifically.

Such a claim, especially the charge that users and practitioners of alternative medicine do not fully understand it, is loaded with politics. Both sides try to use the purported difference between medicine and CAM based on science and nonscience to their advantage. Those who oppose CAM use it to deride the therapies, and those who favor CAM use it to disparage medicine. At the heart of this quarrel are firmly entrenched ideas ranging from the debate over what constitutes evidence and how we know what we know to the debate on the value of cure versus care in treatment versus healing. At the same time, we cannot dismiss the probability that both organized medicine and alternative practitioners feel threatened by the process of mainstreaming. CAM poses huge challenges not only to the dominance of biomedicine, but also to the fruits of dominance – status and power in decision making about health care and in the livelihood of physicians. Mainstreaming means, for some alternative practitioners, a destructive medicalization of their art and an unwelcome cooptation of their livelihoods. These fears are not unreasonable.

Some physicians may be taking their cues about the menace implicit in the growth of CAM from their patients. Many patients are not telling their physicians about their use of alternative therapies. One reason is that to some patients the differences between CAM and medicine are major, and they believe that because of these differences physicians have not yet fully accepted alternative medicine. Accordingly, some physicians see CAM as a true alternative to medicine. They know that patients are spending millions of dollars on untested therapies, money that could be spent on medicine. They are also, in some cases, having to deal with certain negative consequences of the use of alternative medicine, such as the adverse interactions between herbs and drugs or injuries from the improper practice of yoga, chiropractic, or acupuncture. For their part, some alternative practitioners are watching with apprehension as research drags on and/or issues inconclusive findings, and as colleagues are lured into medical environments where their scope of practice is truncated, their services dependent on the approval of physicians, and their skills scrutinized and perhaps devalued.

However, in the evolving relationship between medicine and CAM, we can discern the outlines of a very different scenario. Depending on their exposure to or experience with alternative, complementary, or holistic medicine, either through their patients or themselves, some physicians are becoming positively interested in CAM, perhaps using it themselves, perhaps recommending it to others (friends and family at least), perhaps becoming practitioners themselves. Through medical journals that are publishing more articles on CAM, medical schools that are offering more courses on CAM, and patients who are asking physicians if they should use certain therapies, physicians are gradually learning about CAM. Most of these physicians may still require validation of alternative medicine through scientific research. Some will also include their own or their patients' experiences in their evaluations of specific therapies. Another development is forging remarkably close ties between medicine and CAM. Across the United States, hospitals as well as groups of physicians and practitioners are setting up integrative medicine clinics. Both physicians and alternative practitioners work in these clinics, sometimes as a team. Some are located in hospital settings, others in medical centers, others are free standing. Although a few clinics specialize in the care of people with particular medical conditions, most cater to outpatients who come to the clinics for specific types of CAM therapy. These clinics are still small and few in number, but their appearance indicates that change is happening quickly.

## THE MANY DIMENSIONS OF MAINSTREAMING

This book is organized as an exploration of the various dimensions of mainstreaming. Chapter 2 continues the project of how we understand CAM and its relation to medicine. It elaborates the proposition of a fundamental difference between CAM and medicine based on the scientific framework of one and the nonscientific framework of the other. At its core, this difference is grounded in two kinds of knowledge: formal and informal. Formal knowledge derives from the application of scientific methods of investigation (empirical observation, hypothesis testing) to produce objective, verifiable facts about our phenomenological world. In contemporary society, scientific experts, including physicians, are authoritative figures because they are specially trained in the pursuit of science as an enterprise. Their knowledge is privileged. Informal knowledge encompasses both our everyday, common-sense understanding of our lives as well as the intuition that some of us acknowledge and employ to grasp and interpret bits and pieces of hidden messages. Although everyone, including physicians, draws on informal knowledge, not everyone draws on formal knowledge. CAM exists in the world of informal knowledge to the extent that it consists of belief, something that cannot be empirically tested, verified, and reproduced. Many scholars are now blurring the boundary between medicine and CAM by showing how certain therapies can be understood through scientific lenses. One tool they have employed is language. New names and new definitions are emerging to grasp and explain CAM. Several chapters discuss some of the interests and ideologies that are steering and diverting the endeavor to construct the status of CAM in relation to medicine.

Chapter 3 approaches mainstreaming from the perspective of the people who are using alternative therapies. It discusses a number of reasons for the growing use of CAM and demonstrates how people are not only drawing on informal knowledge about alternative therapies and experiential knowledge about their health and healing needs when they turn to CAM. They are also making rational choices about the role of medicine and CAM in fulfilling their needs. Surveys show that people are not replacing conventional with alternative medicine. They are using both according to their own assessments of appropriateness. In other words, users of CAM are integrating it with medicine, but only for themselves. Nevertheless, their behavior is having an impact on the institutions of health care.

Chapter 4 discusses the growing interest in CAM among physicians. Their attitudes are changing and their previous hostility toward alternative medicine is softening. By taking courses and reading the literature on CAM, physicians are learning that some therapies are not only harmless, but also helpful to patients as well as to those physicians who are trying to treat certain patients with certain kinds of illnesses. But hidden in these discoveries is an interesting complicity between patients and physicians. Along with their patients, many physicians are also becoming increasingly disenchanted with the practice of medicine. They are realizing that their relationships with their patients have suffered under corporatized health care. Learning about CAM may be a route for physicians to rebuild more effective communication with patients and to strengthen their capacity for empathy. In this endeavor, physicians are bridging the two worlds of formal and informal knowledge. Their acceptance of CAM requires scientific proof of safety and efficacy, but their attraction to it is grounded in their embrace of the art of healing.

Arguably, the most important venue for the mainstreaming of alternative medicine is research. The NCCAM at the NIH is funding research projects that are sorting the wheat from the chaff in CAM, establishing which therapies are safe and effective for specific disorders, which are harmful or useless, and why and how certain therapies work. Physicians are reading about this research in medical journals, and it is guiding their acceptance of CAM. However, there is a catch to the critical role of this research. Although much of it is being conducted through the methodological gold standard of randomized and controlled clinical trials, there are a number of problems with RCTs. Medical researchers have become increasingly aware of them and are trying to correct them. These problems are exacerbated in CAM research. Above all, the question of what constitutes adequate controls – whether participants must be blinded and whether treatments must be compared with placebo – pose frustrating conundrums for testing some types of alternative therapies. Some researchers are therefore being creative and flexible in their use of RCTs. It remains to be seen whether the medical community will accept these studies as the kind of proof of safety and efficacy that they want if they are to accept CAM. Chapter 5 presents some of the problems behind research based on RCTs, and Chapter 6 describes the studies that are being conducted at selected NCCAM-funded research centers.

Government has been a central actor in the mainstreaming of alternative medicine. Individual senators can be credited for recognizing that growing numbers of consumers want access to more alternative therapies and that government has a fundamental responsibility in ensuring that the products purchased are safe and effective. Congress mandated the establishment of an Office of Alternative Medicine (OAM) at the NIH in 1991, much to the chagrin of some officials at the NIH. Its beneficence in funding research has been astounding. From an initial budget of $2 million in 1993, the renamed NCCAM received $89.138 million in 2000, the largest percentage increase of any NIH unit that year. Its 2003 budget was $112.547 million. At various times, various government officials (from Congress as well as from the NIH) have tried to influence the course of this research. Different constituencies have different interests in how the research is conducted and what results it produces. In the end, the significance of science in grounding this research has prevailed, at one point over the objection of those government officials that were so central to the initial funding. Government continues to approve increases in the NCCAM's budget, but it no longer meddles in the decisions of experts on the grounds for this one dimension of mainstreaming CAM – the centrality of science in research.

There is one additional dimension to mainstreaming in which government can be an active participant – whether and how CAM becomes a component of contemporary health care. Here, government joins the insurance industry. Although their reasons for supporting CAM's role in health care are complex, both have an interest in the cost-saving potential of alternative therapies. Unfortunately, little research is available at present to support (or disprove) the assumption that alternative medicine can help control escalating health care costs. One reason is that CAM's role in health care is still relatively small. It is entering formally through the doors of integrative medicine clinics. There is no reliable data on the number of these clinics across the United States, but we do know that their numbers are growing. At present, integrative medicine clinics are self-funding; they are not receiving any support from the public sector. As experiments in health care and in controlling health care costs, integrative medicine clinics might warrant government support, justified on the same basis as federal policy regarding health maintenance organizations (HMOs) in general and, specifically, funding for state demonstration projects on the use of HMOs in the Medicaid program (Brown 1983; Ruggie 1996). Policymakers also believed that HMOs would achieve savings, and in some states, they did. The question of whether CAM can also reduce the overuse of medical products and procedures will require more evidence from researchers. Ultimately, however, whether government and third-party insurers facilitate the role of CAM in health care is a political decision. The state of Washington has gone the furthest by requiring health insurance plans to cover the use of chiropractors, acupuncturists, and naturopaths for the treatment of conditions covered by the plans.

Medicine and CAM are becoming partners in health care, although they are not always and entirely comfortable as partners. However, as partners, they are contributing to a new social order in health care. Is this new social order radically different from the old? In the end, my answer is no – different yes, but not radically. The practice of medicine will become, I believe, more humanized by the introduction of CAM, and the practice of CAM will become more rationalized by the process of mainstreaming. But medicine will remain based on science and CAM will remain a disparate set of therapies that summon the subjective powers of healing within those who use it. What is new is the partnership itself, which will become institutionalized, I predict, along with its contradictions and complementarities.

I focused this study on developments in the United States. In the area of health care, as in certain other fields of social policy, the United States

lags behind Europe. CAM has been an integral part of health care in
a number of European countries for decades. By and large, physicians
in Europe have never been as antagonistic to alternative medicine as
their American counterparts, nor have they labeled and conceptual-
ized CAM as an alternative that threatens medicine. Nor were such
practices as midwifery suppressed to the same extent in Europe as in
the United States. In part these differences can be explained by factors in the professionalization and institutionalization of medicine, in
particular, and science, in general. In part they are also due to the relationship between the state and these professions; the regulatory role of
the state has been stronger in Europe, and professional interests have
become more collectivized. As a result, throughout the 20th century,
certain types of alternative and conventional medicine were much more
complementary in Europe, and their coupling has become smoother as
national insurance programs cover more and more therapies. Insurance
companies in the United States are beginning to offer some coverage for
CAM, but it is still minimal. Because insurance companies take their
cues from the market, health care insurers will only respond if and
when consumers demand more coverage. We do not yet know whether
either the demand or the expanded coverage will occur. Physicians and
the research they rely on for information about safety and efficacy are
bound to influence consumer demand. Because some research is finding minimal support for the effectiveness of certain therapies and harm
in others, demand may dampen. At this point, predictions are only
conjectures. I offer some throughout this study.

My overall conclusion is that CAM will remain an adjunct to
medicine, but in this role it will contribute to medicine as a profession as well as to health care as a practice. CAM will also be enriched
by the process of mainstreaming and the legitimacy it promises. As
more people come to understand CAM more fully, from the perspective of various kinds of knowledge, they will be better able to sort for
themselves the kernels of wheat that they choose to consume and the
bits of chaff that they will continue to discard. The forces of change
outlined in this book will improve the relationship between CAM and
medicine, I believe, strengthening the ties and enlightening all health
care actors.

# Understanding CAM: The Problem of Knowledge and the Power of Words

Many of the therapies housed under the rubric of CAM are not new in the United States. In the 19th century and into the early years of the 20th century, practices that we would now consider alternative flourished. Some of these therapies have persisted, and some, such as osteopathy and chiropractic, have even been legitimized by the courts. However, the present practice of these two modalities barely resembles their common roots in bone setting. Other therapies – nostrums and secret potions, exorcism, and mesmerism – fell out of favor long ago. The same is true of medicine. Certain centuries-old methods of diagnosis and treatment used by medical professionals have also experienced lasting value, whereas others have not withstood the test of time. Physicians still examine a patient's temperature to ascertain the presence of infection. They no longer, however, subject patients to bloodletting, purging with calomel, or dosing with strychnine (the latter for post surgery patients), to name a few.

Despite these similarities, the course of alternative medicine and its place in American health care diverged widely from that of conventional medicine as the 20th century progressed. In becoming alternative, these practices also became ostracized. They were no longer part of "regular" medicine because their practitioners were not trained as physicians and their practices were not based on science, which had gradually come to inform the practice of medicine. As the status of medicine advanced, alternative practices seemed to disappear. When some of them began to reappear in the latter 20th century, it seemed at first that their status as alternatives had solidified during their absence. However, the framework of inimical difference structured the relationship between alternative and conventional medicine for only a short time. By the mid-1990s, the notion that some alternative therapies could be complementary to conventional medicine began to change the status of the newcomer – that is, of alternative medicine. The 21st century is witnessing yet another terminological innovation, in which CAM and conventional medicine are becoming integrative. But this new concept of integration is raising new questions about the changing status and future role of what are still considered to be two different approaches to health care.

This chapter explores one underlying feature of the shifting relationship between CAM and conventional medicine – the assumption that CAM and the practice to which it is said to be alternative, conventional medicine, represent two different kinds of knowledge. It identifies certain social actors – patients, physicians, researchers, and government officials – who have been involved in constructing the dichotomy, and it examines how some continue to argue for difference, whereas others have begun to question it. Finally, it asks what is behind these positions – what motivates them, what kind of evidence is used to support the claims of difference, and what judgments are made about the social significance of the difference. We will see that for some individuals in each group, the debate is more than intellectual. It has become a political struggle. Some perceive the dichotomy as a hierarchy and claim superiority for one or the other – CAM or medicine – based on the kind of knowledge represented by each. Others either deny that the dichotomy exists, or they minimize its significance by claiming that these two approaches to health, illness, and healing are compatible and parallel, if not fully and always equal. These debates are immensely consequential for the future of health care. Later chapters explore how the growth of CAM is affecting the institution of medicine and vice versa, and what this means for the delivery of services. Let us turn first to the question of knowledge and how its different forms have become associated with different constituencies.

## KNOWLEDGE IN CONTEMPORARY SOCIETY

For centuries and to the present day, medical knowledge has coexisted with nonmedical knowledge about health and healing. For the most part, although medical and nonmedical knowledge have come into contact and on occasion resided in the same person or the same institution, they have maintained separate lodgings. Medical knowledge has decidedly evolved in the 20th century, becoming more scientific and increasingly based on advanced technology. In contrast, the knowledge base of alternative medicine is diverse and varies by modality. Some of this knowledge can be characterized as traditional, some is religious or spiritual, some intuitive or commonsensical. The knowledge base of alternative medicine is more accessible, in general, to ordinary people than is the science-based knowledge of medicine. Is it correct to claim, however, that science alone distinguishes CAM and conventional medicine?

There are different kinds of knowledge that enable humans to understand the phenomenological world, and every individual uses more than one, perhaps even several, on any given day. In this sense, some types of knowledge are inherently compatible, or can be made to cohere by individuals engaged in the multifaceted activities of their everyday lives. However, other types of knowledge are oppositional or contradictory. Contestations are most likely to occur when knowledge becomes ideological and distorted, that is, used for personal or political purposes.

In saying that there are different kinds of knowledge that are produced, disseminated, and used differently by individuals and groups, we must be careful not to give knowledge a substance and an existence in its own right. Knowledge is not a fixed entity, over and above people. Its content and structure are constantly changing among individuals and experts alike, and its transmission and acquisition are subject to the vagaries of language and communication (Mead 1934). Neither is knowledge pure in any of its forms, for it is embedded in culture and systems of authority (Mannheim 1936). Its meanings signify social meanings; its forms constitute social practices. Nevertheless, some scholars claim that in modern society certain kinds of knowledge have acquired an "autonomy" and "force" in their own right (McCarthy 1996, 20). This knowledge is thereby placed higher on a hierarchy, achieving its status through collective consent or social control. Such superior knowledge rests on the authority of its producers. In the case of contemporary society, these people are scientists and experts, whose work and words embody the spirit of objectivity.

To simplify the journey through this analysis of the role of knowledge in understanding CAM, we can distinguish two main clusters of knowledge: formal, scientific, and professional, and informal, non-scientific, and everyday.[1] The former is rule bound, it derives from objective criteria; the latter is open ended, the information it produces is subjective. Saying that medicine and CAM are founded on different kinds of knowledge places medicine within the fold of formal, scientific, and professional knowledge and CAM within the realm of informal, nonscientific, and everyday knowledge. The dichotomy is useful, but not entirely satisfactory.

Let us elaborate formal knowledge first. Many observers maintain that the "constitutive mechanism of social action and the identity of [modernity] is increasingly driven" by a particular kind of knowledge, one that is based on science broadly understood and the experts who produce and disseminate findings about the phenomenological world (Stehr and Ericson 1992, 3, ff). Scientific knowledge has become a critical resource in contemporary society; its productive potential functions much as labor and capital did in earlier eras. Contemporary society is thus historically unique, representing a new height of progress in learning and a new social condition in which science penetrates every facet of life. Other kinds of knowledge are subsumed within the parameters of logical inquiry, their relevance contingent on rational justification.

In this view science is distinguished from other social institutions by its position of authority and autonomy (Zuckerman 1988). Because people have come to value science, its products are accorded more of an unchallenged measure of truth than other kinds of knowledge. Scientists produce evidence based on tests conducted according to rigorous standards of investigation. Thus derived, evidence can persuade people to change their thoughts and behavior. Although some scholars bemoan the "iron cage" of rationality to which modern society has succumbed (Weber 1958 [1904]), other scholars herald the liberating potential of this new knowledge that demystifies the grip of irrational forces and charts the path of ever greater improvement in the human condition (Bell 1973).

---

[1] For more on the sociology of knowledge, and the history and the debates within it, see Swidler and Arditi (1994).

If someone is claiming that only medicine and not CAM embodies formal knowledge, that person is emphasizing the importance of scientific evidence in the practice of medicine. He or she is at the same time claiming that alternative medicine is not evidence based. Many individuals, among them patients, physicians, lawmakers, and third-party payers of health care, are skeptical about alternative medicine because it has not yet been subjected to scientific investigation. They say they would accept it when and only if scientific evidence proves its safety and effectiveness, and finds it to be a valid form of health care. CAM is understood by these people as embodying elements of mysticism and, although possibly harmless, potentially adverse to the goal of conquering disease. Indeed, any time people use alternative therapies and thereby delay treatment, a potentially adverse effect looms. Saying that alternative medicine is not scientific contrasts one dimension of CAM and medicine. A fuller understanding of the concept of informal knowledge elaborates additional dimensions of difference.

There are two contexts within which informal knowledge is cultivated. One is universal and timeless — everyday life. The other is more specific to contemporary society – the mass media. As a feature of everyday life, informal knowledge is, as Geertz (1983) said, "local." In a chapter titled "Common Sense as a Cultural System," Geertz explored how

vernacular wisdom [or] what the plain man thinks when sheltered from the vain sophistications of schoolmen [is] as much an interpretation of the immediacies of experience, a gloss on them, as are myth, painting, epistemology, or whatever, [and], like them, historically constructed and, like them, subjected to historically defined standards of judgment.... Common sense is ... an elaboration and defense of the truth claims of colloquial reason ... it does not celebrate an unseen order, it certifies a seen one. (76–9)

The knowledge that informs everyday life is fashioned by individuals who endeavor to make sense of their world. It is grounded in experience and social interaction. It is delivered through various media. It is translated, edited, and interpreted by individuals and groups. However, everyday knowledge is none of these alone or even in combination. Everyday knowledge, as knowledge in general, is best understood not as a noun but as a verb, for knowledge is an activity. As Mead (1934) said, mind neither precedes nor follows experience; mind, self, and society are inextricably linked social processes.

Although this understanding of knowledge as rooted in everyday processes does not offer anything novel, ordinary people and their everyday lives have taken on a new significance in contemporary society. The 20th century has witnessed a historically unique context for the reproduction and transmission of informal knowledge – the mass media, including the world of popular culture and the internet or related information technologies. These venues are challenging and perhaps reshaping the boundaries between formal and informal knowledge. To some extent they rely on the formal knowledge that is produced by experts. Yet, they aim to render that knowledge less obtuse and more accessible to laypeople. One could argue that these vehicles of communication reduce information to the level of mass culture, reflecting Tocqueville's concerns about a middling standard for culture that eventually reduces it to a lowest common denominator. Knowledge obtained from the mass media thereby carries the risk of misinformation or misinterpretation. But one could also argue that privileging certain information as above mass consumption, especially in an age of high levels of literacy, casts knowledge into social hierarchies that reinforce class structures and shortchange the useful outcomes of mass cultural information.

It can be argued that informal knowledge does not compete with formal knowledge, but stands parallel to it. Given the cultural base of contemporary society, certain vehicles of informal knowledge subsume formal knowledge, translating theories into everyday language and filtering the abstract for use in everyday life. Knowledge in contemporary society is thus broader than the categories "formal" and "informal" allow. It is derived from human experiences, based on information that is obtained from multiple sources, and rendered practical. It is adopted by individuals and groups who choose among authorities, facts, ideas, opinions, ideologies, and beliefs to create their own "stocks of knowledge."

This broader understanding of informal knowledge, as embodying more than simply the opposite of formal, rule bound, and scientific knowledge, softens the dichotomy between CAM and medicine. We can see that informal knowledge plays a role in contemporary health care, in the actions of people, among them patients, nurses, insurers, and lawmakers, some of whom are bringing their multifarious "stocks of knowledge" to bear on the introduction of alternative medicine in health care. This understanding of informal knowledge also allows us to see that it is not alien to the medical profession. Physicians employ common-sense reasoning in medical decision making and "rely on knowledge sources that are embedded in everyday life experiences," including the patient's (Cicourel 1986, 91).[2] CAM practitioners and patients are not alone in their willingness to accept the value of informal knowledge in matters of health and healing. When physicians solicit family and friends to tend to the needs of patients, they are recognizing the importance of informal knowledge. Family and friends know about the nonmedical dimensions of caring for a sick person at home and can even be instructed on how to administer certain medical care procedures.

Although analytically distinct and even divergent in many ways, the two clusters of knowledge are also linked and possibly concurrent. However, the extent to which they can be concurrent depends on whether everyone has access to formal knowledge, or only a privileged few. In the field of health care, medical professionals clearly use both kinds of knowledge. Their training and their experience, their scientific judgment, and their informed intuition intermingle. For them the dichotomy is more of a spectrum. But what about patients and CAM practitioners? Most of them are not trained in the same way as physicians. Do they therefore lack scientific knowledge of their enterprise? If so, should they receive scientific and/or medical training? What kind, exactly, and how much and why? Can and should the dichotomy become a spectrum for CAM practitioners as well, assuming it is not now? How one answers these questions depends on whether one envisions conventional and alternative medicine as paradigmatic mind-sets and on how one claims these mind-sets are achieved.

Interpreting the relationship between these two approaches to health care is not politically neutral. It rests on what one wants to say about the status of CAM in relation to medicine. Perspectives on these issues are grounded in social location and may be shaped by self-interest. The ideas we hold reflect not only our particular stations in life, but also our social affiliations and the resources these provide, all of which enable us to produce, reproduce, and disseminate knowledge – over and above

---

[2] Studies of laboratory science also demonstrate how everyday reasoning is incorporated into daily activities (Knorr Cetina 1981, 1999; Latour 1987).

opinions. The substance of knowledge, the ideas that different groups of people hold at any given time, express both particular and multiple social experiences and identities. Ideas and the knowledge on which we draw to validate our ideas reveal social differences and social inequalities. Ideas and ideologies guide social action and are sometimes directed toward reinforcing or restructuring social differences and inequalities.

Taking these thoughts further, some observers maintain that "power and interests operate in all domains and that reason itself is not free from the marks of class and group perspectives in its historical and social development" (McCarthy 1996, 28). Both formal and informal knowledge are therefore subject to the play of power and interests. How the purveyors of both present their ideas is, therefore, subject to suspicion. Accordingly, if science constitutes a dominant idea system in contemporary society, it is because scientists exercise their ability to misrepresent their purposes (and sometimes their data) as value free and universal. Or, in a more or less conspiratorial vein, studies of "science in action" reveal how scientists, informed by specialized knowledge and motivated by circumstance, create reality or "fabricat[e] . . . scientific facts and technical artifacts . . . [out of] . . . black boxes," as Latour said (1987, 21). Sometimes their hunches, impelled by pressures to produce, flounder; sometimes they are lucky – until new theories are produced. Similarly, the worlds of mass media and entertainment produce what sells. Belying the notion that individuals exercise choice in the products they consume is the structured and delimited character of the products available for consumption (witness the "variety" of cable television stations or women's magazines). The ideas generated by these sources of informal knowledge in contemporary society are driven by interests – economic, political, social – and the power that certain people have to promote their interests.

Self-interest is, indeed, one of the major driving forces of social life, motivating everyone at some point. It is assuredly present in the social processes at work in the growth of CAM and the possible changes that are occurring in health care. We can detect self-interested behavior on the part of all the actors investigated in this study. We must beware of those who claim to be above the fray, which is itself an interest-based claim (McCarthy 1996, 33). Individuals and groups of people exercise different capacities to influence others and promote their self-interest. Some of these differences may occur for reasons other than status and power. For instance, time and place are key factors in the receptivity of ideas and actions. Examining these differences constitutes an investigation into the dynamics not only of social construction, but also of social change.

As we continue with the project of understanding CAM, we will see that those who have been at the forefront in the effort to explain alternative medicine have particular purposes that drive their analyses. In looking now at how they define CAM, we will see that definitions reflect both ideas and ideologies, knowledge and interest. As a result, definitions confuse our understanding as much as they advance it, for they conjure up questions not just of meaning but also of motive and consequence. At the same time, understanding what CAM is and how it differs from medicine and what the relationship (economic, political, social) is between the two enables us to develop a fuller understanding of the ultimate goal of both health and healing. My interest in this analysis is to see if and how medicine and CAM can work together in this common enterprise. To the extent that there is contention in the relationship between CAM and medicine, cooperation will require some concessions from both sides and considerable negotiation to construct accommodation.

## CHANGING NAMES, CHANGING DEFINITIONS

We can observe at once how the dynamics of knowledge mold definitions of CAM. Before one can define a phenomenon, one must name it. Both of these acts, naming and defining, are social processes. They are the product of social forces that construct meaning. They may rely on authoritative knowledge or everyday understanding. They may entail intermediation or power struggles over competing goals and the means to achieve them. They may result in consensus, or they may broker temporary settlements that await an opportunity to rename and revise. While language fosters communication, it also both masks and reveals divergent interests, biases, assumptions, values, worldviews, and structures of power and authority.

Take the term "alternative." Historical accuracy would compel us to say that it is actually Western biomedicine that has developed as an alternative to, or perhaps an outgrowth of, centuries-old treatments that are still used today. We do not need to go as far back as 2600 B.C.

when acupuncture was first codified in China and travel through the
long history of healing across the globe to make the point that only
relatively recently did biomedicine become a dominant form of modern
health care in the Western world. In the 19th century and even into the
20th century, American health care consisted of a great variety of beliefs and practices. Patients could choose among remedies that predated
medical history (botanicals), several that were new on the horizon
(homeopathy), or such established practices as the "heroic therapies"
that ended the days of George Washington.[3] By the mid-19th century,
certain groups of practitioners began to form "professional societies"
and developed certification procedures for their methods. One group
had begun to rely primarily on allopathic treatments and medicines in
its attempt to cure diseases.[4] Organized as the AMA in 1847, it adopted
labels such as "irregular" and "quackery" to ostracize competing practices and practitioners (Starr 1982; Gevitz 1995).[5] By the 20th century,
the medical profession was basing its claims to superiority on evidence
derived from scientific experimentation; to support them, some state
governments passed legislation that outlawed certain "irregular" practices. The Flexner Report in 1910 sealed the fate of medical training
in the U.S.[6] Also, to check widespread abuse of substances sold as
medicines and cures, the first Food and Drugs Act in 1906 "required
a modicum of accurate data on patent medicine labels," a move that
some hoped would guarantee "the purity and honesty of [medicine]
and deal harmful nostrums a 'death-blow'"(Young 1992, 25). It did
not fully succeed; the legislation was eventually strengthened, but not

[3] Some American physicians in the 19th century considered certain treatments commonly used in the "regular" medicine of the time less safe than such "newer" treatments as Thompsonian botanicals (Gevitz 1988).

[4] The term "allopath" was actually coined by Samuel Hahnemann, the founder of
homeopathy, to distinguish the "like can cure like" premise of his treatments from
allopathy, which is premised on principles of combative contraries (for instance, an-
tibiotics attack and destroy bacteria).

[5] There were also "reputable irregulars," such as bone setters. Porter (1988) discussed
the fuzzy boundaries between quacks and irregulars. As we have seen, some regulars
practiced methods that we would now call quackery.

[6] Commissioned by the Carnegie Foundation, the Flexner Report assessed the educational content, processes of training, and certification of competency in the nation's
medical schools. Its recommendations resulted in, among other things, the closing of
several medical schools and an increased role for the AMA in standardizing medical
education and credentialing.

until 1938. Certain practices whose eccentricities made them magnets for the slur of "quackery" – the seneca snakeroot espoused by John Tennent, and the metal rods, called tractors, that Elisha Perkins used to treat all manner of diseases (Gevitz 1988, 3–6) – died their own death.

Throughout most of the 20th century, words such as "marginal," "fringe," and even "heresy" continued to be used by the medical establishment and its government allies to isolate sundry practices. Some stigmatized modalities disappeared as a result, whereas others went underground. Among the latter were various forms of self-treatment, folk medicine, and home remedies. Medical sociologists have noted that as the 20th century advanced these therapies remained "far and away the major source of healthcare in the United States" (Wolinsky 1980, 291). Medical anthropologists have observed that the old world practices of early 20th century immigrants have persisted in ethnic communities to this day (O'Connor 1995), whereas other "subgroups" in the United States adapted strands of various modalities for their own use.

In the 1970s, the so-called countercultural movement began to use the term "holistic" to describe health care practices based on the interconnectedness of mind (and/or spirit) and body in the healing process. Its members extended the human potential ideas of the 1960s, including feminism, environmentalism, and spirituality, to espouse the merits of non-Western healing systems. Besides their social and political leanings, this group was socially significant for another reason – many were "baby boomers." By the late 1970s, people in their 20s and 30s became interested in holistic medicine, even if they were not card-holding members of the counterculture. The growing numbers provided an attractive market for a new industry, which gradually expanded its product to appeal to a wider clientele. As more people adopted and used holistic medicine, the fringe became a populist fad (Oubré 1995, 41).

Despite these developments, or perhaps because of them, by the 1980s the term "alternative" entered the lexicon. It probably originated within the medical community, which began to notice "certain organized systems of health practices outside the mainstream of Western medicine, as well as procedures not ordinarily associated with health care but nevertheless thought to be useful in the maintenance of health or the treatment of disease" (Relman 1979, 312). Although at first the term was seemingly benign or "morally neutral" (Gevitz 1995, 127), it quickly acquired a more activist meaning for the medical community, connoting a search for "alternatives to what some believe to be a dinosaur – the modern medical system" (Relman 1979, 313).[7] The 1990s brought a new era for these unorthodox, unconventional, and, to some, unusual health care practices. As we will see, within the short span of that decade, several modalities moved from the fringe to a proximate and complementary position alongside the mainstream, and then to a more dynamic and integrative relationship with it. Although the medical profession has been an important actor in this transformation in identification and identity, this time the government is playing a more central and mediating role in bridging the gap between two different approaches to health care.

### THE BOUNDARIES OF CAM AND CONVENTIONAL MEDICINE

When using the phrase "alternative medicine" and when attempting to define its content, focus in the health care literature (both scholarly and popular) is usually placed on the word "alternative,"[8] which in and of itself signifies that what it embodies stands apart from something else, in this case modern, Western, conventional medicine.[9] The

[7] Relman is quoting from the introduction of a book titled *Wholistic Dimensions in Healing*. Interestingly, in the 1960s and 1970s, the term "alternative" was also being used to describe new developments that were outside the mainstream in other fields of social innovation – for instance, alternative schools (Swidler 1979).

[8] Instead of using the word "medicine," some authors complete the adjective "alternative" with such nouns as "methods," "treatments," or "therapies." There has been less attention paid in the health care literature to the meaning and use of "medicine," either in and of itself or in combination with the adjective "alternative." Alone, "medicine" commonly refers to the biologically based Western system of allopathy. But when used together with "alternative," a standard dictionary definition of "medicine" is generally assumed or invoked: medicine is that which helps or heals; it is "predicated on what representatives in a given time and place consider to be disease" (Achterberg 1996, 58). Other terms that are also the subject of definitional debate include health, illness, and disease. Many authors in both CAM and conventional medicine turn to the World Health Organization's unusually broad understanding of health as an ideal state of well-being that goes beyond the mere absence of illness, and of illness as a "rupture in life's harmony." Interestingly, the World Health Organization has long espoused mutual respect and cooperation between traditional and modern health care providers.

[9] Naming and defining Western medicine is less contentious, but some authors also note the biases inherent in the use of such words as Western, conventional, orthodox, traditional, allopathic, and biomedical. The bias pertains as much to the description of medicine as to what is implied about alternative medicine. For example, not all alternative medicine is Eastern – folk medicine, Native American medicine, and homeopathy are a few examples.

juxtaposition is not a simple contrast, however. Involved in the effort to define and explain, one can detect an implicit relationship between CAM and medicine, an effort to situate them as opposing or cooperative, as subordinate and dominant (either one or the other), as coequal despite difference, as coequal and similar, or something else.

Distinctions are the essence of identity, whether of the self, of objects, or of fields of study.[10] Although acts of differentiation can be intellectually useful and politically inconsequential, they become significant when steered toward social purposes. Gieryn (1983) developed the concept of "boundary work" to describe activities that aim to construct difference in order to promote self-interest. His focus was on scientists and how they pursue their professional goals. He argued that when scientists as a group demarcate what they do compared with nonscientists, they are constructing a difference that establishes their superiority. Their quest is fraught with practical issues pertaining to material opportunities and professional advantages. We can extend this concept of boundary work to other groups or individuals. It is applicable when we can demonstrate that groups or individuals seek to distinguish themselves from others in such a way as to gain leverage.

Thus understood, boundary work infuses the contemporary existence of alternative medicine. It is an activity of differentiation performed by both alternative practitioners and medical professionals. It has set up a competitive game between two opponents. However, this kind of boundary work is also imploding upon itself. Although Gieryn limits the concept to the construction of hierarchical relations, we can discern other forms and other goals of boundary work among those who are engaged in constructing a new relationship between CAM and medicine. Some actors are trying to demonstrate that although CAM and medicine are different, they need not be opposed. The result is a blurring of the lines that divide. This process is also political, but it is a kind of politics that involves some yielding of hardened positions, some exchange of ideas, some relaxation of ideologies, and some compromise in interests. Let us look at how the exercise of defining CAM demonstrates the various processes of boundary work and political positioning.

---

[10] Lamont and Fournier (1992, 2) noted a fundamental axiom that informs the work of anthropologists and sociologists of culture and knowledge: "human beings name and classify things and people. They create labels through contrast and inclusion."

## HOW THE MEDICAL COMMUNITY DEFINES CAM

It is not surprising that some medical professionals would adopt a definition of CAM that describes it as secondary to conventional medicine. We can go beyond the occasional pejorative remarks that continue to appear in mainstream medical journals and note more subtle approaches.[11] The most common definition currently used in the mainstream medical literature assumes the primacy of medicine: "unconventional therapies [are] medical interventions not taught widely at U.S. medical schools or generally available at U.S. hospitals" (Eisenberg et al. 1993, 246).[12] The main distinction here is between established practices and those that are currently outsiders. As its authors readily admit, this definition is now outdated, for increasingly more medical schools are offering courses on CAM, although most of these are elective (Bhattacharya 2000), and increasingly more hospitals are offering some access to selected alternative therapies.[13] A significant feature of the definition, therefore, is the possibility it offers for revision in the social location of CAM. Implicit in any change, however, is the centrality of insider premises in grounding the shift from outsider status.

What are these insider premises? Some in the medical community have taken great pains to distinguish the theoretical and practical differences between conventional and alternative medicine in such a way as to uphold the scientific foundation of medicine and denounce any

---

[11] The subtitle of a 1993 AMA publication was far from subtle, however: *Reader's Guide to Alternative Methods: An Analysis of More Than 1,000 Reports on Unproven, Disproven, Controversial, Fraudulent, Quack, and/or Otherwise Questionable Approaches to Solving Health Problems.* Clouser, Hufford, and Morrison (1995, 79) retorted that "with a list of stigmatizing terms, this book attacks the legitimacy of alternative medicine through its influence on language before it offers a single argument or bit of evidence."

[12] Other features sometimes included in definitions of CAM are that it is not generally reimbursable by health care providers and that it lacks documentation in the U.S. for safety and effectiveness against specific diseases and conditions. O'Connor et al. (1997, 50) offered this broad definition of CAM: "all health systems, modalities, and practices other than those intrinsic to the politically dominant health system of a particular society or culture . . . [CAM] includes all practices and ideas self-defined by their users as preventing or treating illness or promoting health and well-being."

[13] A survey of 5,810 hospitals in the U.S. found that 15% offered some type of CAM, most frequently pastoral care, massage therapy, relaxation treatment, guided imagery, and therapeutic nutrition (Health Forum/AHA 2002).

incursions on its superiority by the appearance of alternative medicine.[14] This demarcation between scientific medicine and non-scientific CAM carries more significance than in other arenas of boundary work.[15] Here, it implicitly raises a host of additional descriptive terms that feed definitions and boundary work, and relegate alternative medicine to an inferior position (such as rational/irrational, factual/fanciful, proven/unproven[16]). Possibly only a minority of physicians continues to believe that CAM is nonsense, mystical, hocus-pocus, etc., and thereby not only outside the realm of science, but also contradictory to the principles of science. Yet, many physicians do wonder whether science can be applied to investigating CAM. The issue revolves around the role of belief in alternative medicine. Insofar as belief is subjective, it is difficult to measure objectively.[17] It is a critical issue because the view that science is the central means of legitimacy in medicine is roundly accepted. Science is, therefore, the only means of legitimating CAM – in the eyes of physicians.

Science has played a role in health care since the ancient Greeks rejected the significance of supernatural phenomena and attempted to study the body through rational principles of investigation. When the NIH was founded after World War II, the contemporary role of science

---

[14] Most often cited as a flagship for this view is an editorial in the *New England Journal of Medicine*: alternative medicine relies on "anecdotes and theories" and fails to provide the kind of evidence "that would allow any conclusions to be drawn." Furthermore, it embodies a "rationale that violates fundamental scientific laws" and reverts "to irrational approaches to medical practice" (Angell and Kassirer 1998, 839–40).

[15] It has taken a long time for the social sciences to establish their scientific mettle. Their success in doing so is not altogether clear, however, especially when words such as soft and hard are used to distinguish the two kinds of science. In some universities, the discipline of psychology prefers to be considered a science and not a social science (not part of the Arts, in other words).

[16] Unproven is sometimes taken to mean invalid or wrong when it simply means not tested. A number of commonly used medical procedures are also untested by means of scientific clinical trials, but they are not unproven if one accepts experience as a basis for evaluation.

[17] Belief cannot be directly observed, so it cannot be captured for measurement. Interestingly, one of the founding fathers of sociology confronted a similar problem. Durkheim (1964 [1895]) suggested that, although society cannot be directly observed, its effects can be both observed and measured as social facts. His case studies included suicide, religious ritual, and moral constraint. Chapter 6 shows how some CAM researchers are adopting an analogous approach and investigating the effects of belief on health and healing as well as on the body.

in medicine became increasingly focused on the production of evidence. Chapter 5 elaborates the method of RCTs, which is now the hallmark of scientific studies in medicine. For now, suffice it to say that RCTs and the present demand that medicine be evidence based are not as neutral as some medical researchers profess. There is considerable professional debate about the role of ideologies and interest in determining what constitutes evidence. Research findings have to be interpreted and the act of interpretation is not value free (cf Rodwin 2001).

Several studies by sociologists of science (cf Knorr Cetina 1981; Latour 1987; Shapin 1995) reveal how the quest for status and power figure into the production of knowledge. Their findings "demand revision of the idea that scientists enjoy autonomy from political and economic forces swirling outside [and inside] their laboratories, because such cloistering is essential for objectivity and truth" (Cozzens and Gieryn 1990, 5). Their studies also raise questions about the validity of designations like "science" and "nonscience" in demarcating boundaries, including the one between conventional medicine and CAM. However, to the extent that the terms adhere, we can ask if something other than negative forces are at work. Perhaps the captivating dynamics of the quest for status and power, and the play of ideologies and interests, mask another level of social forces that may be at work, most significantly authority, which is a more systematic foundation of social order.

The term "authority" signifies a willingness on the part of followers to obey, whether a leader, a set of principles, ideas, or institutions. For several decades, the medical profession has exercised unusual authority in formulating our understanding of health and illness and in shaping our health care system. But the basis of this authority has changed. Whereas in the past, the professionalism of medicine granted its practitioners authority, the fact that medicine is a science-based discipline has become the key to its present authority. Science has acquired a hallowed place in contemporary social discourse. As the cultural foundation of contemporary knowledge, science constitutes what Knorr Cetina (1999) calls our "epistemic culture."[18] New ideas and new information

---

[18] Knorr Cetina's term is plural, however. That there are epistemic cultures represents for her the disunity of the sciences. Her focus is not on the construction of knowledge per se, but on the machineries of knowledge, whose diversity disunites the sciences.

are subjected to scientific scrutiny by laypersons and professionals alike, albeit with different methods and depths of sophistication. As a cultural system, science structures several key features of our social order, from the way we work and spend money to the way we build homes and rear children.

Putting it this way allows us to make another important distinction – between institutions and actors. Institutions such as science and medicine command authority; individual scientists and physicians command authority only to the extent that others judge them and their actions to be embodiments of science and medicine. When conducting research or practicing medicine, some scientists and some physicians succumb to external demands (patronage) and internal tensions (competition); others refrain. Some actions are governed by rules and principles, others by self-interest. But the power of scientists and physicians to justify their actions is based on their ability to enlist the authority of science. In this formulation, that science involves politics, ideologies and interests does not reduce its authority as an institution that produces and organizes knowledge.

## HOW THE CAM COMMUNITY DEFINES CAM

Interestingly, the CAM community also draws on science to define itself. However, it is divided on whether to question or accept the authority of science as a social institution. As a result, the understanding of alternative medicine that emerges is not altogether clear. For instance, one group of CAM scholars, mired in the oppositional game between science and nonscience and the competition it fosters, explicitly attempts to reverse the reasoning that demotes alternative medicine. It envisions CAM as a preferable alternative to medicine. Among the tools employed in this group's boundary work is vocabulary that evokes positive attributes of alternative medicine and negative attributes of conventional medicine. Thus, in contrast to the spirituality and holism of CAM, signifying balance and harmony within an individual and

Definitionally, Knorr Cetina (1999) said that "epistemic cultures are the cultures of knowledge settings, and these appear to be a structural feature of knowledge societies" (8). She understands both knowledge and culture as practices (or social actions and processes).

between an individual and his or her environment, biomedicine is said to be infused with a "materialism" that reduces the physical body to its parts (Eskinazi 1998b,1622). The contrasting images are powerful and their appeal obvious. Another formulation: "conventional therapy [aims] at combating destructive forces while alternative healing [seeks] to strengthen constructive forces" (Oubré 1995, 47). The appeal here may be less obvious – the image may be attractive to those who associate construction with something positive and destruction with something negative. Other differences that some members of the CAM community frequently note include the role of patients in healing. Unlike the more or less unidimensional and patronizing process that pervades conventional medicine, alternative medicine embraces the recipients of treatment as active participants in their own health care.[19] The implicit attack here strikes at the heart of discontent with conventional medicine.

Other authors in the CAM community have tried to rise above the invidious subordination of one or the other set of actors. They simply claim equality between CAM and medicine, recognizing the difference but characterizing it as complementary. For example, take the work of a panel on definition and description at a CAM research methodology conference in 1995. Members explicitly attempted to put alternative medicine on more equal footing with conventional medicine and to avoid any biases in doing so. They based their case on the common (or at least compatible) goals of CAM and medicine – health and healing – and on their connection as two kinds of medicine. They therefore proposed the "desirability of moving toward a single definition of 'a medicine'" and developed a "neutral" scheme for describing the fundamental characteristics of both CAM and the dominant healing system (O'Connor et al. 1997, 52).[20] Yet, the vocabulary they used may have

---

[19] A less felicitous rendering of this idea suggests that by placing a measure of responsibility on patients, CAM therapies also implicitly or explicitly blame them for failure to heal. Davidoff (1998) called this the "responsibility paradox." It arises because unlike conventional medicine, which sees the source of disease and its cure outside the patient, CAM locates these within, focusing particularly on mind and spirit. In some CAM therapies (imagery, hypnosis, biofeedback), the patient is primarily responsible for engaging his or her mind and/or spirit in the healing process.

[20] The scheme consisted of a list of parameters for obtaining thorough descriptions of CAM systems. The parameters, which could also be applied to medicine are lexicon (specialized terms), taxonomy (classes of health and illness addressed), epistemology

inadvertently undermined their intentions. They defined CAM as "a broad domain of healing resources that encompasses all health systems, modalities, and practices and their accompanying theories and beliefs, other than those intrinsic to the politically dominant health system or a particular society or culture in a given historical period" (O'Connor et al. 1997, 49). The dominant health care system in the United States is later named biomedicine. Despite disclaimers that the "the terms *dominant* and *CAM* are nonevaluative" (52), one is hard pressed to see how this can be. As the panel elaborated its notion of the dominant health care system, it fell deeper into the hole of imputing that CAM is subordinate insofar as it lacks the characteristics of its dominant counterpart:

identifying a health system as 'politically dominant' does not imply that it achieved its position of dominance through political means. It is rather to recognize the social fact that the dominant system has a reputation for efficacy and broad cultural authority as well as dominant (or perhaps even exclusive) access to legislative and social institutional supports such as medical practice laws, legally recognized accreditation and rights of self-regulation, third party payment, privileged access to public research monies and to prestigious publication venues, high status and so forth. (50–1)

By implication and, of course, in actuality, alternative medicine does not enjoy a reputation for efficacy, carry broad cultural authority, or partake of the privileges bestowed by legal and institutional legitimacy. The claim that this difference does not result in a secondary status is hollow without more substantive argumentation.

Providing this substance was the mission of the first conference held in 1992 and sponsored by the OAM at the NIH. The conference participants had to make several political decisions regarding the status of CAM. They sought to elaborate the definition of CAM, clarify the differences between CAM and medicine, and in so doing establish the grounding for mutuality in the goal of health and healing. A series of workshops produced a categorization of alternative therapies that

(canonical body of knowledge), theories (of interconnections), goals for interventions, outcome measures (success according to the system), social organization, specific activities and *materia medica*, responsibilities, scope, analysis of benefits and barriers, accommodation and views of suffering and death, and comparison and interaction with the dominant system (O'Connor et al. 1997, 54). Researchers are to fill in the blanks using observation, not interpretation.

distinguished among "fields of practice"; the more common therapies were sorted according to these fields, producing the list presented in Table 1.1 (Workshop on Alternative Medicine 1995). The analytical basis for the categories was never clearly stated beyond noting that the divisions are "traditional" and the committee had simply added to them (xlvi). The conference participants could not do anything else because knowledge about alternative medicine was fragmentary and unsystematic at the time. Their goal, therefore, was to establish "a baseline of information on alternative medicine, which may be used to direct further research and policy discussions" (x). The main route chosen was to describe the practices. These descriptions attempted to articulate the essential nature of alternative therapies, while indicating certain similarities and differences among them. The typology has now become a formal system for understanding CAM. It has provided an important basis not only for advancing discourse on CAM but also, as we will see, developing scientific knowledge about it.

Unlike the OAM workshop participants, some scholars focus on the similarities among the various therapies and attribute a more general commonality to CAM as a whole. Take, for instance, the claim that all CAM therapies are characterized by such qualities as a belief in nature, vitalism or vital force, spirituality, and holism.[21] Some authors extend the point and postulate that these "fundamental premises unit[e] the alternative community" (Kaptchuk and Eisenberg 1998,1061).[22]

---

[21] The Report of the NIH Workshop on Alternative Medicine elaborated these common beliefs: humans have built-in recuperative powers; individuals are integrated in the "stream of life"; religion and spiritual values are important to health; there is a causal, independent role to the various "manifestations of consciousness"; the Hippocratic injunction – first do not harm – must be maintained; and use of whole substances (foods and herbs) is preferred. It also suggested these common concepts: holism, balance and imbalance, energy, healing, and curing (Workshop on Alternative Medicine 1995: xxxix–xl). The final report of the White House Commission on Complementary and Alternative Medicine Policy said that the similarities among CAM therapies "include an emphasis on whole systems, the promotion of self-care and the stimulation of self-healing processes, the integration of mind and body, the spiritual nature of illness and healing, and the prevention of illness by enhancing the vital energy, or subtle forces, in the body" (WHCCAMP 2002, II, 3).

[22] Kaptchuk and Eisenberg (1998) also included "science" in their list of commonalities, saying that the "science of alternative medicine is ultimately 'person friendly.' Its language is one of solidarity, unity, and holism instead of the distant, statistical, and neutral conventions of normative science" (1062). Elsewhere these authors developed what they call a taxonomy of CAM (Kaptchuk and Eisenberg 2001). Another author

Their assumption is arguable. Are all practitioners of music therapy interested in the recipient's body? Do all homeopaths inquire about the spirit? As for users, are all individuals who turn to acupuncture for relief of shoulder pain or dong quai to alleviate the hot flashes of menopause even aware of holism?

Other scholars maintain that CAM practitioners "do not constitute a distinct community. Indeed, they represent a heterogeneous population promoting disparate beliefs and practices which vary considerably from one movement or tradition to another and form no consistent or complementary body of knowledge" (Gevitz 1988, 1). For the most part, alternative practitioners strive to distinguish their diverse theoretical and epistemological roots, and resist being lumped into one large category. In other words, they also engage in boundary work among themselves, making distinctions between Shiatsu and massage, or yoga and dance therapy, that resemble professionally constructed distinctions between chemistry and physics, or neurology and psychiatry. We can return to the list in Table 1.1 to elaborate this point. At present, the different CAM therapies can be said to constitute specializations. As specializations, shiatsu and massage are two types of manual healing (a field of practice) that differ in technique and theory. But because they are not professions like academics and physicians, they are not disciplines analogous to physicist and psychiatrist. Other CAM practitioners, such as osteopaths, chiropractors, and naturopaths, are health care professionals (some individuals among them may also be MDs). These distinctions are based on training and certification. The purpose of this boundary work is largely benign – clarification for its own sake, not as a basis for competition. Once the market for CAM services expands, however, these purposes may change.

PUTTING IT TOGETHER

How can we collect and assess these definitional exercises? It is clear that although the medical community prioritizes the role of science in medicine, some medical professionals dismiss CAM for not involving

who is sympathetic to CAM says, however, that "there exists no scientific explanation for how some practices could possibly work" (Eskinazi 1998b, 1622). This debate involves not only the role of science in CAM, but also the very meaning of "science."

science, whereas others are not as certain about the stark difference based on science between conventional and alternative medicine, or are not as dismissive of CAM because it does not embody science in the same way as medicine. One may well be left with a sense of confusion or dissatisfaction after reading how the CAM community defines itself. Some within this community seem to dismiss science as meaningless in understanding CAM. Others, although paying allegiance to the role of science in understanding CAM, are not entirely clear of its role. Resorting to description and calling for observation to elaborate the characteristics of CAM is more ethnographic and social scientific than scientific per se. These latter methods of understanding CAM invite one to venture inside the therapies and discover how they work from the people who practice and use them. They elicit, in other words, an appreciation of the informal knowledge that grounds alternative medicine. Scientific knowledge about CAM requires reliable criteria to validate that the therapies work and to explain how they work in more formal terms. We will see that this kind of knowledge about CAM is now being produced. It is changing not only the words we use to understand the therapies, but also the status of CAM from that of an outsider to that of an insider. A process of diffusion has begun whereby the boundary between conventional and alternative medicine is being challenged and pushed, if not crossed and dismantled.

The work of the OAM and its workshops and panels has spawned more research on CAM that is in turn leading to new and more nuanced definitions, encompassing broader features of the relationship between CAM and medicine. For instance, since 1996, the National Library of Medicine and the Medical Subject Headings Term Working Group, both stalwart medical institutions, have defined alternative medicine as "an unrelated group of non-orthodox therapeutic practices, often with explanatory systems that do not follow conventional medical explanations" (http://www.pitt.edu/~cbw/altm.html). Note the recognition that alternative medicine is therapeutic and that there are explanations for its effects. This achievement rests on the work of the early OAM conferences. Armed with preliminary research findings, OAM directors were able to persuade Congressional allies – in particular, the Senate Appropriations Committee – of progress in filling in some of the lingering gaps in understanding alternative medicine. As noted earlier, Congress has increased the budget for research on CAM. Accordingly, although alternative explanatory systems were once the primary tools for understanding CAM, new scientific research is now also engaging conventional medical explanations.

Another major development, relevant to the topic of this chapter, occurred in 1997 when Congress mandated an important change in the OAM's name, a change that signifies the power of a word. Having shed its initial designation as the Office of Unconventional Medical Practice in 1992, the OAM is now the National Center for Complementary and Alternative Medicine.[23] The change in name carried with it a new jurisdiction (each NIH center is an autonomous unit) and thereby a potentially new social relationship – within the NIH at least. Let us briefly consider the significance of this change; its fuller ramifications unfold in the course of this book.

WORDS AND RELATIONSHIPS: TIMING AND SEQUENCING

Among the many problems researchers and practitioners have experienced when trying to define alternative medicine is its residual nature. As long as alternative medicine is understood in the negative – as something that is not medicine – it is difficult to get a handle on what it actually is. Adding the word complementary revealed the widening recognition of a changing reality in both patient use and physician attitudes (the subjects of the following two chapters). It also facilitated a change in the status of CAM. If CAM practices are complementary, they are *by definition* compatible with conventional medicine. Also mitigated by the new terminology was the concern that an alternative practice might replace medical care because complementary connotes something that is supplemental and not substitutive. However, there's the rub – if CAM is a supplement, it remains secondary. We know that certain alternative therapies are no longer thought of as quackery. Have these therapies now attained legitimacy? If so, what does this mean for the role of alternative medicine in health care?

The answers to these questions are still evolving. They are premised on new developments in research and practice. Research is attempting

---

[23] The NCCAM's current definition of CAM is "a group of diverse medical and health care systems, practices, and products that are not presently considered to be part of conventional medicine" (http://nccam.nih.gov).

to sort out those therapies that are safe and effective for specific purposes. This specificity must be emphasized because, in practice, claims about CAM are becoming highly qualified. By far the majority of alternative and complementary therapies are for purposes of health care or well-being that are auxiliary to conventional medicine. Medicine tends to predominate when conditions are serious; CAM is then secondary. When and where practitioners or users claim superiority for a CAM therapy, it is usually for cases in which medicine has been tried first and failed. However, CAM can be primary, when prevention or well-being are the goals. Exceptions to these timing sequences occur among ethnic groups, especially first generation immigrants or older Native Americans or African Americans. These people may seek traditional providers first. However, it is unclear whether culture or personal finances or poor access to conventional health care underlies their behavior.

In the chapters that follow, I continue to investigate issues of legitimacy and the processes that are constructing the legitimate (and in most cases secondary) status of certain CAM modalities, as well as those that are rendering other modalities illegitimate, meaning that research is demonstrating their harmfulness and/or inefficacy. Although the issues of legitimation and delegitimation differ from those discussed thus far, they are all part of the larger project of understanding CAM, if not through definitional exercises, then through various ways of knowing. The final chapter explores the latest terminological mutation in the relationship between CAM and conventional medicine – the movement toward integration.

# 3

# The Growth of CAM: Patterns of Use and Meaning

CAM has become one of the fastest growing fields in health care. In 1991, approximately 33% of respondents to a survey were using at least one type of unconventional therapy annually and the total number of visits to unconventional practitioners exceeded the number of visits to all primary care physicians in the United States (Eisenberg et al. 1993). Expenditures on these therapies and practitioners at that time were estimated at about $14 billion per year, $10.5 billion of which was paid out of pocket, an amount comparable to out-of-pocket expenditures for all hospitalizations in the United States. The survey was repeated in 1997, and it found substantial increases (Eisenberg et al. 1998). Approximately 42% of the respondents were using alternative medicine and, once again, they were visiting alternative practitioners more than primary care physicians. Also, expenditures on alternative medicine had grown to about $21 billion, $12 billion of which was out of pocket.[1] According to various estimates, Americans are currently spending more than $20 billion on dietary supplements alone.

---

[1] In a survey by Astin (1998), 40% of the respondents used CAM. A Landmark Healthcare, Inc. (1998) survey found that 42% of respondents used CAM. A secondary analysis of the 1996 Medical Expenditure Panel Survey ($n = 16,038$) found that only 9% of the population used CAM, perhaps because the survey did not focus on use of CAM (Bausell, Lee, and Berman 2001). Also, this last survey gave respondents a list of 10 CAM therapies, whereas the Eisenberg et al. (1993, 1998) and Astin (1998) surveys gave them a list of 16 therapies and prayer. Because the Eisenberg et al. and Astin surveys included megavitamins, commercial diet, and lifestyle diet, they have been criticized for overestimating CAM use. These are the only national surveys to

There are a number of other dimensions to the growth of CAM on both supply and demand sides, indicating that it has become a widespread phenomenon. For instance, several new colleges or schools have sprouted across the U.S. to train CAM practitioners, and increasingly more medical schools are offering elective courses on CAM. Professional growth has been accompanied by a proliferation of specialized journals reporting on CAM research and theorizing about the significance of CAM. Information about CAM regularly appears in the mass media, including the Internet; magazines specifically devoted to CAM have multiplied. Health food stores where salespersons act as consultants, CAM fairs where the tools of several trades are displayed, self-help courses available in local communities, and advice in all these venues cater to the demands of consumers. In short, CAM has invaded many corners of contemporary society; at the same time, it is a product of contemporary society.

We know that alternative medicine is not new. But its present manifestation, embedded as it is in the cultural present, entails unique qualities. This chapter seeks to understand why use of CAM has grown so much. It first asks who uses complementary and alternative therapies: What are the characteristics – medical, demographic, ideological, and so on – of the people stimulating its current growth? It then tries to link use of these therapies to broader social and cultural patterns of change in both American health care and American society. Driving the analysis are such questions as what does CAM represent to the people who are using it, how does it speak to them, is the current resurgence of alternative medicine an expression of changing social and cultural patterns, what is it about contemporary society that might be inducing growing use of CAM? As one scholar of culture (speaking of the work of anthropologist Clifford Geertz) put it: "if one pays close attention to apparently marginal practices one might learn some interesting things about the wider society" (Kuper 1999, 118). This chapter gives close attention to current research on the use of alternative therapies, and treats it as an empirical grounding to interpret the broad link between the growth of CAM and changes underway not only in health care but also in American society.

---

date. Other studies are limited to, for example, specific geographic areas, adults enrolled in specific family practices or clinics, or persons suffering from specific disorders.

Research on why more people are now using CAM is still exploratory, but some consistent themes are beginning to emerge. Three umbrella answers are most common: (1) it represents a disenchantment with conventional medicine, (2) it represents a search for self-control, and (3) there is a congruence between the contemporary worldviews of CAM users and the beliefs, values, and philosophy embodied in CAM (Astin 1998).[2] I will use these three explanations to analyze the appeal of alternative medicine to people who use it, while also assessing what we can derive about the relationship between growth of CAM and changes in contemporary society. Each of the three umbrella explanations alludes to some of the broad patterns that characterize contemporary society and that infuse the current (re)emergence of alternative medicine. We will see that empirical research has yielded some support, albeit mixed, for these three explanations. Because the focus of this chapter is on ordinary people, it elaborates the role of informal knowledge in motivating a certain kind of health behavior.

## WHO USES CAM AND WHY?

There is some consistency in the empirical literature to date on the general demographic, socioeconomic, medical, behavioral, and ideational characteristics of people who use alternative medicine. A summary profile (Table 3.1) identifies them as people who, compared with nonusers, are in poorer health; suffer from chronic illness; are more educated and have higher incomes; are more likely to be white women ages 35 to 55 years; and tend to live in the western states (Bausell, Lee, and Berman 2001). We can elaborate these characteristics through an examination of the three reasons most often invoked for using CAM.

### Disenchantment with Medicine

Scholarly studies and mass media reports tell us that patients have become dissatisfied with the quality of health care (Table 3.2). Treatments are intrusive and overmedicalized; physicians speak in the fragmented and fragmenting language of biomedicine; and the disjuncture between medicine, which is oriented toward curing illness, and health care,

---

[2] In a review of the literature, Furnham and Forey (1994) discussed 13 different but related reasons for patients favoring CAM over conventional medicine.

TABLE 3.1. *Who Uses CAM?*

---

Research shows that, compared with non-CAM users, CAM is used more by:
- people who are in poorer health
- people who suffer from chronic illness
- people who have more education
- people who have higher income
- whites
- women
- people ages 35 to 55
- people who live in the western states

---

which is oriented toward wellness and the prevention of illness, is deep and wide. Disenchantment with medicine has been evolving for decades and it has several dimensions. Throughout the 1960s and 1970s, writers were castigating the "insidious" consequences of "medicine as an institution of social control" (Zola 1972), the overbearing power of the medical profession (Friedson 1970), the depersonalization of patients (Becker et al. 1961), and the "oppressive" and "counter-therapeutic" environment of hospitals (Goffman 1961), to name a few complaints. Fox (1977) coined the term "demedicalization" to refer to the "backlash" that was underway among "young physicians- and nurses-in-training interested in change, and various consumer and civil-rights groups interested in health care" (17).[3] In the 1980s, states began to pass laws requiring that medical professionals, facilities and insurers respect patients' rights to treatment, information, and privacy. Congress continues to debate a national Patients' Bill of Rights, aimed above all at the degeneration of personal care in managed care organizations (MCOs)[4] and the ability of patients to demand treatment.

---

[3] Demedicalization is associated with a number of different changes in health care, some structural, others cultural, all associated with an apparent transformation in authority relations. For instance, activists have formed patients' rights groups. These centered at first around the issue of the right to be "allowed to die" rather than "kept alive by artificial means or heroic measures . . ." (Fox 1977, 19). Currently, patients' rights are of primary concern. Other indicators of demedicalization include insurance regulations that circumscribe open-ended treatment decisions and reduce physicians' authority.

[4] I use the term "managed care organization" in this book rather than the more familiar "health maintenance organization" because the former is broader in scope than the latter.

TABLE 3.2. *Why Do People Use CAM?*

---

Disenchantment with Medicine
- Disenchantment does not mean rejection.
- Most people use both CAM and conventional medicine.
- Together CAM and conventional medicine are better than either one alone.
- There are problems in communication between physicians and patients.
- People with chronic conditions in particular use both CAM and conventional medicine.
- People use CAM to seek relief from symptoms.

---

The growth of CAM is due in part, some claim, to these negative developments in the practice of medicine and the delivery of health care. Discontent with them has been building for years and alternative medicine is now offering an outlet. Those who turn to CAM are voting with their feet, showing not only their frustration but also demonstrating a desire for more personal, low-tech health care in which patients are people who have a voice. In this analysis, CAM represents a true alternative. Let us examine more closely the proposition that people who use CAM have turned away from conventional medicine.[5]

The fact is that many patients are using alternative medicine along with, not instead of, conventional medicine. Eisenberg et al. (1998, 1573) found that 96% of patients who saw a CAM practitioner also saw a medical doctor, but not necessarily for the same condition; the results were the same for both the original and follow-up surveys.[6] A different survey conducted in 1997 also found that a substantial

---

[5] Attitude surveys are one of the main tools employed to tap people's dispositions, but they are far from perfect instruments. Besides several other methodological problems, sampling and closed-ended questions can skew results. Because the American literature is so spare, I occasionally supplement it with studies from Britain and Canada, two countries whose general orientation toward health care is fairly closely aligned with the United States, despite their different financing systems (Ruggie 1996). Here and there, Australian studies are also cited. The studies vary considerably. Some look at national data, others are more local. Some of the studies are relatively large surveys, others focus on, for example, a single hospital or practice or even patients with a particular illness. Methodological variations may explain some of the mixed findings I note in the text. At the same time, despite the variations, there are some consistent findings.

[6] In 1991, 20% of patients consulted both medical and CAM providers for the same condition, and 32% in 1997.

number of respondents were using both alternative and conventional medicine (Landmark Healthcare, Inc. 1998).[7] This latter survey also found that since starting to use CAM, the majority of patients reported no change in their number of visits to medical doctors, about one-third reported a decrease and 3% reported an increase. Figures for concurrent use of alternative and conventional medicine are not always so high. Eisenberg et al. (2001) found that two-thirds of respondents used both, lower than before but still impressive.[8]

Even though people are using both alternative and conventional medicine, we cannot yet discard the proposition that they may be turning to CAM because of their discontent with conventional medicine. Studies have attempted to dissect the reasons patients use (and do not use) CAM in relation to their attitudes toward and experiences with conventional medicine.[9] A general finding is that the small proportion of the population who use CAM primarily – that is, those who apparently have rejected medicine – are more distrustful and dissatisfied with conventional medicine than people who use both alternative and conventional medicine. But among those who use both, discontent with conventional medicine is not clear-cut. For example, Astin (1998) found that about one-half of his respondents said they were highly satisfied with conventional medicine. Yet, more than one-third of them used CAM. Only a few (9%) of the respondents reported dissatisfaction with conventional medicine, and many (40%) of them used CAM.

Some British studies have further pursued the issue of what dissatisfaction with conventional medicine means, and they give us another angle from which to view this beast. These studies are reviewed in Furnham, Vincent, and Wood (1995). It seems that in Britain

---

[7] Seventy-four percent of those who used alternative care did so along with conventional medical care, and another 11% used CAM both along with and as a replacement for conventional medicine, leaving 15% who used CAM as a replacement. The number of people who used CAM as a replacement is unusually high compared with other studies, perhaps because only HMO patients were questioned.

[8] There is one study that found very low concurrent use. Based on data collected in 1995, Druss and Rosenheck (1999) estimated that only 6.5% of the U.S. population visits both unconventional practitioners and conventional medical providers and 1.8% use only unconventional care.

[9] One small-scale study specifically asked nonusers why they did not use CAM; most said they were not interested, and a few said they did not believe in it or it was unscientific (Elder, Gillchrist, and Minz 1997, 183).

discontent is focused more on the individual health care provider than on conventional medicine per se. Unfortunately, few American studies separate attitudes toward conventional medicine and toward one's physician.[10] Eisenberg et al. (2001, 346–7) asked respondents to distinguish between conventional and alternative providers of care and the findings were mixed. There was little difference in agreement and disagreement with the statement "[Your] alternative provider spends more time with you than does your conventional medical doctor" (a little more than one-half agreed and a little less than one-half disagreed). There were more differences, though, with the following statements, and they suggest that people who use both alternative and conventional medicine are not displeased with their conventional providers: "[Your] provider(s) of alternative medicine offer(s) a more understandable and useful explanation of your medical problems . . ." (42% agreed, 56% disagreed) and "[Your alternative provider] is a better listener than your conventional medical doctor" (41% agreed, 52% disagreed). We return to the issue of physician–patient relations in Chapter 4.

An Australian study offers another, important factor that might be involved in patients' dissatisfaction with conventional medicine. Distinguishing between confidence in the efficacy of conventional medicine, satisfaction with specific medical practitioners or treatments, and loss of hope in obtaining a satisfactory outcome through conventional medicine, McGregor and Peay (1996) found that users of alternative medicine were less confident in conventional medicine and less hopeful of successful treatment. However, they were not more dissatisfied with their recent experiences than a demographically comparable community group. Perhaps, then, people are using both alternative and conventional medicine because neither alone provides the treatment they are seeking. Another way of putting it is that CAM, when used together with conventional medicine, offers more than the latter alone. What more, exactly, is vague and ephemeral; for now, we might

---

[10] One American study did concur with the British, and added that the personal qualities of doctors are more important than their professional qualities or the services they offer (Dunfield 1996). The author did not correlate this finding with use of CAM, but he did note that women prefer a more subjective, interactive doctor–patient relationship. We might hypothesize, then, that people who are not satisfied with their doctor–patient relationship would be predisposed to seek more congenial relations with CAM providers.

observe that people hope to benefit from CAM. Eisenberg et al. (2001, 346) found that only 21% of respondents who both saw a medical doctor and used CAM therapy agreed with the statement, "Alternative therapies are superior to conventional therapies," but 79% agreed that "Using both conventional and alternative therapies is better than using either one alone [for your problems]." Confidence in CAM providers and medical doctors was similar (81% and 77%, respectively).

These findings suggest that disaffection with conventional medicine and/or physicians may be a by-product of health status. Indeed, surveys have found that people who use alternative medicine are more likely to have poorer health than nonusers and to suffer more from such chronic conditions as back problems, pain, and anxiety (Palinkas and Kabongo 2000; Bausell, Lee and Berman 2001). For many, the failure of conventional medicine to treat their chronic conditions may have led them to seek alternatives, but not necessarily to reject conventional medicine.[11] In fact, some studies report that users of alternative therapies make almost twice as many visits to conventional providers as nonusers, and they still report higher levels of unmet need (Paramore 1997), indicating, perhaps, the presence of chronic illness. It is possible that people who are attracted to CAM have had worse experiences with their regular physicians because of their poorer health status. Perhaps for the same reason, their experiences with alternative medicine may also be mixed. One small-scale survey found that, although most of the respondents reported some improvement in their condition after using CAM, less than one-half were satisfied with their alternative care (Drivdahl and Miser 1998).[12]

There is some merit to the notion that people who have poorer health use CAM more than healthy people and that inadequacies in

[11] One Australian study found that even though users of CAM did not suffer from more persistent medical conditions and were not clearly less satisfied with their recent experiences with medical practitioners and treatment, they showed a substantially lower level of confidence in the efficacy of conventional medicine in general (McGregor and Peay 1996). Another Australian study found that two situations – receiving conflicting information and being worried about their medical condition – were significantly associated with visits to CAM providers (Trutnovsky et al. 2001).

[12] There is a contradictory finding in a Canadian study. It found that, despite more chronic health problems, slightly more CAM users rated themselves as being in good general health compared with nonusers (Kelner and Wellman 1997). This survey may have tapped more people who use CAM for general well-being, including chronically ill people who seek relief from symptoms.

conventional medicine have led them to try alternatives, even though they also continue to use conventional medicine. Consider the case of cancer patients. Their use of CAM is high. Studies of cancer patients generally find at least one-half of the respondents use CAM; in some studies, use is as high as 80% of the respondent group (Richardson et al. 2000). In many ways, cancer patients who use CAM are not significantly different from users in the population as a whole. Among cancer patients, women and those ages 35 to 55 years are more likely to use CAM than their counterparts, echoing findings on CAM use in general. Contrary to findings on general use, however, there is some evidence to suggest that cancer patients who use CAM are not necessarily sicker or more lacking in hope about the benefits of conventional medicine than cancer patients who are nonusers. Oncology outpatients use CAM more for relief of symptoms related to their medical treatment than for purposes of curing (Sparber et al. 2000).[13] In other words, among cancer patients, use of CAM may be a reflection not of severity of illness, or an expression of loss of confidence and hope, but a form of self-management in relation to one's broader needs. Cancer patients are trying to supplement conventional medicine, which is oriented toward acute care, with personal care (especially through the use of mind–body therapies) that goes beyond the capacity of conventional medicine. This is not demedicalization or a condemnation of medicine, even though it recognizes the limits of medicine.

Consistent with this argument, there is mounting empirical evidence that within the general population users of alternative therapies find some "relief from their symptoms" or "feel better" as a result of their alternative treatment (Elder, Gillchrist, and Minz 1997; Astin 1998). Studies are also finding that the number of people using CAM for general well-being (that is, not because of a particular condition) has expanded – in the Eisenberg et al. (1998) surveys, the increase was from 33% of respondents in 1991 to 58% in 1997.

It would appear, then, that most Americans use alternative treatments to complement or extend their medical care. The survey evidence does not point to an abandonment of conventional medicine.

[13] However, one study of patients with advanced cancer in England found that CAM users had a high degree of faith in the anticancer or curative possibilities of CAM (Oneschuk, Hanson, and Bruera 2000).

To be sure, there is discontent with conventional medicine, as there always has been.[14] Studies that probe for complaints about conventional medicine certainly find them, and they are as would be expected. The more common grievances are that conventional medicine cannot meet patients' needs because of the unfriendly modalities it uses (chemicals, surgery); patients think their physicians do not consider their problems serious enough to warrant treatment; and patients want a practitioner who is caring and willing to listen (Elder, Gillchrist, and Minz 1997, 183–4). Although not uncritical of conventional medicine, these findings suggest that we continue our search for a fuller understanding of the growing use of CAM.

### Self-Control and Empowerment

One resolution for patient disenchantment with conventional medicine and its seemingly uncaring physicians is to take more responsibility for one's own health care (Table 3.3). That is what patients appear to be doing when they seek alternative care. However, taking care of one's own needs is also what people do in their everyday lives when they eat nutritious foods, exercise, take vitamins, use over-the-counter products for various minor ailments, and so on. In other words, people have always enjoyed a considerable measure of autonomy for their own health care, especially for nonacute conditions. However, in the last few decades there has been heightened recognition that patients are people with needs, desires, and rights. It has been occurring on the part of medical providers engulfed in the consumer orientation of contemporary medicine, and on the part of patients tuning in to an evolving discourse on the self and making new lifestyle choices. Let us examine the empirical picture first.

Surveys consistently find that many patients are using CAM on their own, and making this and other health care decisions without informing their physicians. Researchers have not yet fully explained this behavior. One study offered some focus group answers: "why would I bother sharing any kind of information that I might know about how

---

[14] Historians remind us that dissatisfaction with the medical profession has existed as long as the medical profession. It has been rivalled by dissatisfaction with alternative remedies, some of which were no more than quackery and as harsh or dangerous as orthodox heroic methods. See Gevitz (1988) and Young (1992).

TABLE 3.3. *Why Do People Use CAM?*

---

Self-control and Empowerment
- There is a heightened recognition that patients are people with needs, desires, and rights.
- People are not informing physicians about their use of CAM.
- Those who use CAM and conventional medicine for different health-related reasons are particularly less likely to inform their physicians.
- People with more education want to think for themselves.
- People with higher income can afford to pay for CAM out of pocket.
- People coordinate their ailment with the type of CAM therapy(ies) they use.
- CAM use also reflects social, cultural, and geographical factors.
- Choice is relative: people do not have complete information about CAM.
- Women use CAM more than men.
- Self-control and empowerment include taking personal responsibility for informed decision making.

---

this seemed to help me – they [physicians] don't want to hear it and I don't want to get yelled at by them" (Elder, Gillchrist, and Minz 1997, 183). Eisenberg et al. (1998, 1575) suggested that a general "don't ask, don't tell" milieu exists in the medical profession. A later survey (Eisenberg et al. 2001) confirmed this hypothesis, and detailed reasons for nondisclosure on the part of patients. Foremost among them: "It wasn't important for the doctor to know" (61%) and "The doctor never asked" (60%).[15] It is unclear from these several studies whether patients had raised the issue of CAM with their physicians and discovered lack of knowledge and interest, or whether patients simply assume that their queries will be met by a frown or a blank stare.

Our uncertainty about patient motivations for nondisclosure, as analyzed in the health care literature, leads to a host of additional unasked questions. Do patients want to discuss their use of CAM with physicians? If so, what would it take to establish communication? If they do not want to discuss their use of CAM, why not – are

---

[15] Other reasons were: "It was none of the doctor's business" (31%); "The doctor would not understand" (20%); "The doctor would disapprove of or discourage CAM use" (14%); and "The doctor might not continue as their provider" (2%). An unpublished focus group study conducted by Sara Warber and reported in Whitmarsh (2000, 367) found that the cancer patient participants were concerned that disclosure might jeopardize their valued relations with doctors, insofar as doctors' reactions to disclosure were so unpredictable, they believed.

patients exerting independence; are they harboring fear of humiliation; or, might patients, knowingly or not, be expressing a preference for accessing CAM in nonscientific terms, in a vocabulary that they understand, and through methods and venues that they control?[16] Can it be that patients who are not informing physicians about their use of CAM are thereby reinforcing the boundary between alternative and conventional medicine?

Researchers have been quick to conclude that patient behavior exhibits a desire for self-control, but there may be more to the lack of communication between physicians and patients. For example, Elder, Gillchrist, and Minz (1997) probed the question of nondisclosure further and found that patients are less likely (57%) to disclose their use of CAM to their physician when they use alternative therapies and see their physician for different health or illness reasons. When patients see both alternative and conventional medical providers for the same health or illness reason, they are more likely to disclose their use of CAM to their physician (73%). This finding encourages us to look again at the fact that many people who use CAM do so for chronic conditions, about which they most likely would also consult physicians. The kind of self-control patients with chronic illness are exercising may be based on sound knowledge about their conditions and needs, and it may indicate an increased aggressiveness in taking advantage of the expanding medical marketplace and the many and diverse options it is beginning to offer.

In contrast, growing numbers of people who are turning to CAM for well-being would not necessarily discuss this interest with their doctors, perhaps because they are associating the domain of conventional medicine with illness alone. This kind of self-control is no different than wellness behavior in general, but its present expression also reflects and perhaps propels the expanding options available to consumers.

Although the studies cited so far have found that aspiring to control one's own health care motivates much use of alternative medicine, other studies have found that the desire for self-control is not a significant predictor of CAM use, except among those few who use CAM

---

[16] As Geertz (1983, 87) said, people don't need (or want) scientific theories to explain why they should stay out of crowds in the flu season – common sense suffices and experience confirms it.

primarily (Furnham, Vincent, and Wood 1995; Astin 1998).[17] This picture may reflect the elusiveness of the term "self-control" and the complex behaviors, needs, emotions, and ideas it envelops. Everyone desires self-control, even the sizeable proportion of the population that does discuss their use of CAM with physicians. We can probe the issue further.

Consider the finding that people with at least some college education use CAM more than persons with lower educational attainment. Also, those in higher-income brackets use CAM more than lower-income persons, and many CAM users are paying out of pocket for their treatments.[18] Although these findings appear frequently in large-scale surveys, we must treat them with caution because most surveys, especially those that require written answers or are limited to English, acknowledge that less-educated, poorer persons and racial and ethnic minorities are underrepresented in their sample.[19] Studies that directly investigate ethnic, racial, and socioeconomic differences find that use of alterative therapies by minorities and patients who are underserved in conventional medicine is high – in one study, it was comparable to use among nonminority and affluent groups (Wolsko et al. 2000).[20] Most studies of minority use of alternative or folk medicine are small scale or ethnographic, and focus on a single, localized group, making generalization difficult.

Nevertheless, one could argue that a higher level of education may predispose people to want to think for themselves, to know more about

---

[17] Furnham and Beard (1995) criticized the way "self-control" is used in most studies – self tends to be counterposed to something else and the two sides are assumed to be mutually exclusive. They showed that CAM users attribute health and illness to both internal and external factors, and while they are more likely to take their health into their own hands, they are also cognizant of the role of environmental factors in future health (1429–30).

[18] One small-scale study that separated college and postgraduate education found higher use of CAM among the latter group (Drivdahl and Miser 1998). However, it also found that those in the highest income bracket (more than $60,000) used CAM to the same minimal extent as those with the lowest incomes (less than $20,000).

[19] This problem is also a methodological by-product of telephone surveys, especially when these are conducted in English only. Minorities tend to be distrustful when nonminorities solicit information by telephone, in person, or by mail.

[20] This study compared use at three sites located in different kinds of communities. Findings in studies that are confined to one community are inconsistent. Studies have not yet adequately disentangled the cause–effect relationship between access to health care and CAM use among racial and ethnic minorities.

their bodies and their health care, and to be more discontent with intrusive treatments and patronizing physicians. But a lingering question is the relationship between these variables – might people be engaging in some measure of self-control aside from their discontent?[21] For instance, an interesting set of studies focusing on the correlation between education and type of therapy used found that respondents with some post–high school education use more relaxation techniques, therapeutic touch, massage, and acupuncture, and those with lower education and income use more chiropractic (Kelner and Wellman 1997; Paramore 1997).[22] The former therapies are mainly adjunctive and enhance well-being. Their use might be expected among a population well served by the conventional health care system, whereas use of the latter could be a replacement for more expensive conventional care when not covered by insurance. Putting the education dimension aside, studies also find that, up to a point, people with certain ailments turn to particular types of CAM – chiropractors for back pain and relaxation techniques for emotional stress (Kelner and Wellman 1997; Astin 1998; Eisenberg et al. 1998; Palinkas and Kabongo 2000). However, there are even more consistent findings in the literature showing that patients use a mix of therapies for the same condition. They shop around when they can; however, as with any product, the availability of different kinds of CAM varies by location.

Take the case of cancer patients once again. A study of 453 cancer patients in Texas found that more than 80% used at least one alternative therapy (Richardson et al. 2000). Of these, 13% used only one, 62% used 2 to 6, and 25% used 7 or more. When spiritual practices and psychotherapy are excluded, nearly 70% of the patients used at least one alternative therapy. Use was greatest for spiritual practices (80.5%), vitamins and herbs (62.6%), and movement and physical therapies (59.2%). Another study of 100 cancer patients in Maryland found that the most frequently reported therapies were spiritual, relaxation, imagery, exercise, lifestyle diet (e.g., macrobiotic or vegetarian diets), and nutritional supplementation (Sparber et al. 2000).

---

[21] It is unclear why less educated people would not also feel this discontent; they may not, however, have the personal and material resources to act upon it.

[22] Paramore (1997, 88) noted that 90% of chiropractic services are reimbursable by insurance and 40% of HMOs cover chiropractic, which may explain its greater use among those with lower levels of education and income. He also cited studies conducted in the early 1980s with similar findings.

From yet another study, we can add "old-time remedies" and chiropractic to the list of therapies used by cancer patients (Kao and Devine 2000). A British study reported that herbs, shark cartilage, and vitamins were used the most (Oneschuk, Hanson, and Bruera 2000); a German study found that pharmacological and dietary approaches predominated (Kappauf et al. 2000). A study that focused on ethnic differences among cancer patients in Hawaii found that Chinese patients preferred herbal medicine, Native Hawaiians preferred Hawaiian healing, and Filipinos preferred religious healing or prayer (Maskarinec et al. 2000). In other words, in being selective in their choice of which CAM modality to use for their ailments, patients may be exercising self-control, but their choices also reflect broader social, cultural, geographical, and practical factors.[23]

Despite the appearance of choice, many patients' knowledge about CAM is incomplete, perhaps even inaccurate, and the disparate sources of the mostly informal "referrals" they receive, ranging from the media and other strangers to family and friends, compounds a potential problem in this exercise of self-control – lack of full knowledge about conditions and treatments. For instance, we do not know the extent to which consumers ask health food store personnel or pharmacists for recommendations, nor do we know how familiar these consultants are with the literature on the safety and efficacy of, most important, herbs, nor whether they ask consumers what other supplements and medications they are taking. However, we do know that a number of herbs have been identified as useless – that is, no better than placebo – or dangerous either in and of themselves or when taken with other supplements and medications. One study of 125 surgical patients who took herbs, vitamins, dietary supplements, or homeopathic medicines found, that, in 27% of the cases, the product could inhibit coagulation; in 12%, it could affect blood pressure; in 9%, cause sedation; in 5%, have cardiac effects; and in 4%, alter electrolytes (Norred, Zamudio, and Palmer 2000).

Because survey research tends to focus on attitudes toward responsibility for health care decisions, other dimensions of the role of the

---

[23] We should also note some possible methodological inconsistencies in the research. Studies may or may not ask people why they choose certain treatments and not others. Some studies may be open ended; others may offer respondents a limited list of therapies.

self in health care are less well investigated. We can explore the issue further by focusing on a singular finding in the literature. When surveys find a gender difference, invariably it is women who use CAM more than men. In part, this difference may be due to women's greater use of the health care system in general, an empirical fact that itself requires explanation. For years scholars attributed women's help-seeking behavior to a "learned helplessness." Feminist reinterpretations point out that as primary caretakers and the link between family members and the health care system, women consult the medical profession as much, if not more, for others as for themselves. Feminists also elaborate the close connection in women's lives between self and other, and the greater self-awareness women experience and develop because of their social roles. Most important with regard to health care is the role of the women's health movement, which continues to enable women to gain a better knowledge of their bodies and to take control of the way conventional medicine treats women's bodies.[24] I would suggest that women's greater use of CAM can be understood as a next step in a progressive line of self-help activities.

To gain more insight into certain dimensions of self-control and the empowerment it brings, we can draw on empirical studies of CAM use among women with cancer.[25] A consistent finding is that a significantly greater proportion of women cancer patients are using CAM than are men with cancer. Some of the behavioral correlates of this use among women cancer patients are noteworthy. For instance, studies show that many women with breast or ovarian cancer are telling their physicians about their use of CAM – almost 40% in one study (Von Gruenigen et al. 2001), almost 50% in another (Boon et al. 1999), and more than 50% in yet another (Adler and Fosket 1999). This behavior does not reflect what happens in the general population, but probing for its reasons illuminates an interesting dimension of self-control. Rather than interpreting confiding in physicians as dependence, I would suggest that it represents a search for information that can lead to an intelligent choice. In fact, one study found that women cancer patients were highly cognizant of their personal responsibility in the decision-making

---

[24] Citations for these points could consume pages. I arbitrarily limit myself to three: Gilligan 1982; Belenky et al. 1986; and Ruzek, Olesen, and Clarke, 1997.

[25] There seems to be more discussion of the self in research on women and health, perhaps because the topic is pertinent to feminists. Many studies are oriented toward dispelling myths about women's health behavior.

process and in making informed decisions; the most common reason for deciding not to use CAM was "a lack of meaningful information regarding safety and efficacy" (Boon et al. 1999, 644, 645–6). Another study found that many of the women who did not disclose their use of alternative medicine to their physicians wanted to coordinate their different healing strategies themselves.[26] The type of CAM used by women cancer patients tells us something about this coordination. Prayer and spiritual healing predominate, indicating that women are seeking respite from the trials of their illness.[27] Overall, breast cancer patients are more likely to use a wider range of alternative therapies than the general population (VandeCreek, Rogers, and Lester 1999).

This discussion demonstrates that the desire to exercise greater self-control in one's health care need not be dismissive of the medical profession. Patients with chronic conditions and certain serious illnesses, such as cancer, recognize that there may be limits to the capacity of medicine to deal fully with their condition. Taking responsibility for self-care becomes an important component in their overall care. Those who turn to CAM are not necessarily seeking self-control per se, but it is up to individuals to find those alternative therapies that offer the benefits they want and to partake in the regimen of these therapies. In this way, self-control becomes a component of self-care. We have to assume that individuals can judge for themselves their various needs and the capacity of specific CAM therapies to fulfill these needs.

### Beliefs, Values, and Philosophies

As we saw in Chapter 1, CAM embodies a philosophical orientation toward health and healing that emphasizes certain beliefs (for instance,

---

[26] This study also found that many participants had already been using CAM before they learned of their breast cancer, "challeng[ing] the stereotype of the 'desperate' patient who is willing to try anything" (Adler and Foskett 1999, 456). There is a generalized and, some believe, false impression within the medical profession and elsewhere that "when people become sick, any promise of a cure is beguiling" (Beyerstein 2001, 230).

[27] In their study of 112 subjects, VandeCreek, Rogers, and Lester (1999) found a large gap between use of prayer (76%) and the next most frequently used therapy, exercise (38%). Twenty-nine percent used spiritual healing, 25% megavitamins, 21% relaxation, and 21% self-help groups. There is considerable debate about referring to prayer as a CAM therapy. Separating prayer and spiritual healing is preferable to many who study the issue.

that healing is a natural process intrinsic to individuals) and certain values (for instance, the relationship between humans and nature is symbiotic and whole). Understandably, surveys consistently find that people who agree with such statements as "The health of my body, mind, and spirit are related, and whoever cares for my health should take that into account" score high in CAM use (Astin 1998, 1551). Beyond agreement on specific beliefs and values about holism, nature, and the relationship between these and health, many scholars argue that the philosophical orientation of alternative medicine has a special meaning for people who use it because the philosophy resonates with their personal beliefs and values (Table 3.4). That is, CAM attracts

TABLE 3.4. *Why Do People Use CAM?*

Beliefs, Values, and Philosophies
- Personal worldviews are compatible with the philosophical orientation of CAM.
- This compatibility constitutes an elective affinity.

Spirituality
- Spirituality includes beliefs, behaviors, and experiences that may or may not be religious.
- Spirituality is a "search for the sacred."
- There is a positive link between spirituality and health.
- Certain religions and CAM therapies encourage a similar holistic health promotion.
- There is a positive link between prayer and health.
- Certain religious behaviors (prayer) and certain CAM therapies (meditation, visualization) induce a similar relaxation response.
- There is significance in the meaning of prayer or a mantra beyond the elicitation of biological processes.
- Meaning provides positive motivation for constructive actions.
- There is a positive link between spirituality and self-esteem.
- Both spirituality and CAM connect an individual with an "other" and summon personal resources.
- A sense of community develops through rituals in spiritual practices.
- Certain CAM therapies also summon collective resources and collective energy.

Cultural Creatives
- There is an elective affinity between attraction to CAM and commitment to, e.g., environmentalism or feminism, or involvement with, e.g., esoteric forms of spirituality or personal growth psychology.
- There is an elective affinity between attraction to CAM and a "New Age" orientation.

people who hold general worldviews that are compatible with holism and/or with thinking outside the box. Two kinds of general worldviews appear most frequently in the literature. One involves spirituality. The second is harder to label; it consists of such political and normative values as a commitment to environmentalism or feminism, or such psychological beliefs as the importance of self-expression or self-actualization in personal growth. A term coined by Ray and Anderson (1997) has been widely used to identify these people as "cultural creatives." Purportedly, their various beliefs and values put them at the leading edge of cultural change and innovation.

Let us look more closely at these two worldviews, spirituality and cultural creativity, to explore what they have in common with CAM. To frame the analysis, I turn to the work of Max Weber, a founding father of sociology. Weber (1958 [1904]) introduced the term "elective affinity" to capture the willingness of individuals to accept the doctrinal strictures of the early Protestant sects, as well as their predisposition to engage in the sort of frugal behavior in their economic lives and livelihoods that led to the accumulation of capital, thereby laying the material foundations of capitalism. A similar process may be at work in the adoption of CAM by people who are spiritual or cultural creatives.

## Spirituality

Studies that test for the relationship between spirituality and the use of CAM invariably find a robust connection, even though the specific measures of spirituality vary. Sometimes spirituality is synonymous with religious beliefs (agreement with statements such as "The Lord is my Shepherd"). Sometimes it pertains to religious behaviors (church attendance or prayer); sometimes to beliefs and behaviors that are not religious per se (a sense of being "one with the universe" or "communing with nature"); and sometimes to experiences that derive from these beliefs and behaviors. Sometimes, beliefs, behaviors, and experiences are conflated, as in this definition of spirituality: "the feelings, thoughts, experiences, and behaviors that arise from a search for the sacred" (Larson, Swyers, and McCullough 1997, 21).[28] Flowing through definitions of spirituality is another variable, faith, which is

---

[28] A panel convened by the National Institute of Healthcare Research to study the relationship between spirituality and health formulated this definition.

often linked with spirituality and religiosity to form a trilogy. However, spirituality, religiosity, and faith are different. Most important, religion usually pertains to formal religious organizations or institutions, whereas spirituality does not depend on a collective or institutional context (Pargament 1997).[29] Also, one cannot assume that individuals who engage in the same religious practice embody the same degree of religious faith or experience their spirituality in the same way.[30] With these caveats in mind, let us pursue the relationship between spirituality, which I employ as a summary concept unless otherwise specified, and use of CAM.

Why would people who are spiritual be drawn to CAM?[31] We can perhaps find one answer in the positive link between spirituality and both physical and mental health (Ellison and Levin 1998).[32] There are several dimensions to this correlation: behavioral, emotional, and social. People who are spiritual tend to engage in healthy lifestyles. Those in certain religious groups are less likely to smoke, drink alcohol, and eat meat. In many cases, this behavior is rooted in explicit prohibitions in doctrines or interpretations of them.[33] In others, it is embedded in such broader values as purity, humility, devotion, and so on. Also, spiritual people are less distressed and depressed. They tend to have higher self-esteem and personal mastery. They have better coping resources, both personal and social, the latter emanating from their

[29] George et al. (2000) maintained that this distinction is arbitrary because religiosity is not confined to institutional settings, and many religions encourage spiritual expression outside typical organizations and institutions.

[30] A person may attend a religious institution because of the wishes of a spouse; that person may but not necessarily feel spiritual, or a person may feel spiritual but not necessarily attend a religious institution.

[31] Although the question assumes a cause–effect relationship, the direction of the causal arrow is often unclear. Presumably, adhering to a belief system precedes and predisposes an individual to use CAM. Sometimes, however, individuals first experience a life-threatening illness, which prompts them to use CAM and as a result they acquire a particular belief or orientation to life and death.

[32] Research on this topic is recent. Interestingly, like research on CAM, the medical community first reacted to the suggestion of a link between spirituality and health with skepticism and hostility (Ellison and Levin 1998). However, there is now growing interest among medical researchers in the nature of the link and, as we will see in Chapter 4, growing acceptance by physicians of the importance of spirituality in health and healing.

[33] Not all religious beliefs or practices are health promoting. For instance, Strawbridge et al. (1998) found that certain denominations may induce obsessive behavior or unhealthy guilt. Other denominations counsel their members to eschew medical treatment in favor of prayer or to be selective about the medical treatments they accept.

spiritual community. These examples emphasize the role of spirituality in precipitating and supporting healthy behavior.

However, Sloan, Bagielli, and Powell (1999) criticized studies that suggested a link between spirituality or religion and health because, they said, the link is not with spirituality per se but with other factors.[34] For example, people may be regular churchgoers because they are more socially active and functionally mobile than irregular or nonchurchgoers. The superior health of people who are spiritual or religious is most likely based on their healthy behaviors first and foremost. Most important, these are behaviors that also occur among people who are not religious or spiritual. The authors conclude that "even in the best studies, the evidence of an association between religion, spirituality and health is weak and inconsistent [and] therefore it is premature to promote faith and religion as adjunctive medical treatments" (667).

Nevertheless, to help us to understand a purported link between spirituality and CAM we can turn to the concept of elective affinity and suggest that both spirituality and CAM are based on the holistic health promotion of both. Many CAM therapies explicitly promote healthy lifestyles (such as Ayurvedic medicine, naturopathy, and yoga, to name a few), some engage as well as improve an individual's sense of self (all the mind–body therapies), and some can be said to tie individuals with a wider community that functions as a social resource (e.g., Native American therapies; also, some individuals may find that such practices as meditation, yoga, and dance therapy offer connectedness with others). Presumably, people who have personal and social health-promoting beliefs and values in one area of their lives would feel an affinity with another area that contains similar features. Conventional medicine addresses healthy lifestyles but, aside from psychiatrists, medical professionals are less concerned with matters related to self-esteem and community. However, certain CAM practitioners may not be closely attuned to issues of self-esteem and community (for instance, massage therapists and acupuncturists). These practitioners are holistic in that they normally consider a patient's emotional, psychological, or

---

[34] They make the case for an independent role in an individual's or group's health of such factors as behavioral and genetic characteristics; demographic characteristics (age, sex, ethnicity, education, and socioeconomic status); health status and functional capacity; and the dietary or lifestyle requirements or habits of different religious groups. All these variables (and more) confound the relationship between spirituality and health.

stress-related conditions together with his or her physical condition. But they do not normally consider a person's meaning system or broader social factors, such as social relations, unless these clearly impair an individual's emotional health. Other practitioners, some naturopaths for instance, are more likely to take a patient's personal and social health-promoting resources into account and even make recommendations about these. The link between spirituality and CAM suggested by a focus on holism and health promotion can be seen as a case of elective affinity in this way: when people whose spirituality promotes good health become ill, they may turn to certain alternative therapies (in addition to conventional medicine) because these therapies are more likely to address a fuller range of the health-promoting factors they are used to and that they want to include in their healing agenda. Moreover, they are more likely to select those therapies that include spirituality as part of their holistic approach, as long as these therapies are appropriate for their particular illnesses.

Although plausible, this link may feel strained because it seems to simply connect functional equivalents in health promotion, yet skirt the more innately spiritual attributes of both belief systems and CAM – that is, attributes that pertain to a "search for the sacred," to take one definition of spiritual. Let us examine other behaviors, experiences, and thoughts that are broader in scope and draw out qualities that are more commonly associated with the word spiritual. We can ask if there is something more innately spiritual that links certain behaviors, experiences, and thoughts with CAM for some people.

The practice of prayer is receiving special attention in studies of health. Some prayer is directly related to health in the sense that individuals explicitly pray for their own well-being or that of others. But prayer can be and often is more general. Although studies find that both explicit, health-directed prayer and general prayer are associated with better health (Ellison and Levin 1998), the latter is of particular interest here. What is it about prayer in general that promotes health – that is, even when it is not specifically focused on health – and how might this relate to CAM?[35] One answer is fascinating. Examining what happens when an individual prays, many studies either impute or find that

---

[35] Much of the interest in prayer in the medical or health care literature takes prayer as a practice in and of itself; that is, without considering whether and how it might

prayer induces a relaxation response. The biology of relaxation has been well studied ever since Herbert Benson first suggested the benefits of relaxation in 1975. Reduced levels of blood pressure, heart rate, and metabolic rate all constitute the relaxation response. Physiologically, there may be little difference between religious prayer and recitation of a mantra as occurs in nonreligious meditation (Bernardi et al. 2001).

Benson himself takes a behavioralist stance. He advises his patients to choose a simple two- or more syllable word or phrase (but not the word "one" or the Buddhist mantra "ohm"), or a prayer. He allows that these choices can be meaningful. As it turns out, about 80% of his patients choose a prayer, perhaps because it is meaningful (Moore 1996). Benson claims, however, that it is the repetition of the phrase that is significant; through repetition the phrase becomes associated with the relaxation response. He dismisses, therefore, the significance of meaning per se and the role of spirituality as a "search for the sacred." In Benson's method, it seems that meaning is both relative and circumstantial. He can be understood to imply that individuals with complicated lives might choose one phrase if they were to be counseled by him on a Monday (for example, the Lord is my shepherd), and another phrase if they were to see him on a Friday (for example, my body is my friend). Either phrase could become a mantra, and either is capable of inducing the relaxation response. Some researchers expand on Benson's insights by suggesting that prayer or other religious behaviors elicit a biological process. For example, Dull and Skokan (1995, 49) hypothesized that "cognition within religious belief systems may be associated with bodily changes in the immune system and lead to particular health outcomes."[36]

Once again, the concept of elective affinity can help to explain the link between prayer as a correlate of spirituality and certain CAM therapies. There is a behavioral dimension to both prayer and such

---

constitute a type of CAM. However, prayer is often included in lists of CAM therapies, such as that developed by the Workshop on Alternative Medicine (see Table 1.1).

[36] We should note that the medical literature conceptualizes visualization and other mind–body therapies in a similar way. Even the first OAM conference discussed in Chapter 1 placed prayer and mental healing under the category of mind–body interventions, and elaborated "the complex interactions between the mind and the neurological and immune systems . . ." (Workshop on Alternative Medicine 1995, xii). This "official" classification may not be congruent with what religious believers think is happening when they pray and heal.

therapies as meditation that elicits a similar relaxation response in patients. Patients whose spirituality is comforting would be drawn to those CAM therapies that offer and create similar experiences of comfort. Besides meditation, such other therapies as visualization, massage therapy, reiki, and tai chi can be said to provide a similar link between spirituality and CAM based on relaxation or comfort. The concept of elective affinity explains this link in terms of the meaning the practices evoke for individuals. A biological explanation ignores the significance of meaning by reducing the link to such functional correlates as heart palpitation.

Other scholars try to capture the fuller meaning of prayer by examining the overarching cognitive framework that spirituality provides for interpreting events (Idler 1995). The implication is that prayers are meaningful because of their words and the ideas they convey. Similarly, the mantras that people use in meditation are also said to be meaningful. Mantras are either given by a facilitator who understands an individual's needs (as in transcendental meditation) or created by an individual for a special purpose. The practice of visualization entails a similar foundation in meaning. Insofar as prayers, mantras, or visualizations are cognitively meaningful to individuals, they have a special significance beyond their connection with physiological or psychological processes that link mind and body. Spiritual cognitions may enable individuals to appraise events or stressors in their lives and the resources at their disposal to cope with, if not actively handle, personal problems, including their own capacity to summon personal resources. Believing that the Lord is one's shepherd may induce hope or faith; deciding that one's body is one's friend may promote optimism.[37] Insofar as certain CAM therapies (yoga and qigong are additional examples) explicitly encourage an individual to actively and meaningfully link body and mind, there may be an elective affinity with these therapies for a person who is spiritual. This kind of elective affinity may occur when a person is ill, or when a person is seeking wellness activities and experiences. Elective affinity between spirituality and CAM at this cognitive level of meaning need not pertain to prayer alone. It can encompass cognitive meaning in other practices or behaviors,

---

[37] It is also possible that cognitive processes include the expression of negative thoughts and feelings, which may result in cathartic release.

experiences, and, of course, thoughts. Thus, people whose spirituality contains a particular meaning may be drawn to those CAM therapies that offer similar meanings, however spiritual they may be. In these formulations, meaning is a positive force promoting optimism, faith, healing, or similar constructive actions.

If indeed cognitive processes involving meaning are at work in prayer or recitation of a mantra, it is understandable that some studies find that spiritual beliefs and practices also have a salutary effect on an individual's self-esteem. Explanations for this positive influence highlight involvement in a relationship with an "other," whether it be a deity, the universe, or the implicit interaction in a quest for solace or guidance that occurs in prayer or meditation (Ellison 1998, 693). Social psychologists have long understood the relationship between a sense of self and a sense of other to be reciprocal (Mead 1934). Furthermore, it makes sense that positive self-esteem would influence a person's self-evaluation of his or her mental and physical health, promoting more optimistic prognoses and assessments. Certain CAM therapies, such as energy healing, also seek to connect an individual with an "other" in his or her environment, whether this "other" is physical and material, social and emotive, or aesthetic and unknown. One can also consider the practices of yoga, tai chi, and qigong as reaffirming a connection between an individual and his or her spatial and sensual environment. These are not simply physical exercises; they also entail a certain mindfulness with regard to a connection between self and "other" or self and environment. Thus, many of the benefits that research has shown flow from connectedness, such as enhanced sense of self-worth, may also flow from these CAM therapies. In some ways, elective affinity between spirituality and CAM grounded in the cognitive meaning of self and other seems to take us away once again from spirituality as a "search for the sacred." However, it depends on how one understands what is and is not spiritual and sacred. For some people, the core of spirituality is the relationship between self and other.

Besides these physical, cognitive, psychological, emotional, and aesthetic processes and the personal resources they entail, spiritual beliefs and practices also provide individuals with social resources. Not only is the fellowship of a community of like-minded individuals important, so too is the spiritual and practical help offered by, say, a congregation when a member needs counseling, comforting, visitors, or meals (Idler 1995). Since Durkheim (1947 [1912]), sociologists have also recognized the independent importance of ritual per se, whether of the spiritual sort, or of events ranging at least from weddings and funerals to parades and sports, all of them affirming the social value of community. Indeed, insofar as a considerable body of literature in the social sciences has established the positive relationship between good health, including mental health, and such social conditions as being married (Simon 2002; Wilson 2002), one could question an exclusive focus on the role of spirituality. Many CAM therapies are also ritualistic and thereby summon collective resources. Whether the rituals in such CAM therapies as yoga, tai chi, qigong, and meditation are individualistic or social, summoning personal resources or those that include others in a group, depends on the interpretations of individuals engaged in the ritual. One can practice all these therapies alone, but for some people the experience of practicing them in a group is different. The collective energy that comes from group practice is similar, functionally speaking, to the collective energy one feels at a wedding. The spirituality or positive spirit of these rituals derives, for some participants, from the collective energy they generate. The result, for many, is personally reinvigorating.

In sum, many of the symbolic ideas and activities that occur in spiritual beliefs, values, and practices resemble those in certain CAM therapies. A significant feature of this equivalence entails the act of linking one's self to something or someone outside one's self. Just as certain spiritual practices actively involve the individual in communion with a deity or lending a helping hand to needy persons, involving the patient in the healing process is central to many CAM therapies. While seeking to connect an individual's mind and body, some CAM therapies also attempt to take that person's mind outside the body and induce a "personal encounter with a higher spiritual power," as occurs in certain "American metaphysical healing [rituals . . . that] assist individuals in regenerating their lives through contact with the sacred" (Fuller 1989, 122–3). Insofar as many spiritual beliefs and practices encourage holism and hopefulness, there is an elective affinity between these and certain CAM therapies. As Fuller said, "it is precisely the sacralizing aspects of these systems that are most responsible for their popular appeal" (120). The context of his statement is the decline of religion in contemporary American society, the "dull habits and lifeless doctrines" of overly secularized religion, and the loneliness or norm-lessness that results. Fuller also suggested that Americans, especially those who are well educated and seeking a way of life that is person-ally meaningful, are drawn more to the ideas of CAM than to the actual healing practices; witness the voluminous consumption of literature on CAM.

### Cultural Creativity

There is a collection of people whose attraction to CAM has a more secular bent, who harbor beliefs and values that are embedded in the context of contemporary society, and who, I would argue, see in CAM an approach to health and healing that is compatible with their world-views. It is not necessary to say that this group of people has rejected conventional medicine, although some may have. They may well be among those who are disenchanted with conventional medicine, but cognizant of its role in health care. However, their turn to CAM cannot be explained primarily by their rational combination of conventional and alternative therapies to promote their health and healing. Nor is it necessary to say that these people are or are not spiritual. But their attraction to CAM seems to contain a secular dimension beyond their spirituality. As we will see, however, there may be a peculiarly contem-porary and, therefore, cultural dimension to the interest among some people in spirituality. There may be, in short, an affinity between CAM and certain characteristics of contemporary society.

We can begin to explore this hypothesis by identifying the world-views of a group of people called "cultural creatives." According to Ray and Anderson (2000), these individuals exhibit any one or a com-bination of the following beliefs and/or values: commitment to en-vironmentalism; commitment to feminism; involvement with esoteric forms of spirituality and personal growth psychology; and love of the foreign and exotic. Astin (1998, 1551) found that 55% of the cul-tural creatives he identified in his survey used CAM, compared with 35% who did not fit this category.[38] We can postulate an elective

---

[38] An Australian survey asked people to identify themselves on a 7-point scale of "con-ventionality." The attributes were "conventional," "spontaneous," "habitual," "orig-inal," "traditional," "conforming," and "uninhibited" (McGregor and Peay 1996,

affinity between each of the culturally creative beliefs and/or values and CAM. Presumably, environmentalists would be drawn to therapies that are more natural, such as herbs, as long as their production does not harm the environment, or to therapies that are based on energy healing. The relationship between CAM and feminist values, spirituality, and personal growth has already been discussed. To be sure, however, not everyone who is an environmentalist or feminist or interested in esoteric forms of spirituality or concerned with personal growth is attracted to CAM. All these values and practices are complex, and their followers are undoubtedly equally complex individuals with many reference points for their health and healing decisions.

The adjective "esoteric" and the category "love of the foreign and exotic" require further discussion. What is being imputed by these terms and similar characterizations is an outlook or set of beliefs and attitudes most commonly thought to belong to the "New Age." The New Age is perhaps best defined as an orientation toward "openness to the universe and a willingness to accept alternative ideas and practices" (MacDonald 1995, 32). While cosmopolitan in general, New Age-ism and New Agers are highly eclectic when it comes to particular beliefs and practices, ranging from those who believe in the occult to those who "commune with nature." Some New Agers share political philosophies on nuclear disarmament and international cooperation, but not all those who hold these political commitments consider themselves New Agers. Some New Age philosophies and practices draw on ancient beliefs and norms. What makes them new is their adaptation to contemporary circumstances or the fact that they have been adopted anew by people who were not brought up with them.

At face value the elective affinity between New Age-ism and CAM is fairly obvious, but it is also very vague, pertaining to a host of beliefs, values, and experiences. Also, the term New Age covers too much territory, and the decision to use CAM is very personal and specific for each individual. Nevertheless, to the extent that studies find a statistical correlation between any of these ideational and normative variables

1321). Those respondents who used CAM rated themselves lower on the scale (that is, less conventional) than did those who did not use CAM (the means were 4.49 and 6.02, respectively).

and use of CAM, the concept of elective affinity helps us to understand why. There is a limit, however, to its explanatory power in this area of explanations for use of CAM.

Take, for instance, another consistent finding in the surveys on the characteristics of CAM users – the age cohort. Among the white, middle-class respondents who seem to predominate in these surveys as CAM users, use of alternative medicine is highest among those ages 35 to 55 years.[39] To call this large group of people "middle-age" may be stretching the rubber band. However, the current generation of fairly active 55-year-olds would prefer not to be thought of as "elderly," a term now reserved for those at least older than 65. They are also sometimes called the "baby boomers," a term that is primarily a demographic term. There is a wide cultural range, however, within this category. Those closer to 35 no longer debated in their teen years the merits of Pat Boone's white shoes versus Elvis Presley's slick hair, nor were they affected as profoundly as those closer to 55 by the Vietnam War, the first flight to the moon, the civil rights movement, and so on. To gather this group of people together, then, as CAM users, and to understand how and why we can do this, brings us to a very broad characterization of contemporary society and its cultural affinity with CAM. Rather than naming specific cultural attributes of contemporary society – since scholars and pundits are far from unanimous on what these are – we can turn the project around and summarize what we have learned about contemporary society from investigating why people use CAM.

## CAM AND THE CULTURAL PRESENT: THE JUNCTURE BETWEEN BELIEFS, VALUES, EXPERIENCE, IDEAS, AND PRACTICE

Is there anything new in people complaining about doctors, wanting more autonomy, and searching for meaning in life? Probably not. But

---

[39] To be sure, people older than 55 and younger than 35 years of age use CAM. Some studies that control for age find that older groups, and especially racial and ethnic minorities, use CAM more than younger groups (Cushman et al. 1999). Kessler et al. (2001) asked respondents at what age they first used CAM. They found that approximately 30% of the pre–baby boom cohort used some type of CAM therapy by age 33 compared with approximately 50% of the baby boom cohort and 70% of the post–baby-boom cohort.

that these phenomena are interweaving as explanations for a new development in health care may have import in the context of contemporary society.

Western medicine assumes a dualism between mind and body and a fragmentation of the body into its parts. The latter 20th century witnessed a surge of interest in identifying links between these disjunctures and reconstructing their unity. Questions about what it means to be a living body, how the self is embodied, and how it finds expression in its phenomenological and biological world go beyond the field of medicine. Although these questions are especially critical to individuals facing the experience of ill health (Kissell 2001, 2), people who are healthy also ask them. Whatever the motivation, underlying the search for a union between mind, self, and body is the sense that one has a familiar, known, everyday body that is not the medical body – that our bodies are not objects of enquiry, rather we are enquiring subjects (Evans 2001, 18). Arguably, feminism has gone furthest in its quest to reclaim the human body and distinguish it from the "known" biological body. Throughout history women have experienced oppression through their bodies – childbirth, rape, and ideologies of anatomy as destiny are among these experiences. One branch of contemporary feminism has explicitly chosen not to decry and reject the body (for limiting women's freedom) or subordinate it to the status of "fixed and presocial" (Birke 2000, 21), which would require women to accept their bodies for what they are and accommodate themselves accordingly. These negative reactions to the body assume a conceptual framework that is faulty.[40] Instead, this feminist perspective sees the body not as "a passive recipient of cultural practices" (34), but as an active partner with the self. The phenomenological meaning we give to our bodies, whether in experiences of illness or health, represents our integration of our biological body, our cultural norms, and the agency of our selves.

---

[40] Masters (1995) critiqued evolutionary theory by arguing that organisms do not adapt to their environment or vice versa, but rather, the two coadapt. Martin (1996) critiqued a male-oriented biomedical perspective. She described how researchers "discovered, to their great surprise," that sperm are not "forceful penetrators"; rather their forward thrust is "extremely weak" because the powerful "sideways motion of the tail makes the head move sideways . . . [A sperm's strongest tendency] is to escape by attempting to pry itself off the egg . . . [Therefore,] the egg must be designed to trap the sperm and prevent their escape" (108).

These thoughts are relevant to the current growth of CAM. The several explanations explored in this chapter for why people use alternative medicine, and in increasing numbers, come together, I suggest, in the phenomenological meaning of CAM in relation to the biological or medical body and the self. When authors speak of the appeal of the holistic philosophy of CAM, they are referring to the various links that specific alternative modalities make between the parts of the body, between the natural body and the world of nature, between the body and the self, and between self and other, regardless of whether any of these links entail spirituality. Beyond philosophy, a core attraction also seems to be the central role CAM bestows on the acting individual. Participation in alternative methods of treatment apparently enables each individual to construct one's own approach to health and healing and to interpret the meaning of health and healing for oneself. CAM provides the context for these acts. The search for identity and self in relation to a world with multiple options, multiple constraints, and multiple interpretations is one of the many projects that people face in contemporary society.

Although people experience their participation in alternative and conventional treatments differently, by and large, CAM users have not rejected medicine. They may, in fact, be broadening its framework. Perhaps modern individuals are better equipped to recognize that both medicine and CAM have special roles in treating their bodies. Perhaps people are responding to their options by picking and choosing for themselves the therapies they believe will best satisfy their needs. Sometimes these choices will be based on information that is becoming more widely available. Sometimes they will be based on hope and faith or fear and desperation. Sometimes the choices will work for whatever their intended purposes, sometimes not. That people even have these choices firmly locates their search in contemporary society. We can derive from this chapter that contemporary society is less hierarchical, at least with regard to the institution of medicine, and that it offers more choice and more information. All these developments empower individuals. Many people in contemporary society are coping with the burden of individualism by seeking an "other." CAM is just one of several avenues in this search.

In one of his many books, Durkheim (1947 [1912]) argued that culture is above all a way of knowing. Although this understanding applies to culture as a universal, we can be more specific about how people in particular cultures come to know particular things. In this chapter, I have emphasized the role of knowledge that is largely informal. Its source is both personal and social. Its content is heterogeneous and fluid. Its validation is popularized and unsystematic. As we will see in the following chapters, however, knowledge about CAM and health is changing as the medical profession, both its clinical and research arms, begins to introduce more specialized, scientific knowledge into the task of understanding of CAM.

# 4

# Physicians: Learning New Ways

As late as 1990, the AMA was still battling the incursion of unconventional practitioners in American health care. It had set up a Committee on Quackery in 1963 to condemn the practice of chiropractic and invoked Section 3 of the AMA's Principles of Medical Ethics to impede medical physicians from associating professionally with unscientific practitioners.[1] By the 1970s, chiropractors had gained a sufficiently strong national organization to sue the AMA on antitrust grounds. The AMA began to make some concessions soon after the lawsuit was first filed in 1976 – begrudgingly, according to the U.S. Court of Appeals for the Seventh Circuit – such as permitting medical physicians to refer patients to chiropractors and officially admitting that some chiropractic treatments are not without therapeutic value. However, these concessions did not satisfy chiropractors. They finally won their lawsuit in 1987, after ten years of legal maneuvering by the AMA. There were more appeals, but the decision was upheld for the last time in 1990. Although the AMA eventually allowed that physicians could make their own judgments, it has never conceded that chiropractic services might be based on scientific standards.

The AMA has frequently used words such as "sorcery" and "voodoo" to refer to unconventional modalities (Cohen 1998, 21);

---

[1] A physician should practice a method of healing founded on a scientific basis, and he or she should not voluntarily associate professionally with anyone who violates this principle.

in 1955, the organization was still claiming that osteopathy was a form of "cultist healing." But as the medical profession confronted the growth of CAM in the 1990s, the AMA began to take a less vitriolic and more nuanced approach. It adopted policies that reiterated the lack of "evidence to confirm the safety and efficacy of most alternative therapies"; urged the NCCAM to determine safety and efficacy "by objective scientific evaluation"; stated that "courses offered by medical schools on alternative medicine should present the scientific view of unconventional theories, treatments, and practice as well as the potential therapeutic utility, safety, and efficacy of these modalities"; and vowed to work with the NCCAM "to convey physicians' and patients' concerns and questions." Yet, the AMA also encouraged its members to "routinely inquire about the use of alternative or unconventional therapy by their patients, and educate themselves and their patients about the state of scientific knowledge with regard to alternative therapy that may be used or contemplated."[2] In addition, the AMA joined the American Academy of Family Physicians in questioning the appropriateness of some continuing medical education courses on CAM taken by physicians and in developing review guidelines for these courses. Said one spokesperson: "We don't pass judgment on alternative therapies. But we will not credit dangerous medical practices" (Greene 2000c, 1). Nevertheless, the Academy accredits about 100 continuing medical education courses each year. In its current stance, the AMA is clearly holding to its demand for scientific proof, but it also seems to be recognizing that the climate of health care is changing – for both patients and physicians.

Even though less than one-half of physicians in the United States belong to the AMA, there is no reason to doubt that physicians as a whole would be cautious in their approach to CAM. Yet, studies repeatedly show that physicians are also increasingly interested in learning more about CAM. International surveys have found positive physician

[2] These quotes are taken from 3 of the 4 policies that have been passed since 1994 to guide the profession's approach to alternative medicine: H-480.973, Unconventional Medical Care in the United States; H480.964, Alternative Medicine; and H295.902. The fourth policy, H285.933, Financial Liability Encountered in Referrals for Alternative Care, "supports legislation that managed care organizations that offer alternative medicine as a covered service not require referral by the primary care physician for that service, and that the primary physician not be held at risk financially for the costs of those provided alternative medical services."

attitudes toward CAM, general perceptions of moderate effectiveness, and greater support among younger physicians (Ernst, Resch, and White 1995; Astin et al. 1998). One national survey of family practice physicians and internists in the United States found "surprisingly high" support, even encouragement for patient use of CAM and referral to CAM practitioners; support was higher among younger physicians, female physicians, physicians practicing in the West, and family practitioners (Blumberg et al. 1995, 32). Another national survey of primary care physicians also found considerable interest, even training in many CAM therapies, and more positive attitudes among younger physicians (Berman et al. 1998). A number of smaller-scale and regional studies in the United States have similar findings. There is no systematic data on the number of physicians who are themselves becoming CAM practitioners, but we do know that there are some and that the number is growing. The AMA estimates that 3,000 to 5,000 physicians in the United States practice acupuncture (Greene 2000b, 2).

To understand what is behind this apparent change in attitudes toward CAM, on the part of some physicians at least, and to elaborate its dimensions and implications, let us explore 3 hypotheses that parallel those presented in Chapter 3 for patients' use of alternative medicine: (1) physicians have to keep up with their patients' growing interest in and use of CAM; (2) physicians, like their patients, have become disaffected with medicine, especially because of the changes resulting from the spread of MCOs; and (3) physicians have a genuine interest in healing, and they turn to CAM when medicine has reached its limits or failed. Although the discussion here takes each explanation in turn, they are by no means mutually exclusive; in fact, they are probably highly interactive in shaping a more generalized and mounting change in American health care. Whereas Chapter 3 necessarily focused on the role of informal knowledge in the understanding of CAM among its users, we will see here a curious blend of formal and informal knowledge guiding physicians' attitudes and behavior, as well as their responses to developments in health care.

## FOLLOWING OR LEADING?

Growth in patient use of CAM by and large preceded and motivated growing interest among physicians. Physicians have undoubtedly responded with alarm to survey findings that a remarkable majority of

TABLE 4.1. *Why Are Physicians Interested in CAM?*

---

Physicians have to keep up with their patients.
  • Physicians are concerned about growing use of CAM.
  • There is a lack of communication between physicians and patients about patients' use of CAM.
  • This reflects a more general problem in physician–patient relations.
  • There is more emphasis on patient-centered health care and effective communication skills.
  • Talking about CAM is one vehicle for improving physician–patient relations.
  • Talking about CAM encourages physicians to take a more holistic approach to health care.

---

patients visit alternative practitioners more frequently than they visit primary care physicians, spend considerable amounts of money on CAM, do not inform their physicians about their use of CAM, and may be putting themselves at risk, especially with regard to adverse herb–drug interactions (Table 4.1). Two national surveys that asked people whether they had discussed their use of CAM with a medical doctor found little difference in disclosure rates over a 6-year period – 38.5% in 1990 and 39.8% in 1997 (Eisenberg et al. 1993; Eisenberg et al. 1998).[3] It seems that if not directly asked, patients do not raise the issue because they believe physicians are either uninterested in or disapproving of CAM. Rather than risk a negative response from their physicians, patients prefer to keep their two worlds of health care separate. Because studies also find that physicians tend not raise the issue of alternative medicine,[4] medical associations and journals are increasingly

---

[3] Some regional studies find that patients do by and large tell their physicians about their use of CAM and initiate the discussion (Elder, Gilchrist, and Mintz 1997; Sikand and Laken 1998). An online AMA newsletter reported on a large, national survey conducted by *Consumer Reports* in 2000; it found that of the 35% or 16,000 "well-educated and shopper-savvy readers" who used CAM, 60% "told their doctors, and most [doctors] approved (55%) or were neutral (40%). Only 5% said doctors disapproved" (Greene 2000a, 1–2). However, the reporter misrepresented the two academic surveys, saying there was an increase in disclosure rates from 28% to 40%.

[4] In a Denver area study, Corbin Winslow and Shapiro (2002) found that 52% of their physician respondents asked patients about their use of CAM less than half of the time and another 17% never asked. Physicians' propensity to ask patients was directly associated with their attitudes toward and comfort level in discussing CAM.

advising physicians to ask patients about their use of CAM. Some articles offer practical suggestions on how physicians might broach the issue (Eisenberg 1997).[5] Remove the references to "alternative medicine" and these strategies for physician–patient interaction reflect a broader issue that is troubling the medical profession, namely, a recognition that too many doctors are not communicating well with their patients. It is a problem that not only goes beyond CAM but also strikes at the heart of medical culture and medical authority.

For decades, medical anthropologists and sociologists have been studying doctor–patient interaction and identifying difficulties in communication (Mishler 1984). The most common themes involve the condescending medical worldview of the patient as a "case" or "diagnosis"; the obscure medical language of symptoms and disease; and the physician's lack of sensitivity toward a patient's vulnerable situation, social and personal background, and role in discourse and decision making about health care. Physicians themselves now voice concern about the "arrogance" that remains "regrettably, common" among them (Berger 2002, 145). In part, arrogance is an occupational hazard. Because of their special knowledge, physicians exercise power over patients, and the "longing for an omnipotent physician/parent/God" among some patients "taps into the latent arrogance/grandiosity/hubris of some physicians" (147). Berger also pointed to the contemporary commodification of health care, which has created a situation in which "the patient is no longer seen as a human being but simply as a job to be done cost-effectively" (146).

These criticisms have not fallen on deaf ears. The Association of American Medical Colleges recently issued a statement of objectives for medical student education, specifying 4 main attributes that graduates should possess. First among them is that "physicians should be altruistic," which is elaborated as being compassionate, empathetic, trustworthy, and truthful; act with integrity, honesty, and respect for patients' privacy and dignity as persons; have the capacity to recognize and accept limitations in one's knowledge and clinical skills; and have character traits, attitudes, and values that underpin ethical and

---

5 The letters received in response to this article ranged from supportive, to "ask, note, and advise against potential adverse affects," to advise patients not to use alternative medicine.

beneficial medical care (Medical School Objectives Writing Group 1999, 15–16). The guidelines also stated that physicians must be knowledgeable, skillful, and dutiful.

By now, most medical schools have begun to abandon the traditional model in which students learned the "art" of medicine through apprenticeship and trial and error, leaving the task of gaining competence to their experience as physicians (Haber and Lingard 2001). They have adopted a more proactive role through courses that explicitly teach physicians-in-training how to communicate effectively with patients. Instruction on patient-centered interviewing and oral presentation skills help medical students and residents to learn how to elicit information while establishing rapport and how to convey information effectively and compassionately. Students learn the value of a narrative, including when and how to listen, and when and how to use closed versus open-ended questions. Formats are both didactic and problem based, ranging from lectures and workshops to simulations (some use computer-generated or "virtual" patients, others use real patients) and demonstrations (or role modeling, usually followed by discussions or debriefing). Students are videotaped or observed; sometimes those having difficulty are identified and given remedial training (Lin, Barley, and Cifuentes 2001). Teaching these courses is a new venture for many faculty, who themselves require assistance in developing curricula and training in how to teach elusive concepts, behaviors, and values (Lang et al. 2000).

Reports on the results of these programs are consistently positive. One study that compared patients' perceptions before and after a hospital resident training program found statistically significant improvement (Sliwa, Makoul, and Betts 2002).[6] Even experienced clinicians are confronting their deficiencies in communication skills and attending conferences and continuing medical education courses that offer awareness training and practice (Vanderford et al. 2001). Although some training programs and courses concentrate on physician–patient communication and/or relations in general, others focus on new clinical

---

[6] To be sure, successful and satisfying communication flows in two directions. When patients are better prepared for consultations, in terms of both knowing what information they are seeking and what preferences and fears they may be harboring, both patients and physicians benefit (Sepucha et al. 2002).

situations and ethical dilemmas that physicians now face, such as dealing with drug and alcohol problems, end-of-life decisions, and ethnic diversity.

It is widely accepted that formal education alone can only go so far in changing a well-entrenched culture of medicine. However, it is not widely acknowledged that an informal and hidden curriculum permeates medical education, reinforcing established medical culture whether intentionally or not. A study of participants at a 1998 conference on physician–patient communication sponsored by the American Academy on Physician and Patient found considerable evidence of the tacit and callous messages residents receive. Administrative hierarchies reward efficiency over time spent with patients and their families, senior physicians fail to look at let alone listen to their bedridden "cases" and use dehumanizing language to discuss patients during teaching rounds (Branch et al. 2001). The study also collected examples of techniques for teaching, learning, and constructing a climate of humanism in an active clinical setting – that is, in real time not a classroom – based on sensitivity to and respect for patients through simple words and actions.

Physicians who are disturbed by the deterioration in physician–patient relations have been vocal and provocative, whether in their roles as teachers or authors, about the need to "return to the basics of medicine," which is understood as embracing an ethic of caring or humanism (Branch 2000; Weiss 2000). Although some medical schools include medical humanities somewhere in the curriculum, it is more likely to be considered enriching and supplemental, a desirable option but not an integral component of medical education, except where it serves as a handmaiden to bioethics (Friedman 2002, 320–1). Advocates of the importance of teaching humanities in medical school stress that the "humanities inculcate a tolerance for ambiguity, provide a basis for the reconciliation of competing values, and foster the ability to discern the narrative thread in the setting of illness" (Weiss 2000, 559).

These concerns with communication and humanism in physician–patient relations have undoubtedly been influenced by a change among patients themselves. Spurred on, perhaps, by the mass media – which not only publicize instances of physician errors, but also offer a wealth of advice and information for health care consumers – patients have become more knowledgeable about health care and more assertive about their needs and desires. They demand information on treatment options, want to be involved in decision making, and harbor a degree of personal autonomy. Patients are insisting on changes in traditional medical culture, and physicians are learning how to accommodate them. Physicians are changing not only their styles of personal interaction, but are also learning how to bring patients' everyday lives – their knowledge, behavior, and values – into the clinical setting. This includes a patient's interest in CAM.

In the context of a sensitive physician–patient relationship, physicians have to weigh their own predispositions toward CAM in accordance with their patients' needs for information and advice. We can surmise that a physician who is opposed to alternative medicine would do a better job of maintaining a patient's trust by cloaking his or her distaste and, perhaps, providing evidence on safety and efficacy, rather than revealing his or her bias. A physician who is favorable toward the use of alternative medicine would also maintain a patient's confidence better by providing information on safety and efficacy, as well as on the laws regarding the credentialing and licensing of practitioners, rather than advocating any particular therapy. Learning about CAM (or about any other interests or concerns that patients have) is central to effective physician communication with patients. In their study of physicians in the Denver area, Corbin Winslow and Shapiro (2002) found that 60% of their respondents wanted to learn more about CAM, and physicians who had positive attitudes toward CAM were more interested in learning more about it. In general, the desire to better communicate with patients about their use of alternative therapies was the strongest reason for wanting to learn more about CAM.[7]

There is another angle to the relationship between physicians' interest in CAM and physicians' relationships with their patients. Talking about CAM encourages physicians to take a more holistic approach to their patients' health.[8] The job of primary care physicians in particular

---

[7] The researchers offered 5 statements of reasons for wanting CAM education. The percentage responding somewhat or very important to each are as follows: "Want to dissuade if unsafe and/or ineffective," 94%; "Want to recommend if safe and effective," 90%; "Want facts," 87%; "Patients asking," 82%; and "Insurance coverage," 34%.

[8] Graham-Poole (2001) argued that there is a distinction between holistic medicine and CAM. As defined by the American Holistic Medicine Association, "the art and science of healing the whole person – mind, body, and spirit – in relation to every person's

is to understand the whole person. Despite complaints that the dominant medical paradigm is still based on Cartesian dualism, general medical education now encompasses the biopsychosocial model, and science is providing evidence of the molecular connection between the nervous system and, for instance, the immune and cardiovascular systems (Marcus 2001).[9] Introducing CAM into this knowledge base offers, advocates believe, an evolving science (to be discussed in following chapters) and, as important, a philosophy that supports a holistic approach to health care. To play their roles as comprehensive caregivers, primary care physicians are learning that they need to do more than refer patients to specialists and coordinate, if not integrate, the fragmentation in modern health care. For some time now, primary care physicians have been including healthy diet, dietary supplements, and exercise as part of their recommendations for everyday self-care. Increasingly more believe that it is not a far stretch to also consider herbs or yoga, if patients are themselves considering these. Physicians have also become more interested in mind–body therapies, such as relaxation techniques, biofeedback, and meditation, not only because of patient interest but also because of a growing appreciation of the role of the mind in healing the body (Blumberg et al. 1995; Berman et al. 1998). We can conclude, then, that physicians want to learn about CAM primarily to keep up with and guide their patients and to maintain their confidence. However, they also want to learn about CAM to improve their own understanding of health care, to be fully informed on how they can best meet their patients' needs, and to improve their communications and relationships with patients.

Adopting a strategy of holistic, patient-centered care is not an easy task, however. It takes personal motivation, and it uses up a scarce

community and environment" integrates not only conventional and unconventional methods of promoting optimal health, but also integrates nutritional, environmental, and behavioral medicine with psychoneuroimmunology and social and spiritual health (663). By implication, CAM, or at least certain CAM modalities are not as integrative as holistic medicine. I agree. However, my point here is that CAM may be a route toward holistic medicine, and holistic medicine may be a route toward CAM.

[9] Some still complain, however, that "conventional medical education addresses the problem of how to handle the so called *soft* problems of complex interactions between social, somatic, and psychic factors" only marginally and late in the program (Burger 2001, 81).

commodity in what has become our fast-paced health care system – time, time to talk, reflect, learn, and practice. Many physicians believe that as much as they may want to change the culture of medicine, their ability to do so is no longer under their control. Reports of "a disturbing trend among residents toward cynicism and self-protective strategies as their training progresses" are commonly taken to reflect the intense and exhausting process of becoming a physician. However, these reports may also be revealing unfortunate developments in the evolving system of health care (Shapiro 2002, 323).

THE CORPORATIZATION OF HEALTH CARE

The majority of physicians in the United States now either work for MCOs or accept patients covered by a managed care plan, and the majority of Americans are covered by some form of managed care insurance.[10] Managed care has brought unprecedented change to the American health care system and unprecedented dissension and debate among physicians and patients about its benefits and future (Table 4.2). Although there is no end to complaints about managed care in all corners of the medical profession, intensity of hostility varies. Two general issues trouble physicians and both are related to their growing interest in CAM: loss of autonomy and deterioration in the physician–patient relationship. Both are due to the increasing bureaucratization of health care. Regardless of whether corporate health care is primarily responsible for declining applications to medical school and growing numbers of physicians withdrawing from medical practice, there is little doubt that it is contributing to rising disenchantment with the practice of medicine among physicians.[11]

---

[10] Managed care is another one of those huge umbrella terms that covers as many items outside as under it. The prototype system consists of capitated, salaried, or discounted fee-for-service payment to physicians; flat annual or monthly fees for members; comprehensive services; gatekeeping efforts to control diagnostic testing and visits to specialists; and other limits on numbers and extent of services (such as length of hospital stay).

[11] The problem of physician withdrawals from the medical workforce is worse in California and directly attributable to dissatisfaction with MCOs (Greene 2001). For various reasons, the forecast is now for an impending shortage of physicians (Cooper et al. 2002).

TABLE 4.2. *Why Are Physicians Interested in CAM?*

---

Corporatization of Health Care
- MCOs put physicians in an adversarial position vis à vis patients.
- Patient trust is jeopardized.
- Trust can be rebuilt through renewed emphasis on physician empathy.
- CAM emphasizes a personal relationship of respect and trust between practitioner and patient.
- Learning about CAM is one vehicle for improving physician empathy.
- Physician recommendations about CAM are hampered by many factors, including lack of knowledge, sense of competition, and the licensing and credentialing of CAM practitioners.
- MCOs help by creating networks of practitioners.
- MCOs are interested in CAM because:
  - offering CAM helps to maintain patient satisfaction and attract new members.
  - CAM promotes health maintenance and preventive care.
  - CAM emphasizes self-care for wellness and healing.
  - self-care includes shared decision making.
  - there are positive cost–benefit implications of prevention and of CAM's supportive role in healing.
  - CAM may help MCOs to prioritize health care resources.

---

Physicians by and large agree that cost is an important factor in health care, but they also feel strongly that the overriding concern of MCOs with cost control lowers the quality of care, restrains physicians from providing optimal care and, in general, impairs physicians' independence (Hojat et al. 2000). Limits on number of visits, diagnostic tests, lengths of hospital stay, referrals to specialists, and overall expenditures per physician are the main culprits. In addition, because MCOs employ more generalists than specialists, they are influencing the choices of medical students and raising concerns about an oversupply of specialists in a market experiencing severe competition and declining opportunities. To be sure, physicians are not unanimous in these views. One survey of 1,011 primary care physicians in Pennsylvania's MCOs found considerable agreement about the provision of preventive medical care and some agreement that MCOs do not affect physicians' overall ethical obligations, such as providing information, obtaining informed consent, and maintaining confidentiality. However, the survey also found considerable agreement that MCOs adversely influence physicians' relations or communications with their patients (Feldman,

Novack, and Gracely 1998).[12] Another survey of internal medicine residents found one-fourth of the respondents agreeing with the statement,
a managed care system or HMO is the best model of health care for
the United States, and one-third agreeing that they would be satisfied
working in an HMO (Nelson et al. 1998). Two-thirds said that time
for family life was a major influence on their choice of speciality. With
the caveat that there are many different dimensions to managed care
that these surveys are not capturing, they are finding that there may
be greater, albeit not large, support for managed care among would-be
physicians than might be expected.

Despite the presence of sanguine attitudes among some physicians,
there is a generalized theme in the literature that MCOs put physicians in an adversarial position vis à vis their patients. Gatekeepers are
at particular risk, especially if there are financial incentives linked to
restricting medical care, but all physicians are affected by the shorter
office visits and demands for increased productivity. Moreover, because physicians in MCOs on occasion compromise patients' interests
(Feldman, Novack, and Gracely 1998; also see note 12), patient trust in
physicians has eroded. There is some evidence, however, that patients
can distinguish between the confidence they have in their own physicians, based on their personal experiences, and their antipathy toward
the regulations of MCOs. Patients may even absolve their physicians
from blame (Mechanic 1998). However, the issue of declining patient
trust in physicians is not confined to MCOs. Both Medicare and Medicaid reimburse physicians and hospitals only a portion of their fees,
thereby creating a similar incentive to underserve that jeopardizes the
fiduciary relationship between physician and patient. The media regularly inform us of physicians' links with pharmaceutical companies
and medical device manufacturers and the potential influence of these

[12] The question, what effect does managed care have on the ability of the physician to
carry out ethical obligations, contained the following 6 subcategories (avoid financial
conflicts of interests, place patients' best interests first, respect patients' autonomy,
respect patients' confidentiality, obtain informed consent, provide patient with information). The overall response was 34% negative effect, 59% no effect, and 7%
positive effect. There were 5 questions about physician–patient relations. The negative
responses were highest for increased productivity leaves too little time with patients
(69% agreed), and physician gatekeeper is seen as adversary by patient (66% agreed).
Sixty-two percent of respondents agreed that MCOs provide preventive medical care
frequently.

market interests on physicians' treatment recommendations. One could say that the commodification of health care also strains relations of trust and therefore patient confidence in providers.

As noted earlier, patients have begun to take a proactive role in identifying what they can and cannot tolerate in their health care options and in changing traditional physician–patient relations. Incensed by developments in corporate health care, they are lobbying at both state and national levels for legislation that specifies their rights as patients and requires health care providers and insurers to comply with contractual obligations. The changing role of patients as their own advocates and as consumers is a substantial building block in the transformation of physician–patient relations. In general, the direction of change is toward increased transparency in provider decisions and an increased role on the part of patients in their own health care decisions. The medical profession is responding positively for the most part. Just as there are medical school courses on improving communication skills for both students and experienced physicians, so too is there increasing discussion in academic settings and medical journals on how to train physicians to increase patient trust (Thom 2000). The themes are closely related. Thom and his colleagues are developing a training program that helps physicians to increase patients' trust by thoroughly evaluating problems, understanding patients' experiences, expressing caring, providing appropriate and effective treatment, communicating clearly and completely, building partnerships, and demonstrating honesty and respect (248).

How might these developments affect physicians' attitudes toward CAM? Consider the training program in trust just mentioned. What is being attempted here, it seems, is to teach physicians the elusive but critical quality of empathy. Whether empathy can be taught or evolves from experience is debatable. One small qualitative analysis found that some physicians maintain that empathy is an attitude, others maintain that it is a skill, and most maintain that it is both (Shapiro 2002). The respondents all described empathy with such phrases as "putting myself in the patients shoes"; distinguished empathy from sympathy (feeling what the patient is feeling, not what you would feel in the same circumstances); and agreed that "empathy is more than an intellectual understanding or cognitive analysis ... [it] involves a personal relatedness" – even one respondent who described himself as "not big on touchy-feely language" (324). It seems that empathy is both a means and an end, a tool that lends a helping hand when diagnosing, a quality that improves the physician–patient relationship. Whatever its definition or function, there can be no question that empathy is the heart and soul of the medical profession.

CAM enters this picture in its emphasis on the interpersonal relationship between practitioner and patient, beyond effective communication. In all CAM therapies that involve a practitioner, the practitioner–patient relationship is based in principle on respect by the practitioner for the patient and trust by the patient in the practitioner. Although these values also ground most conventional physician–patient relations, there are other factors that support this relationship in CAM. For instance, in certain complementary and alternative therapies (especially the mind–body and biofield therapies), both practitioner and patient must believe in the value of the modality for it to be effective and must willingly embrace emotions and intuition.

Physicians who are not themselves practitioners learn about the values underlying practitioner–patient relations when they learn about CAM, whether in continuing education courses or in the literature.[13] CAM courses induce physicians to reflect on their own relationships with patients and, perhaps, to change their behaviors. As physicians understand what CAM is all about, they understand at the same time why their patients are using or are interested in using alternative medicine. In this way, knowledge about CAM becomes a vehicle for improving physician empathy. Physicians do not need to practice alternative medicine or fully accept its validity to acquire these lessons. However, their open-minded exposure to the principles of CAM cannot but influence, at the least, their attitude toward their patients. How physicians respond to sensitivity training and practice empathy in the rushed environment of an MCO is another matter.

Some physicians have begun to refer their patients to CAM practitioners. In fact, surveys are finding that a majority of physicians are or are willing to make referrals (Borkan et al. 1994; Astin et al. 1998). Although patient requests are the driving force, experience with or knowledge of a therapy is positively associated with referral patterns

---

[13] This paragraph is based on informal interviews I conducted of approximately 10 physicians attending 3 different Continuing Medical Education courses on CAM.

and acceptance of alternative medicine (Berman et al. 1999).[14] Physicians gain knowledge not only by taking courses and reading the literature on CAM, but also from patients who report on their experiences. Primary care or family physicians make referrals more often than specialists. They are also more knowledgeable about CAM, more likely to practice one of the therapies themselves and somewhat more likely to use these therapies for themselves or their families (Borkan et al. 1994). It is difficult to generalize about which therapies physicians favor in their referrals. Among others, factors such as a patient's desires, needs, and illness; the availability of practitioners in the area; and, again, a physician's knowledge of and experience with a therapy, enter into physicians' referral decisions. In general, biofeedback, relaxation, hypnosis, spiritual healing or prayer, massage, spinal manipulation, and acupuncture top the lists of physicians' referrals.

We can assume, up to a point, that physicians who approve of their patients' use of CAM or refer their patients to CAM practitioners would not consider these therapies to be competitive with their own medical practice. Whether CAM does compete with medicine, in either the eyes or wallets of physicians, depends on a number of factors in a physician's practice – for instance, the size of practice (those with smaller practices are more likely to consider CAM competitive) and type of reimbursement (those with fee-for-service practices are more likely to consider CAM competitive). Perhaps most important, however, is the degree of success in treating a patient. Physicians who have not been able to help their patients to the satisfaction of both are more likely to be open to alternative forms of therapy.[15] We can conjecture

---

[14] Borkan et al. (1994) also found that the synergy between the alternative therapy and patients' cultural beliefs, patients' lack of response to conventional treatment, and the belief that patients have a "nonorganic" or "psychological" disease were high among the reasons given for making referrals. Other studies have also found that younger physicians and women physicians are more likely to accept and refer patients to CAM practitioners (Berman et al. 1999).

[15] There is another interesting possibility in this scenario that raises the question of how physicians respond to what they perceive as psychological problems in patients. For some time, there has been concern that primary care physicians underrecognize and underdiagnose mental health problems. A recent survey, showing an increase in outpatient treatment of depression, indicates that detection may be improving (Olfson et al. 2002). Nevertheless, another survey found that both family physicians and internists continue to express "considerable uncertainty in their knowledge of psychotherapy and in their evaluation of the effectiveness of other strategies for the prevention of

that physicians who lean toward or embrace CAM, for whatever reasons, are likely to believe that alternative and conventional medicine can become partners in health care. However, when patients are using both forms of treatment, the effectiveness of each, as well as their synergy, is enhanced if, and perhaps only if, both providers communicate with each other as well as with the patient.

There is a scarcity of research on the topic of physician–practitioner communication. What little we have is not positive. One study found that family physicians and chiropractors share information in only about 25% of the cases in which they referred to one another (Mainous et al. 2000). When cross-referred and self-referred patients were combined, chiropractors sent reports to family physicians for 48% of the cases and family physicians sent reports to chiropractors for 25% of the cases. Family physicians were more likely to feel they were in competition with chiropractors than vice versa and less likely than chiropractors to feel comfortable sharing information. It seems that family physicians are still under the influence of the AMA's historic posture toward chiropractors.

One area of concern that physicians might have in making referrals to CAM practitioners is licensing and credentialing. State governments vary considerably in their regulations (Cohen 1998). The only therapists that are systematically recognized as licensed practitioners by state governments are chiropractors and osteopaths (licensed throughout the United States), acupuncturists (licensed in more than one-half of the states),[16] massage therapists (licensed in about one-half of the states), and naturopaths (licensed in about a dozen states). In general, MDs can legally practice any CAM therapy in which they are trained as part of their practice.[17] An additional constraint, however, for physicians who are considering a referral to a CAM practitioner

recurrence of depression" (Gallo et al. 2002, 1). To the extent that physicians do not know what to do with patients who might be having mental health problems and to the extent that these same physicians consider CAM to be "psychological," they may be supportive of their patients' use of CAM.

[16] Some of these states limit the practice of acupuncture to licensed physicians, osteopaths, and chiropractors, whereas others require that nonphysician acupuncturists be supervised by or collaborate with physicians (Cohen 1998, 43).

[17] Among the restrictions: insofar as herbs are not regulated by the FDA, physicians may recommend but cannot prescribe them. In the same way, physicians cannot prescribe drugs or medical devices that are not approved by the FDA. Also, California

comes from practitioner associations, which vary in their credentialing requirements. For instance, the American Massage Therapy Association now has a National Certification Board that conducts a national certification exam on an optional basis. A number of states, but not all, that license massage therapists have adopted the exam as a requirement for licensure. In addition, states have different scope-of-practice limitations for most CAM therapists; these specify what credentials a practitioner needs, what supervision or accountability is required, and what, exactly, the practitioner can and cannot do (38). These specifications, which include definitions of the modality, vary considerably across the states. We can assume that physicians are aware of state requirements, but there are no guidelines for physicians in those states that do not license practitioners, or where requirements for licensure are weaker than in other states, or where the scope of practice limitations is vague. It is not surprising that liability concerns would make physicians hesitant to recommend a therapy, let alone refer patients to practitioners.

Some insurers have made it easier for physicians by offering some type of CAM coverage and, in the case of MCOs, creating a network of credentialed and/or licensed practitioners. Oxford Health Plans was the first major insurer to launch a CAM program in 1997; others now include Kaiser, Aetna, Prudential, and certain Blue Cross and Blue Shield plans. Chiropractic, acupuncture, massage therapy, and physical therapy are most likely to be covered, but one also finds biofeedback, hypnotherapy, and acupressure among the offerings at some MCOs. Most commonly, enrollees pay out of pocket at discounted rates when they use these practitioners. Some third-party payers also provide discounts for selected herbs and other supplements. Consumers pay for the services (and products) directly insofar as they are considered an embedded benefit or supplemental rider. Some plans include certain therapies as covered benefits. These generally require a physician's authorization and include a restricted number of visits, subject only to the plan's usual copayment. National surveys indicate that about two-thirds of MCOs offer some type of coverage for at least one CAM therapy (Landmark Healthcare, Inc. 1999). Insurers are motivated to

does not allow physicians to treat cancer with anything except surgery, radiation, or chemotherapy (Sturm and Unützer 2000/2001, 424).

introduce CAM coverage by market factors.[18] MCOs expect to attract new members and to maintain, even increase, patient satisfaction by catering to their interests, desires, and perceived needs.

Whether intended or not, incorporating CAM into their health care plans may also be reintroducing the lost idea of health maintenance into managed care. The original purpose of an HMO was preventive care. In principle, regular check-ups, screening, and information about lifestyle choices and disease detection were expected to reduce health care costs in the long run by contributing to a more health-conscious and healthier population. In practice, however, prevention programs proved to be a costly enterprise in the short run. Also in principle, managed care was intended to reduce costs by instituting a rational and ethical system of resource distribution – the substitution of less expensive care for milder illness was ethically justifiable, it was argued, in an era of fixed resources (Boyle and Callahan 1995; see also Strom-Gottfried 1998). In practice, however, instrumental rationality (bureaucratic, administrative decision making) overrode substantive rationality. It appears to many observers that erosion of the vision has destroyed the potential of managed care to both realize cost effectiveness and contribute to a healthier population through preventive care. Enter CAM, which may well be reinvigorating the original vision.

One of CAM's core features is self-care. Its meaning in CAM differs from its practice in medicine. In medicine, self-care refers to such diverse activities as taking aspirin for a headache, monitoring one's blood pressure, injecting oneself with insulin for diabetes, and so on. Efforts to enlist patients in self-care remain central to the management of many chronic conditions, and self-diagnosis is critical for the early detection of a number of diseases. Studies consistently find that when a self-care component is added to standard treatments, compliance is less problematic and patients' improvement is speedier and more significant; some studies even report cost effectiveness (Corless et al.

---

[18] Some states have mandates for coverage. Legislation in the state of Washington is the most far reaching: as of 2000, MCOs and insurance companies must cover all licensed and certified alternative therapy practitioners. The majority of states (42) require coverage for chiropractors, following the 1990 federal court ruling. That aside, 8 states have mandates for at least 1 CAM therapy (Alaska, California, Florida, Montana, New Mexico, Nevada, Oregon, Washington); 2 states (Florida, Washington) mandate coverage for at least 2 CAM therapies. These are most likely to be acupuncture (in 7 states) and naturopathy (2 states). These data are for 2000 (Sturm and Unützer 2000/2001, 423–4).

2002; Jacobsen et al. 2002; Shoor and Lorig 2002). However, CAM provides a broader rationale for self-care that can strengthen its practice in conventional medical regimens. A core principle in many CAM therapies is that healing is a natural process. Individuals foster their own healing by summoning the natural forces of their mind, body, and spirit. Practitioners are assistants or partners in healing. Physicians do not need to accept this philosophy of healing to recognize that patients who are interested in using CAM want to do something for themselves that they think may help them. Patients who are motivated to engage in self-care help physicians in the common goal of health care – assuming, of course, that physicians approve of what it is patients are doing for themselves.

Insofar as self-care is ipso facto potentially empowering for patients, it raises an issue in physician–patient relations that has been receiving increasingly more attention – shared decision making. This new development destabilizes the traditional authority of physicians by suggesting a more substantial role on the part of patients in knowing about, conducting, and deciding on their own health care. At the same time, it is a necessary component of a patient-centered, consumer-oriented health care system. Researchers have identified a number of different models of medical decision making, ranging from more or less complete control by either physician or patient (or, sometimes, the third-party payer) to fluid forms of collaboration between physicians and patients within the parameters of insurance coverage. There is little question, though, that within the last few decades decision making has shifted away from physician paternalism toward greater involvement if not autonomy on the part of patients (McKeown et al. 2002). However, insofar as some physicians find it difficult to yield clinical control and some patients prefer that physicians decide on medical matters, shared decision making may be an abstract ideal in many cases.[19] Shared decision making is legislated, in part, by the requirement for informed consent

[19] McKeown et al. (2002) found that in nonspecific medical situations patients from a disadvantaged population indicated a desire for slightly less than equal control in decision making, whereas residents believed that patients should have a more than equal role. Conversely, in certain specific medical situations, patients wanted equal and residents wanted more control, whereas in other specific situations their desire for control was in agreement (more for patients, less for residents). In all situations, both patients and residents had a strong desire for information sharing. In some cases, information was more important to patients than actual control over decisions.

before any procedure. Obtaining informed consent is good practice, at any rate, in a litigious society, especially one in which buyers rule. Accordingly, how to develop shared decision making is part and parcel of communication training. It is well placed under the broad rubric of physician–patient relationships because shared decision making goes beyond information sharing. A large part of a physician's ability to engage in shared decision making rests on empathy – drawing out and understanding patients' preferences and values – as well as on recognizing one's own preferences, values, and limits of knowledge. This situation occurs in the medical domain regardless of CAM. So, a patient's interest in CAM may be no more than another instance of or vehicle for shared decision making. Discussions about alternative medicine may also raise for the first time tensions in the practice of shared decision making. In other words, the issue of CAM is a venue for revealing the quality of the physician–patient relationship. At the same time, physicians who themselves have experience or knowledge of alternative therapies know the role and value of self-empowerment in many of these therapies, as well as what particular therapies may or may not do to enhance a patient's sense of self.

The idea behind much of CAM is preventive health care, maintenance of well-being, and improved healing. For instance, echinacea keeps the flu at bay; yoga and tai chi loosen stiff muscles and keep people fit; acupuncture eases pain; and reiki and meditation maintain physical, mental, and emotional balance. Research, as discussed in Chapter 5, is testing these and other claims. CAM is widely seen as an adjunct to conventional medicine, as I note throughout the book, but the supporting role it plays in health care can also contribute to reduced medical costs. There are only a few cost–benefit studies on CAM available thus far – studies of safety and efficacy must come first. What they tell us is promising, however. One cardiosurgeon who employs music therapy and energy healing during surgery claims that his patients heal faster and have shorter lengths of hospital stay (Oz, Whitworth, and Liu 1998). In controlled clinical trials, patients who use stress management techniques, guided imagery, and therapeutic massage improve biological functioning and/or leave the hospital sooner than control groups. Both outcomes have significant cost-effectiveness implications (Sobel 2000). Much thought will have to go into cost–benefit analyses as more are mounted because they run the risk of focusing on the capacity of CAM to withstand off-loading, that is, of investigating the extent to which MCOs can use alternative medicine to delay treatment. CAM makes a greater contribution to chronic care than to acute care. MCOs falter when they delay urgent care and, once again, CAM's role in acute care is secondary to and supportive of medical treatment and the healing process that follows it. CAM can also play another role by assisting MCOs in the prioritization of health care resources. If certain therapies are wisely used to help healthier or less ill patients stay that way, MCOs could use their resources more effectively in treating patients who are sicker. Whether this practice becomes a form of off-loading or further exacerbates delays in treatment requires further research, along with all these speculations. To avoid the risk of using CAM to "skim the cream" and to make it a true partner, whether within an MCO or any other delivery format, CAM must be well and fully integrated into a comprehensive system of health care. Chapter 7 examines the development of integrative medicine in greater detail.

There is no question that physicians are dissatisfied with corporate health care, but it is not at all clear that their interest in CAM is a reaction against the new system of social relations in MCOs. Instead, I would suggest that both physicians and MCOs may be turning to CAM for more positive reasons. Physicians may be finding that what they have lost in their relations with patients, regardless of whether this loss is directly attributable to managed care, can be rediscovered and nurtured through learning about CAM and discussing it with patients who are so inclined. MCOs may also find that their lost mission can be revived through inclusion of CAM in the project of health care. There is yet one more way in which CAM can be a restorative vehicle for physicians. Not only can it lead them to reexamine their relations with patients, but it may also be involved in a turn inward by individual physicians who are allowing their spirituality to become part of their practice of the art of medicine.

## THE ART OF HEALING

Some physicians may be changing their attitudes toward CAM for primarily defensive or instrumental reasons – to keep up with their patients, to improve their relations with patients and enhance patient satisfaction, and/or to protect patients from possible harm or fraud (Table 4.3). At this point, we can only speculate about the circumstances whereby increased knowledge about CAM softens an initially

TABLE 4.3. *Why Are Physicians Interested in CAM?*

---

The Art of Healing
- There are more courses on CAM and healing.
- There is growing interest in the link between spirituality and health.
- There is growing debate about a physician's role in spirituality.
- In learning about patients' spirituality, physicians learn about patients' interests in CAM.
- In learning about patients' interests in CAM, physicians learn about patients' spirituality.

---

defensive posture and positively influences physicians' behaviors and attitudes toward their patients and health care in general. We do know, however, that some physicians are more genuinely interested in CAM, and a growing number are themselves becoming practitioners.

There is also rising interest in CAM among medical students. Medical schools are responding affirmatively to them, as well as to the changing scene in health care. In a 1997–1998 survey, 64% of the medical schools responding offered some form of education in CAM (Wetzel, Eisenberg, and Kaptchuk 1998).[20] By 2000, 91 of all (125) medical schools in the United States included CAM in required courses, 64 offered CAM as a stand-alone elective, and 32 included CAM as part of an elective; some schools included CAM in more than one type of course (Wetzel, Eisenberg, and Kaptchuk 1998; Bhattacharya 2000). Also, almost three-fourths of the 50 pharmacy schools responding to a 1998 survey said they offered coursework in herbal medicine or some other area of CAM (Rowell and Kroll 1998). The surveys on alternative medicine in medical schools reported tremendous heterogeneity and diversity in content, format, and requirements in the courses. In the main, these are general courses on the philosophy of and research on specific modalities; they are not training courses. There are no formal guidelines systematically in place yet for CAM courses; however, a number of medical associations have developed guidelines and are encouraging medical schools to adopt them, despite an AMA report

---

[20] There are 125 medical schools in the United States; 117 (94%) responded to this mail survey. Of the 123 courses reported, 84 (68%) were stand-alone electives, 38 (31%) were part of required courses, and 1 was part of an elective.

saying that medical schools should be free to design their own courses (Wetzel, Eisenberg, Kaptchuk 1998).[21]

It is not surprising that lack of standardization would breed inconsistencies in the quality of these courses. One critic, who conducted an unpublished survey, condemned them for being "ideologically or advocacy-based" and for failing to adopt a critical stance for evidence of efficacy of CAM (Sampson 2001, 250).[22] One is hard-pressed to find disagreement that courses on CAM should emphasize scientific research. Curiously, however, in response to a survey question, "what methods might best prepare you to advise patients on the use" of alternative medicine, first-year medical students in a large, public, Midwestern school rated observation of alternative medical practitioners (58%) and hands-on experience with patients in clinical settings (46%) higher than articles on clinical trials (32%) and lectures (30%) (Greiner, Murray, and Kallail 2000, 233). These methods are not mutually exclusive; nevertheless, some medical students may be as interested in experiential, informal knowledge as in formal, science-based knowledge.

What medical students are seeking may be similar to what experienced physicians are seeking when they attend continuing education courses on CAM and read the growing literature on its many modalities – knowledge that will help them to keep up with the times and be better doctors by providing informed responses to patients' questions and by listening empathically to their patients' needs, desires, and values. Although formal knowledge about CAM is becoming increasingly important to experienced physicians and those in training, another kind of knowledge – call it emotive or intuitive understanding – is also becoming important. Witness, for example, the increasing number of medical school courses on the link between spirituality and health.[23]

---

[21] The Association of American Medical Colleges, the Society of Teachers of Family Medicine, and the American Public Health Association have all developed separate but similar guidelines (cf Kligler et al. 2000).

[22] This author outlined the topics covered in a course he teaches on CAM at Stanford Medical School. It emphasizes critical thinking about claims of proof and disproof and developing tools to investigate these claims.

[23] The Rosenthal Center at Columbia University maintains the most comprehensive database in the U.S. on CAM and CAM-related courses. It indicates that about 20% of medical school courses are now devoted to the topic of spirituality and health (http://cpmcnet.columbia.edu/dept/rosenthal).

Studies on the healing power of spirituality, such as those discussed in Chapter 2, have piqued the interest of the medical profession. Indeed, surveys reveal a widespread belief among physicians that spiritual well-being is an important factor in health (Ellis, Vinson, and Ewigman 1999; Wilson et al. 2000). Judging by the increasing number of articles in mainstream medical journals on spirituality in medicine, the topic has expanded beyond healing to include the role of physicians in addressing and responding to patients' spirituality. An oft-cited study of hospital inpatients reported that 70% believed physicians should consider patients' spiritual needs, 37% wanted their physicians to discuss religious beliefs with them more often, 68% said their physicians had never discussed religious beliefs with them, and 48% wanted their physicians to pray with them (King and Bushwick 1994). In light of reports like this, physicians have begun to debate exactly what they should do. Some advocate that insofar as spirituality promotes health it is a legitimate part of clinical practice, and physicians should become comfortable addressing the basic spiritual/religious needs of their patients and including a religious history as part of the initial patient assessment (Larimore 2001). Mainstream medical journals seem to have taken note of this sentiment because they are providing "how-to" advice. Some articles suggest general guidelines that include developing self-awareness of one's own spiritual perspectives and becoming familiar with the religious worldviews of cultural groups in one's patient population (Barnes et al. 2000). Other articles suggest using such open-ended questions as "Are there aspects of your religion or spirituality you would like me to keep in mind as I care for you?" (Dehaven 2001, 374). Still others offer explicit questions that physicians can use to conduct a "spiritual assessment" as part of a medical interview (Anandarajah and Hight 2001). Even among those who agree in general that physicians should discuss spiritual issues, there is disagreement about physicians praying with their patients or offering spiritual counseling. Those who support physicians praying with their patients distinguish between physician-led prayer, which is not advised, and patient-led prayer, which is difficult to refuse when patients request that physicians join with them (Koenig 2000). Those who disagree that spiritual counseling is within the domain of doctoring fear that physicians may impose their views on vulnerable patients.

Despite their interest, many physicians remain uncomfortable with the spiritual dimension of their job. A growing number of continuing education courses devoted to the topic are now available for physicians who are simply unsure about their communication and empathic skills. Uncertainty among some physicians about their spiritual role is related to concern about opening a Pandora's box filled with patients' emotional complications or introducing bias into scientific medical judgment (Barnes et al. 2000, 903). Many physicians admonish their colleagues to recognize their limits. Physicians are not trained to perceive "clues that a patient may be struggling with spiritual issues" and, in fact, may be responsive to psychosocial clues in general as little as 20% of the time (Dehaven 2001, 373). Cautious physicians favor leaving religious matters to chaplains or family-preferred spiritual care providers. Other physicians are openly hostile to "facile...ill-defined...misguided...inappropriate [and] simplistic" proposals to link spirituality and medicine that result in the "denigration" of both (Lawrence 2002, 74). There is also an interesting debate about the role of science in this issue. Although many physicians inevitably call for more studies, a few argue that an instrumental approach to religion tends to trivialize it by reducing it to its psychosocial dimensions and equating it with other cultural practices. In this view, religion "does not need science to justify its existence or appeal" (Sloan et al. 2000, 1915).

Whether spirituality, especially in its more religious sense, can be considered part of CAM is the subject of much debate. If the two have their unique domains, they are nevertheless closely linked, by a slippery slope at the least. If physicians are learning that they must be sensitive to and respect patients' spirituality, they are learning at the same time the value of understanding and respecting patients' interests in CAM. Some physicians who heed suggestions that they learn about the religious diversity of their patients may encounter the subject of prana or chi or the personage of a shaman or similar kind of healer. Or they may have to confront the difference between rosary beads and crystal stones or prayers and mantras. In some ways, it may be easier for physicians to cross the boundary between medicine and healing through spirituality because its practices are more commonplace; how physicians contend with faith healing or voodooism no doubt varies by individual and circumstance. In the same vein, some critiques of and ethical objections to studies on distant healing or intercessory prayer claim that researchers have no way of assuring that those who pray are performing their roles as required – that is, to benefit patients.

Alternatively, it may be easier for physicians to confront their dilemmas about their spiritual roles by coming to terms first with their attitudes toward CAM. Some physicians will accept the kind of research on CAM discussed in Chapter 6, especially those studies on modalities that entail elements of belief or subjectivity, as confirming that science and nonscience are compatible. Others will see this research as confirming their view that science and nonscience are separate domains, each with specialized practitioners who can respectfully interact without necessarily integrating. These conclusions are as applicable to spirituality in the more religious sense as to CAM. And the exercise may lead some physicians to consider their relationship to their patients in a new light. As Waldfogel (1997, 973) put it: "The modern health care provider is a powerful therapeutic agent in the clinical setting. [But the] physician's power to heal within the patient–practitioner relationship is no less magical and mysterious than the dance of the shaman, the charm of the witch doctor, or the water of Lourdes."

As they face the issues raised by both CAM and spirituality, physicians are learning more than methods of treating patients. Exposure to CAM and spirituality is drawing physicians out of their strictly medical confines and encouraging them to examine their predispositions and values toward issues their forefathers took for granted and rarely considered, even though these values are at the core of the medical profession – empathy, above all. This chapter has focused on the relationship between physicians and patients as an indicator of physicians' interests and abilities in social and emotional understanding. It implicates a kind of knowledge that differs from the usual fare for physicians, but it also enhances an individual's capacity to be a physician. In Chapter 5, we will see how the centrality of formal knowledge may be hampering the acquisition of these broader and looser approaches to health care.

# 5

# Medical Research: Science and Interpretation

Do herbs heal? Does acupuncture relieve pain? How do these and other modalities work? Why aren't they effective for everyone with the same condition? These questions and a host of others motivated major new research initiatives in the 1990s, most of them funded by the NIH. This research has begun the process of legitimizing CAM in American medicine. At the same time, however, certain types of CAM have become delegitimized. Some have been shown to be harmful, others useless. This chapter explores how processes of legitimation and delegitimation have evolved within the political and, most important, scientific institutions of American society. As social institutions, government and science each have distinctive sets of norms and values and both affect and are affected by their social and cultural contexts (Zuckerman 1988).

In 1991, the Senate Appropriations Committee held hearings on the use of "unconventional medicine" in the United States. The result was the establishment at the NIH of, first, an advisory panel on unconventional medical practices, and then, officially in 1992, the OAM, which began operations with a budget of $2 million.[1] The politics behind the

---

[1] The charter for what was first called the Office of Unconventional Medical Practices is in Section 404E of the NIH Revitalization Act of 1991. PL 102-170 provides $2 million in funding for FY 1992. The NIH Revitalization Act of 1993 established a Program Advisory Committee to advise the director of the new OAM. This committee (many of whose members were drawn from the original advisory committee) officially began in 1994.

creation of the OAM are a classic example of the vagaries of legislative initiative, highlighting in this case the role of individuals and their personal interests. Senator Thomas R. Harkin, a Democrat from Iowa and Chair of the Appropriations Committee, had recently been converted to the benefits of alternative medicine when he used bee pollen to treat his allergies. Similar stories, aired in committee hearings, convinced other senators that the NIH might be in need of an external nudge to enrich its understanding of health. It was no secret that the NIH leadership disapproved of the new office that linked research scientists with "believers" (Young 1998, 281). Although there was "an undercurrent of anger and distrust" of orthodox science among panel members (Brown 1992), reputable academics and MDs were selected to lead and participate in a series of preparatory workshops. The first, held in September 1992, resulted in a major publication that provided a "baseline of information on the state of alternative medicine . . . [to further] the dialogue between the alternative-complementary communities and the biomedical research establishment" (Workshop on Alternative Medicine 1995, vii). By October 1992, the OAM had its first director, Dr. Joseph Jacobs, in place, and the work of planning a research agenda began.

The early years of the OAM were beset by tensions between supporters of various schools of thought regarding what exactly the new office should research and, more bitterly, how that research should be conducted. Jacobs and other medical and research professionals insisted that rigorous scientific methods were necessary to establish the safety and efficacy of any CAM modality. Senator Harkin's appointees on the advisory panel favored "quick field studies that would validate alternative treatments" and bypassing the "excessive" deliberations and safeguards imposed by more rigorous studies (Young 1998, 285). They wanted information about and access to certain therapies to be available to the public as soon as possible.[2] In one of its later Fact Sheets, the NCCAM elides this early dissension by noting that "the congressional mandate [was] to study and disseminate information about the safety and effectiveness of CAM therapies and facilitate the integration of safe

---

[2] There are parallels here to the perennial debate, both between Congress and the NIH as well as within the NIH, that hounds scientific research: what should the balance be between basic and applied research?

and effective treatments into an interdisciplinary health care delivery system" (NCCAM 2001, 4).

The fundamental argument over the virtues of speed versus rigor in research continues to this day, and it has both steeled prior dispositions and produced several efforts to bridge sides and soften stances. Stubborn divisions marked the early years of OAM development, and mounting tensions eventually led Jacobs to resign in September 1994. For a time it seemed that politics and the power of the purse would win over science – Harkin had threatened to allocate new funding specifically for the purpose of speeding up studies (Young 1998, 290). However, a new director, Dr. Wayne B. Jonas, appointed in January 1995, reaped the benefits of timing and ushered in a promising new wave of research that both assuaged Harkin's allies and reinforced the centrality of science. Among the major initiatives were the research centers that are the focus of Chapter 6. Jonas tried to reach out to both sides by proposing that scientific rigor could be "flexible" and "creative," and that it was possible to "bring together the best of healing with the best of science" (*Complementary and Alternative Medicine at the NIH* 1995, 5). However, his belief that new approaches promised to produce "new kinds of knowledge that could transform science" may not have entirely pleased the medical community (Young 1998, 292). Medical researchers embrace creativity in research design, but prefer that it be confined to the introductory and discussion sections of reports, and not muddy the methods (The Standards of Reporting Trials Group 1994, 1930).

This chapter focuses on the debate over methods of research. The heart of the issue is the question of what constitutes evidence. All scientists hold that evidence results from the application of scientific methods of research that include the deductive construction of hypotheses and experimental testing. The medical community has refined the scientific method and imposed a particular form of it – RCTs – on biomedical research. This method of investigation was declared the "gold standard" in 1962 by the FDA, which will not approve a medical product for licensing and/or marketing before an RCT has been conducted.[3] Furthermore, the medical community has indicated that if CAM is to

---

[3] On occasion, the FDA approves the use of trials that do not conform to RCT protocols. The U.S. Code of Federal Regulations 21, Section 860.7 allows the Commissioner

be recognized as a legitimate complement of medical treatment, its safety and efficacy must be proven through rigorous scientific evaluation – that is, testing by means of RCTs.

However, the RCT method has limitations. Even in medical research, it is far from a perfect tool; accordingly, debates have arisen about RCTs, and modifications of its form are being developed in certain kinds of medical research. When applied to the study of CAM, certain limitations of RCTs are amplified and confounded. In particular, not all participants in trials of certain CAM therapies can be blinded (in most cases, the practitioner cannot be blinded, nor, in some cases, can the patient). Nor do all CAM therapies lend themselves well to a placebo control. A question that arises, then, is what constitutes a flexible and creative use of RCTs (to use Jonas' words) or, perhaps, of the scientific method? How can research both maintain scientific rigor yet rise above the constraints of RCTs? The discussion below begins with some basics, proceeds to issues under contention, and then turns to the significance of the discussion for both CAM and medicine, namely, the current emphasis on evidence-based medicine in the practice of health care.

THE SCIENTIFIC METHOD OF RESEARCH IN MEDICINE

Certain criteria guide scientific research across the academic disciplines. In developing an experimental design, researchers must first specify their research question and the population and treatment to be studied. They must then develop appropriate methodological techniques to assure that the purported causal relationship between the intervention (or independent variable) and the outcome (or dependent variable) is as free as possible from extraneous factors, above all, bias. These extraneous factors must in some way be "controlled for" to eliminate their intrusion. How researchers do this depends on their research question, to be sure, but it also involves preferences and predilections. Nevertheless, certain criteria regarding methods have become so standard in medical research as to be obligatory in order to say that the research is "methodologically sound."

of the FDA or a designee to determine on a case-by-case method whether nonstandard or other types of evidence are suitable.

The core feature of an RCT is random assignment of a study population into at least two groups. One group, the experimental group, receives the treatment being tested; the other, the control group, receives either another treatment or a placebo. Random assignment to the two groups advances the internal validity of the experiment by, presumably, equally distributing the effect of extraneous (and sometimes unknown) factors that might account for the treatment outcome. For instance, if the study population is breast cancer patients, random distribution helps to assure that the experimental and control groups will be similar with regard to medical history, current health status, age, and a number of other factors that could in and of themselves influence treatment outcomes. Some researchers assume that randomization, especially of large numbers of participants, suffices to control for equal distribution of relevant confounding factors.[4] Other researchers carefully examine their two study groups to confirm that equal distribution has indeed occurred, and if not, they may incorporate additional controls, again depending on the research question and the researcher's assessment of methodological rigor. Over time, certain strategies have developed to enhance the reliability of similitude between the experimental and control groups (Leber and Davis 1998). For example, in selecting the initial group of subjects, researchers may exclude patients with certain possibly confounding characteristics, such as severe illness, concomitant illnesses, advanced age, and so on. A major problem arises, however. The more selective the initial criteria are for participation, the more the external validity of the study's findings is jeopardized, because the study population becomes less representative of the population as a whole, even the population with the illness being treated.

Related to the technique of randomization into two groups is the expectation that relevant participants are unaware or "blind" to the assignment, both before and after the treatment begins. There are three main participants in a clinical trial: patient, clinician, and investigator. The idea of blindness was originally intended to refer to patients (but as we will see, patients are not always blind in an RCT). The clinician

---

[4] Among the many threats to internal validity are changes in policy or personnel during the study; undetected problems in instrumentation or calibration; and attrition, dropout, or noncompliance by patients (Gatchel and Maddrey 1998). It is unlikely that randomization alone can control for all these, but the larger the number of patients the more likely it is that confounding variables are factored out.

administering a treatment should also be blind (but as we will see, this is not always possible either).[5] The investigator who is evaluating the effect of the treatments on patients should always not know which patients are receiving the treatment under study and which are receiving the comparison treatment or a placebo. When at least two of these participants are blind, the trial is commonly referred to as double-blind. But it is sometimes unclear before reading the section on research methods who, exactly, is blind. Since the investigator is always blind, either the patient, or the clinician, or both can also be blind.[6] Muddled specification is exacerbated by statistical techniques that allow researchers to factor out inconsistencies in large trials.

Although an RCT does not require any particular population size, most trials attempt to recruit a sufficiently large group to allow for greater generalizability, or external validity, of the results of RCTs. Enrolling insufficient numbers of patients may result in a finding of no difference between treatments when in fact there is one, or a finding of equal value when in fact one treatment is superior. Having large numbers of randomized subjects also facilitates the use of appropriate tests of statistical significance. Small clinical trials are nevertheless useful in research, as long as they demonstrate methodologically rigorous controls (Sackett and Cook 1993, 25). Their value tends to focus on the early stages of clinical trials, when information is being built about the safety and potential effectiveness of a new treatment.[7]

---

[5] It is standard practice to have certified personnel administer and/or standardize the treatment in order to control for extraneous circumstances that may occur, for example, when subjects take a pill at home and do not fully follow instructions with regard to the liquid to be used when swallowing the pill, the time of day to take it, and so on.

[6] Park et al. (2001) reviewed 48 articles on RCTs of nonpharmaceutical interventions published in leading journals. There was no consistency in the use of the term "double blind." Even single blind was used to refer to either patient/subject or clinician or investigator/data analyst. Because of the potential for confusion, CAM researchers Caspi, Millen, and Sechrest (2000) coined the term "dual blind" to refer to studies in which the provider of the treatment under study is not blind but the patient and investigator/data analyst/evaluator are. They argue that double blind should refer to a study in which the patient and provider are blind, with the assumption that the investigator is always blind. When all the participants – patient, clinician, investigator – are blind, the study should technically be called "triple blind," but this practice is rare in medical and even current CAM research.

[7] A comprehensive list of the features of an RCT includes random assignment; experimental and control groups; carefully defined populations, interventions and endpoints; double blinded; prospective; adequate size; and approved in advance by an

For decades there was little criticism of the RCT in the medical literature, enabling its ascent to the pinnacle of research methodologies. Recently, however, the imperfections of the RCT have become the subject of greater scrutiny. It is worthwhile to review some of the concerns that are beginning to appear in medical journals because they raise issues pertinent to understanding the applicability of RCTs to research on CAM. I will focus on the two most fundamental features of an RCT – randomization and the existence of a control group – and add consideration of blinding, which is a factor central to each.

RANDOMIZATION

Randomization is an unpredictable mathematical sequencing, in this case, of the order in which the individuals participating in a study are assigned to two or more groups. By definition the assignment sequence is unknown to all involved, or at least should be. Studies have shown, however, that true randomization is "rare" (Schulz 1996, 597). For various reasons, human nature being the main culprit, someone – the investigator, the clinician, the patient, or anyone else directly involved in the study – frequently discovers who is being placed in which group. Sometimes, after an initial randomization procedure, the groups are manipulated so as to maximize internal validity (elimination of confounding factors), but at a cost to external validity (generalizability). From the beginning, then, the problem of selection bias can compromise RCTs to some unknown degree. Weak randomization can result in either exaggerated or diluted effects of the treatment being investigated. One study that was attuned to these potential problems discovered that even before the start of an experimental treatment, patients' well-being improved measurably because of their enhanced hopes and expectations (Kemler and de Vet 2000).

Despite its potential for contamination, little methodology exists for the detection of selection bias.[8] Published studies do not commonly

Institutional Review Board and monitored by a Data Safety and Control Board (Brody 1997, 602). It is generally agreed that the existence of a treatment and a control group is the most important of these features. Small clinical trials can conform to these features.

[8] However, some scholars have begun to develop various statistical techniques that promise to enhance the ability of researchers to detect selection bias (Berger and Exner 1999).

discuss the methodology used to assign participants, so readers have no way of detecting weaknesses in the quality of randomization. There is widespread agreement that inadequate reporting of a number of items related to the internal validity of an RCT (sample size, type of randomization used, how intervention assignment was concealed until the treatment began) reduces confidence in the results, confirming the suspicion that "sloppy reporting reflects shoddy methods, and that with sloppy methods come biased results" (Schultz 1996, 596). Since the early 1980s, leading journals have been publishing guidelines, checklists, and admonitions – the most recent is the CONSORT statement (Moher, Schulz, and Altman 2001) – yet the problem persists.[9] To be sure, the criticism leveled against poor reporting of procedures used in randomization is not directed at the RCT itself or the concept of randomization, but at the lack of information that would allow readers "to estimate the likelihood that the trial results provide a valid (unbiased) estimate of the 'truth' – something we can observe" (The Standards of Reporting Trials Group 1994, 1927).

Arguably, the paramount criticism of RCTs, waged especially by physicians, is their limited usefulness to clinical practice. The main problem is the selectivity of the study populations. The design of RCTs calls for the recruitment of patients with very specific characteristics – in fact, the more specific the better so as to enhance the internal validity of the experiment. Prerandomization run-in periods are increasingly being used to select or exclude patients in clinical trials. Although the effects of these run-in periods have not been systematically examined, one study analyzed illustrative examples of reports of clinical trials in which run-in periods were used to exclude subjects who were either noncompliant, "placebo responders," could not tolerate active drugs, or did not respond to active drugs (Pablos-Méndez, Barr, and Shea 1998). It found that while the reported results of the trials were valid, they

---

[9] An international group of clinical trial researchers, statisticians, epidemiologists, and biomedical editors revised and updated earlier statements to help authors to improve reporting of RCTs and to enable readers to understand a trial's conduct and assess the validity of the results. There is now a 22-item checklist "selected because empirical evidence indicates that not reporting the information is associated with biased estimates of treatment effect, or because the information is essential to judge reliability or relevance of the findings" (Moher, Schultz, and Altman 2001, 1987). Also, a revised flow diagram "depicts information from 4 stages of a trial (enrollment, intervention allocation, follow-up, and analysis."

overestimated the benefits and underestimated the risks of treatment. Moreover, because of the selectivity of subjects in RCTs, clinicians rarely see patients with precisely matched characteristics. They must decide for themselves, therefore, whether differences in, for example, severity of illness, personal medical history, other concomitant illness, and so on warrant application of the RCT findings to their individual patients. The specificity of the study population raises questions about the efficacy of the treatment under study because the RCT offers only an "average value" of efficacy for an average patient (Feinstein and Horwitz 1997, 531). Whether it can or should be generalized to any individual patient is to be judged by the physician.

Randomization is not always necessary or desirable. There are non-randomized studies that investigate the effects of one treatment on one group of patients in one place. These investigations, which can be large or small, are generally used in pilot studies, that is, the early phases of research. They may be replicated on additional patients in the same or different locations to test for generalizability. The findings may lead to the development of RCTs if warranted and feasible.

## EXPERIMENTAL AND CONTROL GROUPS

The second core feature of an RCT, the designation of an experimental and a control group, is plagued by some of the same problems as randomization. The RCT is inherently a comparative investigation, usually of the effectiveness of a new treatment. The main question that arises is, what should it be compared with? Most researchers prefer, whenever possible, to compare the new treatment with a placebo administered to the control group. An important literature is developing on the issue of placebo – as a control *and* as a treatment itself. Throughout recorded medical history, physicians have been administering sugar pills, bread pills, colored water, and so on, in fact, more frequently "than all other medicines put together," to provide "peace of mind" or "more to please than to benefit the patient" (Kaptchuk 1998, 1722).[10] If not entirely inactive, placebos were considered innocent

[10] The word "placebo" derives from the Latin word for "I shall please." It was used in church vespers for the dead. By the 12th century, laypersons were being paid to sing the vespers and, as a result, placebo came to mean "false consolation."

at least. However, with the onset of the era of scientific investigation in the 1940s, the placebo transformed from a "humble humbug" to "an entity with occult-like powers that could mimic potent drugs" (1722). Studies attempted both to specify and to quantify the effect of placebos, and the findings were disturbing. Beecher (1955, 1602–6) concluded that the influence of placebos is not merely psychological; they "can produce gross physical change" and, in some cases, can even be more effective than the known pharmacological drug. By the time RCTs became the norm in medical research, the "placebo effect" came to represent all the "nonspecific" effects that did not depend on the treatment actually under study (Kaptchuk 1998, 1723). Advocates of RCTs began to argue that the only way to capture and control the distortion inherent in the "placebo" effect was through the blinded and randomized protocol of an RCT.

An axiom now permeates medical research: once a clinical trial is underway, it is essential that, whenever possible, all the relevant participants remain unaware of who is receiving the experimental treatment and who is receiving the comparison. A failure in blinding can compromise the study in unforeseen ways. If patients, treatment providers, or both come to know the placement group – for instance, when side effects occur – they are supposed to disclose their awareness. They may not, however, because disclosure generally results in withdrawal from the study, and this either denies patients the possibility of benefiting from a new treatment or contributing to its testing, or it may result in low participation rates that may compromise the study's generalizability.

The reasoning behind the insistence on blinded administration of the treatment under study and a placebo involves a sleight of hand, however. Insofar as a trial is randomized and the administration of the treatment and placebo is blind, it is assumed that all the factors and variables in the "placebo effect" are themselves randomly distributed or averaged and thereby of limited significance, if not insignificant, in the results. The problem with this reasoning is that the "placebo effect" ranges from 0% to 100%, on both the positive and negative (nocebo) sides (McQuay, Carroll, and Moore 1995). Also, patients may react differently to the same placebo administered at different stages in a clinical trial (Reilly 2000). Moreover, there is an assumption that the placebo effect is monolithic and works in the same direction as the treatment under study. However, there are several factors involved in the placebo effect, many of which are unknown, and there is no basis for assuming their unidirectionality. In addition, the specific and nonspecific effects of placebo may not be additive, as is commonly assumed (Eskinazi 1998a, 678). The placebo effect is not, in other words, a mere "dummy" variable, as it has come to be known. It has a life of its own.

Nevertheless, the prevailing assumptions about the placebo have become routinized. Based on them, studies have found, for instance, that on average about one-third of the people taking a placebo in a clinical trial report a benefit. Statistical techniques have been developed to take this estimate into account, eliminating its interference and refining the analytical power of an RCT. RCTs now require that treatments under study must perform significantly better than a placebo before they are declared effective. To say, however, that a treatment performs "no better than placebo" is not necessarily disproving the efficacy of the treatment, but this understanding appeals to a broader appreciation of the placebo effect, which is not common in medical research.

Recently, some researchers have begun to question the basic assumptions of RCTs and have turned their attention to direct investigation of the placebo effect, untangling its diverse features and multiple dimensions as active variables that are not only masked in RCTs but significantly affect the findings. These new studies are revealing some of the innumerable factors that play a role in the placebo effect. Among them are such variables as the natural course of a disease; unidentified parallel interventions, ranging from other treatments to the counseling that occurs in any clinical trial; information given in the consent form; patients' knowledge about the trial and/or the treatment under study; attitudes or latent suggestiveness of doctors and those who administer the study treatments; attitudes and expectations of patients; suggestibility of the patient; the meaning that patients associate with treatment; concomitant conditions of patients, including stress or mood; a patient's prior experience with treatments and possible concomitant conditioning; culture; and so on, including the many factors that change over the course of the study. Any of these variables can have a positive or negative effect, ranging from 0% to 100%, on the outcome of the study.

To elaborate a few of these variables, some studies have built on a 1955 study suggesting that "an injection is thought to be more effective than something that is taken by mouth" (Lasagna 1955), and investigated the effect of type of treatment, specifically, whether a device or procedure produces a heightened placebo effect compared with a pill. Most studies have found that they do (Kaptchuk et al. 2000). Also, placebos that people think are brand-name drugs or powerful drugs such as morphine work better than placebos disguised as generic drugs or common drugs such as aspirin (Christensen 2001). Also, different conditions produce different placebo effects; for instance, people with pain and depression experience greater placebo effects than people with other conditions (Richardson 1994). The context of a clinical trial is also important. One study asked "whether patients rate the efficacy and toxicity of a drug therapy differently in the setting of a placebo control trial as opposed to the same drug therapy administered in a comparative drug trial" (Rochon et al. 1999, 114). The answer was yes. Evaluating published studies, the authors found that in a placebo trial patients are more likely to rate the drug under study as "less efficacious" and "less toxic" than when they are in a comparative drug trial. The presumption is that patients know they are receiving some form of active treatment in a comparative drug trial, whereas in a placebo trial "there is up to a 50% chance that they are receiving an inert therapy" (114). In short, placebos may be pharmacologically benign, but they are arguably not clinically inert.[11]

What are conscientious researchers to do with all this information? How do CAM researchers in particular get a handle on the relationship between a certain CAM modality and placebo? The questions are important because CAM therapies are often dismissed as equivalent

---

[11] The controversial reintroduction of sham surgery is also confirming the power of placebo. It has been unclear whether surgery itself is a placebo or whether the expectations surrounding it influence the outcome or both (Johnson 1994), although there is considerable debate about the inertness of the sham, let alone its harmlessness. Thus far, studies of sham surgery have focused on patients with Parkinson's disease. In one clinical trial, 40 patients had tiny holes drilled into their skulls; one-half received the experimental injection of fetal cells, and one-half received nothing. A year later, 3 people in the placebo group reported improvement in their symptoms (Stolberg 1999). These experiments are proceeding despite the conundrum of ethical issues because existing treatments for Parkinson's are ineffective, and RCTs are needed to demonstrate the efficacy of fetal cell injections. For more on ethical questions in sham surgery, see Macklin (1999). It is interesting to note that clinical trials are not always preceded by basic scientific (laboratory) studies. This is especially the case when there is urgency in finding a treatment.

to placebo. Ernst and Resch (1995, 551) suggested that if one were to treat the various contributing factors as a "perceived placebo effect," one could subtract them from the response observed in the placebo group of an RCT to obtain the "true placebo effect." Although an improvement on the assumption that on average one-third of patients respond positively to placebo, this approach still begs the question of how researchers can capture and measure all nonspecific placebo effects to get closer to the truth. However, the point of the exercise for Ernst and Resch was to establish the distinction between placebo and no treatment. Unfortunately, few studies have both a placebo and no treatment group because the understanding that a placebo may not be inert has become lost over time – at least, in medical research. The approach also points to the possibility of different magnitudes of placebo response as well as of response to the treatment under study. Although "the observed effect of drug administration is ... a combination of the pharmacological effects and the placebo effects," few researchers today appreciate that "active drugs [themselves] always act, in part, as placebos" (Dinnerstein, Lowenthal, and Blitz 1966, 103).

A recent, highly publicized study analyzed 114 published trials comparing placebo groups with groups that were given no treatment. It found that the rate of improvement was about the same (Hrobjartsson and Gotzsche 2001). However, placebos appeared to have some benefit in trials that used continuous subjective outcomes and treated pain. Perhaps because the studies were weak and inconsistent, the authors conclude that there is no justification for the use of placebos outside clinical trials, but we should emphasize the word "outside." A major contribution of the study was to establish the importance of including a no treatment group in clinical trials, something that has been rare.

The ethics of using placebos in clinical trials has also raised issues that can encumber research. A question that can reasonably be asked is, if a known treatment exists, wouldn't any doctor "wish to know whether a new treatment is more, or less, effective than the old, not whether it is more effective than nothing?" (Hill 1963, 1043). In certain situations, it is neither possible nor desirable to administer a placebo. Above all, it is unethical to assign certain patients to a (presumed) no-treatment placebo group when a known treatment exists and could benefit or save lives. Certain cancer patients, for instance, must receive chemotherapy. Various research designs have been developed to tackle the dilemma. For instance, based on informed consent, patients who are willing to participate in a study may be given a known, commonly used drug whose efficacy has been established or the new experimental drug whose potential efficacy has been tested only in pilot studies. Or, all the patients may receive the standard treatment and one subgroup may receive the treatment under study as an addition. These clinical trials may or may not be blinded; the participants may even choose which group they want to be in. In other words, when placebo-controlled trials are difficult or unethical, researchers develop other creative and flexible methods. Insofar as these studies are published, we can assume that they have been accepted by the medical profession.

Certain ethical principles contained in the Declaration of Helsinki, authored by the World Medical Association's Committee on Medical Ethics, can and have been interpreted as effectively proscribing the use of placebo as a control in a clinical study when a proven treatment exists. However, the AMA, the World Health Organization, and the Council for International Organizations of Medical Sciences reject the position that the declaration bars placebo-controlled trials when proven therapy is available (Temple and Ellenberg 2000, 456). The declaration states:

In any medical study, every patient – including those of a control group, if any – should be assured of the best proven diagnostic and therapeutic method. This does not exclude the use of inert placebo in studies where no proven diagnostic or therapeutic method exists . . . . In research on man [sic], the interest of science and society should never take precedence over considerations related to the well-being of the subject. (World Medical Association 1997, 926)[12]

Some commentators, employing a strict interpretation of the declaration's principles, charge that its injunctions are frequently overlooked by institutional review boards and researchers or manufacturers seeking FDA approval (Rothman and Michels 1994).[13] One could say that

---

[12] The declaration was originally drafted in 1964 and based on the Nuremberg Code. It was amended and updated in 1975, 1983, 1989, 1996, and 2000. Each time the rights of individuals in clinical trials were reaffirmed and strengthened.

[13] In describing the general characteristics of adequate and well-controlled studies, the FDA recognizes four different kinds of concurrent control – placebo, dose comparison, no treatment, and active treatment – as well as historical control. The elaboration of active treatment as concurrent control states that this comparison occurs "where the

any study participant who is not receiving the established treatment is not getting the best, proven treatment, which is unethical (Temple and Ellenberg 2000). However, instead of slipping into an antiscience stance, most researchers, review boards, and regulators have adopted a looser interpretation of the declaration's guidelines, maintaining that there are situations in which its apparent strictures can be relaxed. In particular, even though an effective (or partly effective) treatment is known, it may be withheld from the control group as long as the trial "does not place the patient at increased risk of irreversible harm or cause unacceptable discomfort" (Stein and Pincus 1999, 400). In some cases a clinical trial that includes the possibility of unpleasant side effects, such as vomiting, may be justified, but not beyond the point at which these side effects become harmful. In practice, therefore, "the line between ethical and unethical use of placebo is a matter of judgment and subject to change with medical advances" (400).

The ethical requirement of informed consent further entangles judgments about the ethics of placebo. Other than the clause on informed consent in the Declaration of Helsinki,[14] since the 1970s, all funded research in the United States involving human subjects must be approved by institutional review boards that require provisions for informed consent. It should be noted that this requirement does not apply to clinical settings in which physicians can suggest treatments to their patients or order diagnostic tests that may be invasive and uncomfortable, while providing only general information about the treatment or test and receiving only informal consent (Truog et al. 1999).[15] Although there is no question about the obligation to obtain informed consent in RCTs, research has shown that subjects respond differently when they know they may receive a placebo than when they are taking drugs in non-experimental settings (Kirsch and Rosadino 1993, 437). We can

condition treated is such that administration of placebo or no treatment would be contrary to the interest of the patient" (*U.S. Code of Federal Regulations* 2001, 151).

[14] Additional clauses elaborate procedures for cases in which subjects are in a dependent relationship to the physician or are legally incompetent and cannot grant informed consent.

[15] These authors argue that general consent could pertain to RCTs with low risk and high benefit, that specific and formalized procedures be reserved for riskier trials, and that the same reasoning be applied to doctor–patient relations in clinical settings. For a discussion of variations in court rulings regarding lapses in full physician disclosure and informed consent, see Cohen (1998, 60–2).

surmise further that when patients are told that a new treatment may have undergone only single-case trials or may have been tested only on animals or human tissues in laboratories, responses would be affected even more. All these considerations raise questions about the results (and external validity) of RCTs.

In sum, there are a number of shortcomings in the RCT. Most of the efforts aimed at improving its precision and rigor have focused on issues of internal validity. One is hard-pressed to say, however, that these efforts have resolved the criticisms leveled at the reliability of RCTs. Take, for instance, the issue of objectivity, which arises, for one, in problems of measurements. Central to the success of an RCT is the validity of the measurements used. Yet, there is no "gold standard" for the many measurement problems that vex all research. How to measure, say, pain prior to and after experimental treatment, whether to use only biological factors, how to include self-reports if these are used, and so on are all decisions based on the judgment and interpretation of the researchers. The subjectivity of researchers' decisions is rarely acknowledged. Equally obscure are the pragmatic decisions that have to be made because some measurements are more feasible than others. All these irregularities compromise the objectivity of measurements. Even clinical readings that rely on technologically-based (and therefore presumably objective) data on biological markers require some interpretation (Gatchel and Maddrey 1998, 38). The main vehicle for testing the reliability and validity of measurements is reproducibility. Once a trial has been reproduced, the objectivity of its measurements is assumed and questions about the role of interpretation in those measures fall by the wayside.

The debate about RCTs within the medical community has gained momentum recently, signaling a renewed concern with the centrality of this instrument in medical research (Herman 1995; Horton 2001). There are two interrelated parts to this concern. One part pertains to what has come to be known as the hierarchy of evidence (Table 5.1).

In the field of medicine all other research methods are considered, if not inferior, then antecedent to the RCT. Anecdotes have the least validity, although they may stimulate research questions. Case studies, which amass data on several factors over time, and observational studies, which employ different observers who use similar criteria, are useful, but primarily if and when they contribute the building blocks

TABLE 5.1. *The Hierarchy of Evidence*

---

Anecdotes
Case Studies
Observational Studies
Uncontrolled Trials
Small Randomized Clinical Trials
  • Phase I: Evaluates the safety of an experimental treatment.
  • Phase II: Assesses its clinical activity; that is, establishes that there is some efficacy.
Large Randomized Clinical Trials
  • Phase III: Determines clinical efficacy.

---

of preliminary evidence that lead to clinical trials. Both of these latter two methodologies can be either quantitative or qualitative; they can also focus on one patient at a time or several at once. Because they are not experimental, these methods, in and of themselves, are generally believed to overestimate treatment effects. However, anecdotes, case studies, and observations have value in and of themselves. Not only do they spark curiosity, but they can also be helpful in guiding clinical care. Mainstream medical journals have been publishing case and observational studies for years. Some are now publishing reports that observational studies and RCTs make similar estimates of treatment effects (Benson and Hartz 2000; Concato, Shah, and Horwitz 2000). Although not directly criticizing RCTs, the medical research community may be beginning to recognize the independent value of these alternative methods, in addition to their possible importance as building blocks in the construction of RCTs. Nevertheless, despite growing interest in methods of research that are clinically more relevant than RCTs, mainstream journals also continue to publish comments about "the considerable dangers to clinical research and even to the wellbeing of patients" emanating from studies based on anecdotes, case studies, and observations (Pocock and Elbourne 2000). These remarks also indicate that the debate will continue for some time.

A second criticism of RCTs has persisted since its inception. The logic behind the RCT contrasts the kind of knowledge obtained through scientific investigation with the everyday knowledge of clinicians, which is based on anecdotes, cases, and observations. As use of the RCT became more frequent in medical research after World War II, doctors were not only skeptical of its value for clinical decision making. They were also concerned that this method of investigation would displace the role of clinical judgment. Although the two modes of reasoning are not necessarily contradictory, they are distinct, and within institutions of scientific research, they are placed on a hierarchy. As the RCT and the scientific ethos it embodies gained ascendancy in medical research, the discomfort of physicians, especially but not only those in the more general practices, remained an undercurrent – albeit a quiet one, given the growing prestige of scientific medical research. Questions that are increasingly being raised now about the several imperfections of RCTs compound questions about the assumptions of pure objectivity in science. They return our considerations to the less tangible factors involved in any treatment – the role of intuition, experience, judgment, ideas, hopes, expectations, and so on, all of which can be said to represent a different kind of knowledge.

Several efforts are underway to restore both the integrity and the utility of gold standard research. One is the CONSORT statement, which provides a checklist for authors to help them to improve their reporting (see note 8). Another that has become very prominent is a call for what has come to be known as "evidence-based medicine." It began first and foremost as an attempt to sort methodologically sound and weak clinical trials. With closer attention to scientific methods, the value to clinicians of findings that could be certified as "evidence" was obvious, at least to the working group that set out the new course of action. Its manifesto stated that evidence-based medicine "de-emphasizes intuition, unsystematic clinical experience, and pathopsychologic rationale as sufficient grounds for clinical decision-making and stresses the examination of evidence from clinical research" (Evidence-Based Medicine Working Group 1992, 2420). The authors conceded that clinical experience and the development of clinical instincts are "a crucial and necessary part of becoming a competent physician" (2420). However, they also warned physicians that unless acquired through systematic observation and corroborated by the clinical literature, informal knowledge could be "misleading" (2421).

The proclamation stirred the old debate in medical research. Yet, this time, instead of dichotomizing and structuring hierarchically the role of science and experience (including interpretation) in medical decision making, some medical scholars attempted a reformulation of the route toward knowledge. Evidence-based medicine, in this view, consists of

integrating individual clinical experience with the best available external clinical evidence from systematic research . . . [The information clinicians use] is not restricted to randomized trials and meta-analyses . . . [It contains] clinically relevant research, often from the basic sciences of medicine, [and it includes studies of diagnostic tests, prognostic markers, and] the efficacy and safety of therapeutic, rehabilitative, and preventive regimens. (Sackett et al. 1996: 71)

Expanding on this statement, an adherent of the integrative view said that evidence-based medicine is "an approach to decision making in which the clinician uses the best evidence available, in consultation with the patient, to decide upon the option which suits that patient best" (Gray 1997, 9).

Even though the working group claimed that evidence-based medicine represented a paradigm shift, their understanding of it was less a revolution than a validation of what physicians already do. Similarly, the newer version is not saying simply that RCTs may guide physicians in the right direction, but also that clinical "problem-solving represents the art of medicine" (Kassirer 1992, 60), something physicians have known for some time. It is also saying that evidence of efficacy can be obtained from methods other than RCTs. For, "practicing evidence-based medicine involves integrating the medical professional's expertise and the patient's right to choose among diagnostic and treatment alternatives with the best available clinical evidence from systematic research" (Mulrow and Lohr 2001, 253). These statements would seem to have a greater impact on scientific medical researchers than physicians per se.

The significance of evidence-based medicine was taken one step further by the rediscovery of an earlier attempt to systematize knowledge. In 1976, a British physician, Iain Chalmers, organized a search of leading journals going back to the 1950s for studies of pregnancy and childbirth. The group also wrote to physicians requesting unpublished data on the subject. The effort came to be known as the Cochrane Collaboration, named after the late British epidemiologist, Archie Cochrane, with whom Chalmers had studied. Over time, researchers and physicians from Canada, Australia, and the United States joined the effort, and the collaboration expanded to include systematic reviews and meta-analyses of clinical trials on several medical conditions. Those who work on the Cochrane Collaboration evaluate studies, discarding those that are methodologically weak and sorting the rest into different kinds of trials. Affirming the hierarchy of evidence, only RCTs are included. However, the Cochrane Collaboration recognizes various kinds of RCTs – those that are single blind and unblind, those using placebo and other controls, and even trials without controls. There is potential value in all these, both to the clinician and as part of the hierarchy of research evidence. A Cochrane Collaboration report summarizes the best information available and presents it in a clinically relevant form. Based on this best available evidence, practice guidelines can be issued and further research specified.

Despite the centrality of RCTs in medicine, it has been estimated that "only about 15% of medical interventions are supported by solid clinical evidence" (Smith 1991, 798). This figure has persisted for some time – in 1978, the Office of Technology Assessment stated that only about 10% to 20% of the techniques that physicians use have been subjected to clinical trials (Congressional Office of Technology Assessment 1978, 7). One of the reasons may be that many current treatments, even the ubiquitous aspirin, were introduced before the era of RCTs, and because their efficacy, as well as their side effects, were already known clinically, there did not seem to be any need for gold standard testing.[16] The FDA only requires that new investigational drugs be subjected to RCTs. Some CAM therapies, although not as widely used, are much older than aspirin, but they have not withstood the test of time according to the medical community. The medical community is also requiring that CAM therapies be tested scientifically, which means through large, randomized, and controlled clinical trials, even though these therapies are not new investigational drugs. In the process, all the recent developments in scientific research, from criticisms of RCTs to the establishment of evidence-based medicine and the Cochrane Collaboration, are having an impact on CAM.

---

[16] Eventually, aspirin was subjected to clinical trials. Besides confirming many claims for its benefits, these trials led to new medical knowledge that was serendipitous to the purpose of the trials, such as the fact that heart disease in women is different than in men.

## RESEARCH ON CAM

Although CAM research is justified by its growing use, coupled with insufficient knowledge about safety and efficacy, it is driven mainly by the persistent refrain of skeptics that alternative medicine is unscientific and unproven. The only way to address this charge, many believe, is to submit CAM to scientific methods of investigation culminating in well-designed RCTs. Only through gold standard testing can the kind of evidence of efficacy be derived to quiet, if not fully satisfy, critics. The CAM community is divided, however, on the appropriateness of using research methods developed in a biomedical context to investigate treatments that embody different understandings of such fundamental questions as how the body works and what can help it to work better.[17] Nevertheless, many CAM practitioners are interested in putting their knowledge to the test and ultimately to legitimate their work. Whatever the motivation – pragmatic, political, financial, intellectual – scientific research on CAM is proceeding, and its producers are gaining widespread recognition.

The OAM decided early on that, to the extent possible, CAM therapies should be investigated in accordance with established scientific methods of research, even though the evaluation of some therapies would present challenges to the research design (Jonas 1997). Furthermore, insofar as there is some anecdotal and observational evidence for effectiveness, the CAM community has an obligation to put this evidence to more rigorous testing. Whether the obligation extends to explaining the causal mechanisms of effectiveness is questionable. Regardless of complaints, RCTs remain "the best method to answer

---

[17] Federspil and Vettor (2000, 241) argued that "alternative modalities lack many of the minimum requirements of scientific discourse . . . [because] they violate the principle of falsifiability." Along the same lines is the assertion that there is no scientific theory to account for the healing that occurs with certain CAM therapies, thereby limiting their insertion into the empirical, causal, replicable model of proof and disproof that guides science (Pillemer 1999, 324). It should be noted, however, that Western scientists have either developed theories for or applied existing ones to therapies that were once believed to be paradigmatically outside the realm of Western science (such as acupuncture). Some in the CAM community continue to hold that the complexity and uniqueness of certain CAM therapies requires different or even entirely new research and statistical methodologies to capture their health and healing benefits (Levin et al. 1997, 1080).

questions about effectiveness" (Linde 2000, 253) and "to allow infer-
ences about causality" (Gatchel and Maddrey 1998, 36).[18] However,
as in medical research, RCTs, strictly understood, are not always desirable or feasible, even as a final stage of investigation. For such cases,
the OAM adopted the NIH convention: nonstandard research designs
are supported as long as they are fully within accepted standards of
objectivity and rigor as judged by a panel of experts. In other words,
passing peer review of the proposed research design is central. We have
seen that clinical trials in the field of medicine can be deemed rigorous
without having all the standard features of an RCT. In some cases,
ethical concerns require that placebos not be used or that blinding be
suspended. As we will see in Chapter 6, some CAM research is engaging in similar methodological modification. It remains to be seen
whether the medical community will accept it, in light of the argument
that CAM is being held to a higher standard of research and proof
(Cassileth, Jonas, and Cassidy 1995, 293).

A number of the problems raised by RCT-type research on CAM
replicate those in biomedical research. The difference, however, is that
whereas these issues have received scant attention in biomedicine, insofar as they are assumed away by the logic of an RCT, they are at the
forefront of CAM research. Because at least some part of the mechanisms of action in many CAM therapies involve or are purported to
involve subjective factors, CAM researchers have to confront head-on
the boundary between subjectivity and objectivity, belief and science.
Moreover, as we will see, new problems arise at each stage of research
on CAM. Some of these problems can be addressed in conventional
terms, others require the kind of creativity and flexibility that may
push the boundaries of convention. CAM researchers therefore have
to straddle a very narrow fence.

THE PROCESS OF RESEARCH

Before exploring how they go about their task, we should start with
the preludes to research. Reports from a panel on CAM research

---

[18] However, RCTs do not explain causality or mechanisms of action. To answer these
questions, researchers most commonly turn to basic scientific (laboratory) investigations.

methodologies at a 1992 NIH conference presented a clear set of guidelines that emphasized careful thought about and meticulous attention to every step of the research process (Workshop on Alternative Medicine 1995). Also, the current Director of the NCCAM, Dr. Stephen Straus, a renowned clinical investigator who specializes in infectious disease, pragmatically encourages researchers to study those therapies that are widely used by the public and for which there is preliminary evidence about safety and efficacy to justify researching them further (Stokstad 2000, 1569). Without dredging up the past, Straus' aim may be to remind researchers of some early problems experienced by the OAM, when politically and ideologically motivated research on such therapies as magnets brought gasps of disdain, even from some people favorable to CAM. That CAM researchers must be cautioned to heed the requirements of a broad audience, one that includes but is not limited to the scientific medical community, speaks not only to the need for rigorous research but also to the politics of research.[19]

By now, most CAM researchers have heard these messages and are cognizant of the imperative of scientific objectivity. However, many are also concerned that their research remain true to the therapy they are studying. CAM researchers are walking a tightrope. Some worry that approaching a therapy as though it were a new investigational drug or procedure – that is, without a deep understanding of the philosophy behind the therapy, its modes of implementation, issues in its codification, etc. – might produce an inappropriate research design, leading most likely to findings that underestimate efficacy. In contrast, mainstream investigators wonder if CAM researchers who are fully acquainted with a therapy run the risk of bias in their research design, leading most likely to exaggerated findings. At issue is the scientific requirement of "clinical equipoise," which is a condition of genuine clinical uncertainty on the part of the researcher about the benefits of the treatment under study. Although this is a danger for any researcher, those investigating CAM therapies must be especially careful

---

[19] The question of whether scientific research is "pure" or whether funding flows toward areas where patent and profit possibilities exist is perennial. Journalists and scholars alike criticized an early decision in the Bush administration to reduce funding to the National Science Foundation and increase funding for biomedical research at the NIH as short-sighted ignorance of the prerequisite of basic science before applications could be expected.

because of the suspicion within the medical community that their interest in CAM makes them "believers." These considerations are critical in research on CAM modalities, most of which do not have standard practice guidelines; that is, there is more of a consensus among practitioners than a standard protocol for treatment. However, even with modalities that are more or less standardized, such as acupuncture or chiropractic, it is important to air any issues that may appear to cast the researcher in an ideological and, therefore, less than objective light.

Consider first the case of acupuncture, where despite a certain degree of standardization, there are different schools of thought about the proper body points for different ailments and the preferred techniques of needling.[20] Researchers must be clear about the precise kind of acupuncture they are studying and the precise ailment at which it is being directed. Full description and complete disclosure reduce exaggerated claims about the effectiveness of the treatment and enable successful replication. Consider next other therapies, such as reiki, a form of energy healing, that are very individualistic. Not only do practitioners have their own styles, but they may also vary their approach for different patients or even the same one in different sessions. In their everyday practices, some reiki practitioners may combine a variety of therapies (including counseling) or recommend a variety of behavioral changes to patients (such as diet and meditation). A good research design with appropriate controls should be able to capture these particularities and monitor their effect on treatment outcome. The more rigorous, objective, and detailed the research design, the more likely it is to be accepted in mainstream medicine.

Another preliminary task critical to all research but especially important to CAM given its early stages of development is to ask an appropriate research question. One panel report at a 1995 NIH

---

[20] Differences occur within traditional Chinese acupuncture, which individualizes the points, as well as within Western acupuncture, which uses the points formulaically according to the disorder with no variation across patients. Even though Western acupuncture is used in research, one school may insist that needles be inserted deeply and twirled until the patient feels the effect, which would indicate that the correct point has been stimulated. Another school may hold that needles should be placed barely below the skin. There are also different teachings and opinions regarding the use of electrical stimulation. Moreover, it is highly likely that in their everyday practice acupuncturists' choice of points include intuition and formulae (Ergil 1999).

conference on CAM research methodology emphasized a somewhat obvious point – that a question is more "likely to be answerable if it is explicit, focused, and practicable" (Vickers et al. 1997, 113). This advice is intended for CAM researchers who may tend toward questions that focus on the global effectiveness of a treatment. Better than the question "is acupuncture effective in treating addiction" is one that specifies the kind of acupuncture (the body points to be manipulated, needle size, and type of manipulation used), the kind of addiction, the patient population, and the definition of terms such as "effective" and "treat." Such specific and detailed studies can be replicated more easily and, accordingly, contribute more readily to cumulative knowledge.

There is no doubt that the NCCAM is committed to establishing the evidence base for the safety and efficacy of CAM. The agency's annual reports repeat the priority of rigorous scientific research. Its five-year strategic plan, published in 2000, presents a table on the hierarchy of evidence: anecdotes, case studies, observational studies, uncontrolled trials, small randomized clinical trials, and large randomized clinical trials, with systematic reviews across the spectrum (NCCAM 2000, 8).[21] Program officers and directors at the NCCAM acknowledge that "information regarding the efficacy and safety of CAM therapies spans a continuum ranging from anecdotes and case studies through ... data derived from small, well-developed Phase I and II clinical trials" (7).[22] They appreciate that several panels at the NIH conference on research methodologies concluded that the articulation of clear research questions should precede the choice of methods and that different questions have different clinical purposes and require different methods and analytical approaches. Nevertheless, it is also clear that phase III trials (determining clinical efficacy in large RCTs) are a capstone. Nor is there any question that evidence derived from case studies

---

[21] Survey research methods and other questionnaires, although not included in the hierarchy, are increasingly employed in medical research as supplementary tools to gather preliminary evidence. These and large observational studies are the core of epidemiology. It should also be noted that aside from the ethical issues involved in RCTs, large observational studies are sometimes preferable in medical research because they are expedient and less expensive.

[22] Phase I trials evaluate the safety of an experimental treatment; phase II trials assess its clinical activity, that is, establish that there is some efficacy.

and observations, which use less rigorous methods, although suitable for pilot studies, is less useful in and of itself than in its contribution toward the development of an RCT. The ultimate goal of research, then, is to establish causality in the effectiveness of a therapy using large-scale RCTs.

OUTCOME MEASURES

Although the research design of an RCT focuses on randomization, blinding, and placebo controls, another item creeps in to stamp the label of "proof" on studies of efficacy – how the outcome is measured. As we will see in Chapter 6, many CAM researchers rely on objective measures of biological markers that have been developed in medical research as indicators of such subjective phenomena as stress and relaxation. For medical researchers, these markers prove whether an intervention is having an effect. However, CAM researchers are concerned about the implications of equating bodily sensations that have a large subjective component with biological correlates. These correlates do not fully capture what is happening in the body. Nor do they fully explain the process of healing. So how does one measure what biological markers miss?

Medical researchers have also come to realize that something more than can be measured by objective biological factors is at work in health and healing. They have developed a number of methods of measuring subjective outcome, sometimes borrowing from the work of social scientists. Because these methods have been used in conventional medical research, CAM researchers are urged to use them as well, as long as they are appropriate, have been validated, and have had some measure of success (Levin et al. 1997). Perhaps the most relevant for CAM research are various scales that measure "quality of life" or "global health." Most of these scales require patients to evaluate their condition; the questions resemble those in the patient self-reports that physicians regularly employ. Although some of the scales were developed for specific conditions or diseases, and some for purposes of rationing health care to the chronically or terminally ill, they have been adapted for more general usage. CAM researchers are adapting these quality-of-life scales even further to make them more appropriate for use in CAM studies by expanding their emphasis on disease and physical well-being and including consideration of mental, emotional, and spiritual well-being (cf Bell et al. 2001).[23]

There are also a number of more objective measures of quality of life already in use in medical research that are applicable to CAM research. These include such items as activities of daily living, cognitive functioning, physiological functioning, and observations of overt behavior; some of these items are measured by medical personnel, others involve technology. Depending on the research question and the issue or treatment under investigation, researchers in both conventional and alternative medicine supplement these measures with patients' subjective evaluations. Although CAM researchers are regularly encouraged to use existing measures that have been used in other fields, preferably medicine, some unique features of quality of life may be elusive to scales that are less sensitive to the philosophy of CAM. For instance, the measures discussed here may or may not tap the distinction between improvement in symptoms and in other factors of mind and body that make an individual susceptible to symptoms.

There are many reasons why patients improve after treatment (CAM and conventional), and some of these may have little to do with the treatment per se. As noted earlier, because skeptics dismiss CAM as equivalent to some of these other factors, CAM researchers are sensitive to their role in improvement. Most important is time; that is, many conditions heal spontaneously.[24] The only way to test for this is

---

[23] This effort has an ally in work by the World Health Organization (WHO) to develop a culturally sensitive quality-of-life assessment (WHOQOL Group 1995). Its principles hold, first, that assessments of quality of life are subjective, consisting of both positive and negative global evaluations of behaviors, states, capacities, and dis/satisfaction with these. Second, the WHOQOL Group maintains that quality of life is multidimensional, including at minimum both positive and negative physical, psychological, and social perceptions, which are best supplemented by a usual activities or role functioning dimension, as well as by a spiritual dimension – the person's perception of meaning in life. The WHO's definition of quality of life is "individuals' perception of their position in life in the context of the culture and value systems in which they live and in relation to their goals, expectations, standards and concerns" (1405). After constructing questions to operationalize the concepts, the WHOQOL Group conducted pilot and field tests. They have produced a highly workable instrument to measure a devilishly elusive phenomenon.

[24] What appears to be spontaneous healing may also occur when, for instance, an earlier measurement of a condition suggested a pathology that the patient did not in fact have. The error may have been due to factors such as chance, previous physical activity, and stress (Linde 2000).

to compare a treatment to no treatment, something that is rarely done in medical research because only a placebo control allows for blinding. However, this alternative research design is increasingly finding its way into CAM research. When possible, a cross-over methodology can be added whereby patients are randomly assigned to two groups (one receives the experimental treatment and the other no treatment); they first receive what they have been assigned, and then they switch to the other (that is, treatment or no treatment). Finally, being in a study invariably affects participants in unknown ways. Whether this is due to the "Hawthorne effect" first unearthed by a sociologist (the attention that subjects receive when participating in a study influences their performance), the hope of contributing to a cure, the reassurance and caring given by nurses and staff, or whatever else is involved in receiving a treatment, all research on human subjects involves unknown effects.

THE FRUITS OF RESEARCH

The accumulation of RCT research on CAM has caught the eye of the Cochrane Collaboration group. Among others, researchers at the University of Maryland, one of the centers discussed in Chapter 6, have applied the Cochrane Collaboration to CAM. The first step – collecting all the published and unpublished RCTs on CAM worldwide – is a formidable task because Medline, the most frequently used index for medical research, references only about 23% of all serial medical journals and only about 10% of all CAM journals worldwide (Ezzo et al. 1998).[25] Nevertheless, by mid-1998 only about 20% of the CAM RCTs collected were not in Medline. By now, systematic reviews and meta-analyses have been conducted on several CAM therapies and they, or references to them, are available on the University of Maryland's website.[26] Because assessment of methodological quality is central to the Cochrane Collaboration, considerable trust can be put into the validity of its studies. Nevertheless, because there is skepticism about

---

[25] Understandably, there is debate about including unpublished studies in the Cochrane Collaboration. Nevertheless, locating this research is important for CAM because of publication bias.

[26] There are also some systematic reviews of studies that are not RCTs because these were either unavailable or too scarce (Ernst 2001).

CAM and CAM research in the medical community, the researchers are comparing the quality of CAM trials with those found in conventional medicine for the same disorders (Ezzo et al. 1998). Medical and CAM researchers and providers are the main consumers of these reviews, but the public is not far behind.

The Cochrane Collaboration has raised the status of CAM, putting CAM research on a par with conventional medicine research as appropriate for systematic reviews and meta-analyses. Cochrane Collaborations establish the current base of evidence for safety and efficacy. This is not to say that there is evidence of safety and efficacy for those CAM therapies that appear in Cochrane Collaborations because the findings on certain therapies are inconclusive. However, with knowledge about the inadequacies in past research, more research is proceeding. If it is to be considered by the Cochrane Collaboration, it necessarily involves the methods of an RCT.

We can now turn to examples of how CAM researchers are addressing these many issues. Chapter 6 focuses on research that is underway at centers funded by the NCCAM. It examines how researchers are coming to terms with demands for scientific rigor and the need to be flexible and creative when applying standard methods of research to investigating CAM.

# 6

## Investigating CAM: What Works?

The NIH has become the most important source of funding for research on CAM, and the key to its legitimacy, both scientific and political. Although several divisions at the NIH fund CAM research, the most important is the NCCAM. It now undertakes a wide range of activities, including funding for both extramural and intramural research, research training, the development of scientific databases, and public information; it works with educators and researchers in the United States and worldwide. The portfolio of projects funded is broad and both short- and long-term, ranging from exploratory investigations to large multicenter clinical trials. These activities and others grew slowly at first, reflecting a limited budget. But once the transformation from an office to a center was underway in 1997, a change directed by Congress, the growth curve spiraled. From an initial budget of $2 million in 1992, the NCCAM administered $89.1 million in FY 2000, the largest increase that year of any NIH center or institute. In FY 2002, the budget was $104.6 million. The director of the NCCAM testifies before both the Senate and the House Committees on Appropriations at least once per year, and thus far, Congress is responding favorably to developments at the center.

This chapter focuses on the kind of research that the NCCAM funds and that is at the core of its growing reputation. A large portion of these funds is allocated to, currently, 16 CAM research centers located at universities and medical or other specialized centers across the U.S.

The idea for these research centers germinated at the first workshop on alternative medicine held in 1992 before the OAM was an official agency. Reasoning that the peer review process, which governs funding at all scientific research institutions, "promotes conventional research over novel research," the panel on research infrastructure recommended the establishment of centers that could provide a freer environment for the development of CAM research (Eisenberg et al. 1995, 275, ff). The panel members also suggested certain priority areas for research; these became the specialty foci of the centers. The first director of the OAM was favorable to the idea, and a request for applications (RFA) was issued in 1993. Based on earlier workshops and discussions among program officers and the advisory counsel, the RFA specified certain medical conditions and broad health care issues as focal points for the centers. By 1994, 10 research centers were in operation. In 1997, an 11th was added in response to a new RFA specifying chiropractic. Table 6.1 lists the first wave of centers, their specialized areas of research, and other characteristics.

Although all the centers were newly created by the grants, some were offshoots of centers that were already or were just beginning to work on CAM-related issues. For instance, the centers at Columbia University[1] and the University of Maryland[2] had recently received private donations for the study of CAM when the RFA appeared. Other centers were part of larger research institutions – such as the Minneapolis Medical

---

[1] When Richard and Hinda Rosenthal first suggested a grant to the Dean of the Medical School at Columbia, they did not have a clear idea of how the funds should be used. In discussions with Dr. Fredi Kronenberg and others, an idea for a center focusing on research and education emerged and was accepted. However, the Rosenthal grant was small and could cover infrastructure only, requiring a search for additional funding. The OAM RFA came at an opportune time. The Richard and Hinda Rosenthal Center for Complementary and Alternative Medicine now includes the NCCAM center with a focus on aging and women's health, and a number of other projects funded by various sources, such as the NIH (for a national, multiethnic survey of women's use of CAM) and private foundations.

[2] Dr. Brian Berman became acquainted with the Laing Foundation (and Mr. Laing himself) while he was practicing medicine at a private integrative clinic in England. When he relocated to Maryland, the Foundation continued to support his research on pain and allowed Berman to set up a new integrative clinic, in addition to the NCCAM center devoted to research and education. The research center is therefore funded from more than one source.

TABLE 6.1. *First-Wave Centers*

| Institution, Location, Center Name | Director | Specialty | Duration, Amount (Total) | Cofunding Agency |
|---|---|---|---|---|
| **Bastyr University** Kenmore, WA *BU AIDS Research Center* | Leanna J. Standish, ND, PhD (naturopathy) | HIV/AIDS, cancer, hepatitis C, neurological diseases | 1994–8; $920,000 | NIAID |
| **Columbia University** New York, NY *Center for Complementary and Alternative Medicine in Women's Health* | Fredi Kronenberg, PhD (physiology) | Women's health (menopause, hot flashes, fibroids, minority health) | 1995–8; $1,159,737 | ORWH |
| **Harvard University** Boston, MA *Center for Alternative Medicine Research* | David M. Eisenberg, MD (internal medicine) | General medical conditions, alternative medical therapies | 1995–8; $935,696 | NIAMS |
| **Kessler Institute for Rehabilitation** West Orange, NJ *Center for Research in Complementary and Alternative Medicine for Stroke and Neurological Disorders* | Samuel C. Shiflett, PhD (psychoneuroim-munology) | Stroke and neurological conditions, acupuncture and movement therapies | 1995–8; $1,089,922 | NICHHD |

| Institution | Director | Focus | Dates; amount | Funding |
|---|---|---|---|---|
| **Minneapolis Medical Research Foundation** Minneapolis, MN *Center for Addiction and Alternative Medicine* | Thomas Kiresuk, PhD (psychology) | Addictions, major treatment outcome research | 1994–9; $924,000 | NIDA |
| **Palmer Chiropractic University** Davenport, IA *Consortial Center for Chiropractic Research* | William C. Meeker, DC (chiropractic), MPH | Chiropractic | 1997–02; $2,000,000 | NIAMS |
| **Stanford University** Stanford, CA *Complementary and Alternative Medicine Program at Stanford* | William L. Haskell, PhD (human physiology) | Aging, lifestyle factors and pharmacological therapy | 1995–98; $864,150 | NIAMS |
| **University of California, Davis** Davis, CA *Center for Alternative Medicine Research in Asthma and Immunology* | M. Eric Gershwin, MD (rheumatology) | Asthma, allergy, immunology | 1995–8; $899,021 | NAID |

(continued)

TABLE 6.1 (continued)

| Institution, Location, Center Name | Director | Specialty | Duration, amount (Total) | Cofunding Agency |
|---|---|---|---|---|
| **University of Maryland** Baltimore, MD *Center for Alternative Medicine Pain Research and Evaluation* | Brian Berman, MD (family medicine) | Pain | 1995–8; $900,000 | NIAMS |
| **University of Texas** Houston, TX *Center for Alternative Medicine* | Guy S. Parcel, PhD (behavioral sciences) | Cancer, aging, health promotion | 1995–8; $1,040,585 | NCI |
| **University of Virginia** Charlottesville, VA *Center for the Study of Complementary and Alternative Therapies* | Ann Gill Taylor, RN, MS, EdD (nursing) | Pain | 1995–8; $1,103,486 | NIDCR |

Research Foundation, which had been conducting CAM-related re-search for several years.[3] The Palmer Center, which is a consortium, the first of several, had been conducting research on chiropractic for some time.[4]

The initial funding for the centers was relatively small.[5] The start-up funds allowed the centers to survey the field and construct a research agenda. However, the grants were not large enough for the centers to do more than begin to conduct pilot studies of feasible and fruitful areas of research. In 1997, the centers were invited to respond to a new, significantly larger RFA with a modified list of specializations; all but one did.[6] Funding was renewed for 3 of the original 10 centers (Columbia University, the University of Maryland, and the Minneapolis Medical Research Foundation). They had made significant progress in pilot studies and were able to propose well-designed continuing or new projects. In 2003, the NCCAM renewed the Palmer Center's grant for another 5 years. Most of the first-wave centers whose funding was not renewed are still in operation and conduct CAM-related research that is funded through other types of NCCAM, NIH, and private foundation grants.[7]

---

[3] The Minneapolis Medical Research Foundation is an acute care research and teaching hospital operating within the Hennekin County Medical Center. For several years prior to receiving the OAM award, the founding director of the new Alternative Medicine Clinic had been conducting research on acupuncture for the treatment of substance abuse with others at the foundation.

[4] The Palmer Center in Davenport is the headquarters for the Consortial Center for Chiropractic Research. Almost all chiropractic colleges in the United States belong to regional and national associations. When the RFA for chiropractic was issued by the NCCAM, 5 of the more successful colleges (in terms of research efforts) formed the consortium. This group now has a pool of about 125 reviewers and an advisory committee to review and select proposals for seed funding. At present writing, the consortium has funded 18 pilot or preclinical studies in 13 institutions. The grant to Palmer was more than the others because it came late in the first wave of funding and signaled a second wave characterized by larger-scale projects. In 2003 the Palmer Center responded to a new program announcement, and was awarded a new grant.

[5] Most of the centers (in both waves) were cofunded by the OAM and other centers or institutes at the NIH. All grant proposals that come to the NIH now go to a central office that sends them to the appropriate centers or institutes. There is an effort throughout the NIH to have joint funding of projects when the topics so lend themselves.

[6] Applicants were required to submit 3 to 6 research proposals, as well as plans for building administrative infrastructure and conducting educational programs.

[7] There are many vehicles for funding research through the NIH and elsewhere. With a combination of grants, some former centers have survived as virtual if not real centers.

Applications to the NCCAM for funding as research centers undergo the same review process as exists throughout the NIH; that is, they are peer reviewed by experts who are selected by staff at, in this case, the NCCAM. The second wave of funding came in pieces because the NCCAM did not announce the new specializations all at once; additional RFAs followed. Also, some proposals had to be revised and resubmitted. Table 6.2 presents the basic characteristics of centers that I have collapsed into the category of second-wave centers. The grants are all for 5 years; differences in the amounts reflect different administrative and infrastructural needs. The relatively large amounts, compared with the first wave of funding, reflect the largesse of Congress and the reinvigorated mission of the NCCAM: the pursuit of sophisticated scientific research. As before, newly funded centers in the second wave were newly created for the most part.[8] Four of the new centers – Kaiser, Maharishi, Oregon Health and Science, and Purdue – join Palmer in being consortia.[9] Among each center's responsibilities is administering a pilot study program, in which review committees distribute about $100,000 per year to 3–5 projects, as well as a career development program, which funds 1 or more postdoctoral fellows training to become CAM researchers. Each center (both waves) has an advisory board, whose role tends to be supervisory and related to the overall mission of the center.

### SCIENCE AND INNOVATION

The discussion below on CAM research focuses on the second-wave centers and the Palmer Center. It also focuses specifically on those projects that are part of the center grant. Table 6.3 summarizes the studies. Many of the projects are ongoing and others are as yet unpublished, so results are not always presented. When appropriate, therefore, the discussion is supplemented with other research. Even so, it is

---

A review of grants and other activities indicates that by and large CAM research at the first-wave centers or at their universities continues and, in some cases, is thriving.

[8] The center at the University of Pennsylvania is an exception. It began in 1968 to study the effect of hyperbaric oxygen therapy for "the bends" that some deep sea divers experience. A similar kind of research continues now.

[9] There is some overlap in membership between the Oregon Health and Science University and Kaiser centers.

TABLE 6.2. *Second-Wave Centers*

| Institution, Location, Center Name | Director | Specialty | Duration, Amount (Total) |
| --- | --- | --- | --- |
| **Columbia University**[a]<br>New York, NY<br>*Center for CAM Research in Aging and Women's Health* | Fredi Kronenberg, PhD (physiology) | Aging | 1999–2004, $7.2 |
| **Emory University**<br>Atlanta, GA<br>*Center for CAM in Neurodegenerative Diseases* | Mahlon R. Delong, MD (neurology), DC (chiropractic)<br>Codirector: Steven Wolf, PhD (anatomy), FAPTA (physical therapy) | Neurodegenerative diseases | 2000–5, $3.2 million |
| **Johns Hopkins University**<br>Baltimore, MD<br>*Johns Hopkins Center for Complementary and Alternative Medicine* | Adrian S. Dobs, MD (endocrinology), MHS | Cancer | 2000–5, $8 milliom |
| **Kaiser Foundation Hospitals**<br>Portland, OR<br>*Oregon Center for Complementary and Alternative Medicine Research in Craniofacial Disorders* | Nancy Vuckovic, PhD (anthropology) | Craniofacial disorders | 1999–2004, $7.9 million |

*(continued)*

TABLE 6.2 (*continued*)

| Institution, Location, Center Name | Director | Specialty | Duration, Amount (Total) |
|---|---|---|---|
| **Maharishi University of Management** Fairfield, IA *Center for Natural Medicine and Prevention* | Robert H. Schneider, MD (preventive medicine, vedic medicine) | Cardio, aging in African-Americans | 1999–2004, $7.9 million |
| **Minneapolis Medical Research Foundation**[a] Minneapolis, MN *Center for Addiction and Alternative Medicine Research* | Thomas J. Kiresuk, PhD (psychology) | Addictions | 1998–2003, $4.8 million |
| **Oregon Health and Science University** Portland, OR *Oregon Center for Complementary and Alternative Medicine in Neurological Disorders* | Barry S. Oken, MD (neurology) Codirector: Dennis Bourdette, MD (neurology) | Neurological disorders | 1999–2004, $7.8 million |
| **Purdue University** West Lafayette, IN *Botanical Center for Age-Related Diseases* | Connie M. Weaver, PhD (nutrition) Codirector: Stephen Barnes, PhD (pharmacognosy) | Botanicals | 2000–5, $7.9 million |
| **University of Arizona** Tuscon, AZ *Pediatric Center for Complementary and Alternative Medicine* | Fayez K. Ghishan, MD (pediatrics), DC (chiropractic) | Pediatrics | 1998–2003, $5 million |

| Institution | Director | Focus | Period, Funding |
| --- | --- | --- | --- |
| **University of Arizona** Tuscon, AZ *Arizona Center for Phytomedicine Research* | Barbara N. Timmerman, PhD (natural products chemistry) | Botanicals | 2000–5, $7.9 million |
| **University of California, Los Angeles** Los Angeles, CA *Center for Dietary Supplements Research on Botanicals* | David Heber, MD (endocrinology), PhD (physiology) | Botanicals | 1999–2004, $7.5 million |
| **University of Illinois at Chicago** Chicago, IL *Center for Botanical Dietary Supplement Research in Women's Health* | Norman R. Farnsworth, PhD (pharmacognosy) Codirector: Richard B. van Breeman, PhD (pharmacology) | Botanicals | 1999–2004, $7.8 million |
| **University of Maryland**[a] Baltimore, MD *Center for Alternative Medicine Research on Arthritis* | Brian M. Berman, MD (family medicine) | Arthritis | 1999–2004, $7.9 million |
| **University of Michigan** Ann Arbor, MI *CAM Research Center for Cardiovascular Diseases* | Steven F. Bolling, MD (cardiosurgery) Codirector: Sara Warber, MD (family medicine) | Cardiovascular diseases | 1998–2003, $6.7 million |
| **University of Pennsylvania** Philadelphia, PA *Specialized Center of Research In Hyperbaric Oxygen Therapy* | Stephan R. Thom, MD (emergency medicine), PhD (microbiology) | Cancer | 2000–5, $8 million |

[a] Also a first-wave center.

TABLE 6.3. *Research Projects*

| Centers, Projects | Researchers' Specializations[a] | Type of Research[b] | Outcome Measures |
|---|---|---|---|
| **Columbia University** | | | |
| 1) Effects of Black Cohosh on Menopausal Hot Flashes | PhD (physiology)<br>MD (reproductive endocrinology)<br>PhD (neuropsychology) | Randomized trial, $n = 64$<br>Double blind<br>Placebo control | Hot flashes and other menopausal symptoms, sex hormones, ultrasound, bone density, cognitive function, quality of life |
| 2) Chinese Herbal Formula: Beneficial or Harmful for Breast Cancer | PhD (molecular biology) | Basic science | Estrogenic, antiestrogenic, growth activity in various assay systems |
| 3) Macrobiotic Diet and Flaxseed: Effects on Estrogens, Phytoestrogens, and Fibrolytic Factors | ScD (nutritional epidemiology)<br>MD (cardiology), PhD (education: nutrition) | Randomized trial, $n = 96$<br>Unblinded<br>Control = American Heart Association Diet | Biochemical and other cardiovascular parameters (endothelial function, fibrolynic variables, lipid profile, antioxidants); sex hormone profiles (including estrogen and phytoestrogen metabolites) |
| 4) Dietary Phytoestrogens and Bone Metabolism | MD (endocrinology)<br>MD (endocrinology)<br>MD (endocrinology) | Same population, design, etc., as above (operationally 1 study) | Bone mass; markers of bone formation and resorption (urine, blood); estrogen and phytoestrogen metabolites, as above |

## Emory University

| | | | |
|---|---|---|---|
| 1) Transmagnetic Cranial Stimulation (for Depression) in Parkinson's Disease | MD (neurology)<br>MD (neurology) | Nonrandomized trial, $n = 4+$<br>Unblinded<br>All receive TMS initially, those who fail to benefit proceed to ECT | Depression (HAM-D, Beck; psychiatric status; neuropsychological status; dementia; attention; quality of life |
| 2) Polysomnographic Assessments of Alternative Treatments (valerian) for Sleep Disturbances in Parkinson's Disease | PhD (behavioral science)<br>MD (neurology), PhD (neuroanatomy)<br>PhD (anatomy) | Randomized trial, $n = 80$<br>Double blind<br>Placebo control | Polysomnographic measures of sleep time, efficiency, and latency; EMG measures of muscle activity during sleep; clinical assessments of motor function |
| 3) Chinese Exercise Modalities (tai chi) in Parkinson's Disease | MD (neurology)<br>PhD (anatomy), FAPTA (physical therapy) | Randomized trial, $n = 60$<br>Unblinded<br>Controls = qigong, aerobic exercise | Clinical measures of Parkinsonian disability, motor disability, behavior, mood, quality of life |

## Johns Hopkins University

| | | | |
|---|---|---|---|
| 1) Effects of CAM Interventions (green tea) on Oxidative DNA Damage in Cancer Cells | MD (oncology), PhD (pharmacology and molecular sciences) | In vitro | |
| 2) Complementary Therapies (soy and sour cherries) for Cancer Pain | MD (anesthesiology and critical care medicine) | Animal | |

(continued)

TABLE 6.3 *(continued)*

| Centers, Projects | Researchers' Specializations[a] | Type of Research[b] | Outcome Measures |
|---|---|---|---|
| 3) Chinese Herbs Intervention in Men with Prostate Cancer | MD (endocrinology), MHS | Randomized trial, $n = 111$<br>Double blind<br>Placebo control | Biological (oxidative DNA damage in cancer cells, immune system, PSA, stress); quality of life |
| 4) Prayer in Black Women with Breast Cancer | ScD, MPH | Randomized trial, $n = 40$<br>Unblinded<br>Control = attention placebo | Biological markers of stress (blood cortisol), quality of life (living with cancer scale) |
| **Kaiser Foundation** | | | |
| 1) Complementary Medicine Approaches to Temporomandibular Pain Management | PhD (anthroplogy)<br>CD (dentistry), MSc (experimental pathology), PhD (public health)<br>DDS, DrPH (health policy and management)<br>DDS<br>PhD (neurosciences)<br>LAc[c]<br>DC[d] | Randomized trial, $n = 250$<br>Unblinded<br>5 arms: acupuncture, traditional Chinese medicine, massage, chiropractic, usual care | Research diagnostic criteria for TMD (self-report of pain and psychosocial measures) |
| 2) Alternative Medicine Approaches Among Women with Temporomandibular Pain | BA (social work)<br>PhD (anthropology), MPH<br>PhD (neurosciences)<br>ND, MPH<br>DDS<br>LAc[c], MD (traditional Chinese medicine) | Randomized trial, $n = 150$<br>3 arms: naturopathic medicine, traditional Chinese medicine, usual care<br>Unblinded | Research diagnostic criteria for TMD (self-report of pain and psychosocial measures) |

| | | | |
|---|---|---|---|
| 3) Complementary Naturopathic Medicine for Periodontitis | DDS, PhD (immunology and microbiology) CD (dentistry), MSc (experimental pathology), PhD (public health) ND, MPH | Randomized, $n = 136$ Double blind Placebo control | Biological (blood, pocket depth, gingival index, detachment level); quality of life |
| **Maharishi University** | | | |
| 1) Basic Mechanisms of Meditation and Cardiovascular Disease in Older African Americans | MD (preventive medicine, Vedic medicine) PhD (psychology) | Randomized trial, $n = 102$ Single blind Control = health education | Biological (endothelial dysfunction via brachial reactivity testing [BART], heart rate variability, ambulatory ischemia via Holter monitoring, blood pressure, diet, exercise, lipid profile); quality of life; psychosocial stress |
| 2) Effects of Herbal Antioxidants and Cardiovascular Disease in Older African Americans | MD (preventive medicine, Vedic medicine) MD (cardiology) | Randomized trial, $n = 138$ Double blind Controls = placebo, vitamins as "active comparison" | Biological (carotid intima medial thickness [a surrogate marker of atherosclerosis] via B-mode ultrasound, endothelial dysfunction via BART, LDL oxidation resistance [a marker of oxidative stress], blood pressure, diet, exercise, lipid profile); quality of life |

*(continued)*

TABLE 6.3 (continued)

| Centers, Projects | Researchers' Specializations[a] | Type of Research[b] | Outcome Measures |
|---|---|---|---|
| 3) Clinical Trial of Meditation and Cardiovascular Disease in Older African American Women (Multicenter – 3 sites) | MD (preventive medicine, Vedic medicine) MD (family medicine) MD (cardiology) | Randomized trial, $n = 196$ Single blind Control = health education | Biological (carotid intima medial thickness [a surrogate marker of atherosclerosis] via B-mode ultrasound, glucose tolerance, insulin, urinary hormones, catechoamines, cortisol, blood pressure, lipid profile); quality of life |
| **Minneapolis Foundation** | | | |
| 1) 13AR: Botanical Compound of Treatment of Hepatitis C Symptoms | MD (gastroenterology) MD (internal medicine) LAc[c], DC[d], herbalist PhD (toxicology) PhD (chemistry) MD (addictions) | Randomized, $n = 45$ Double blind Placebo control Laboratory and animal | Biological (viral load), quality of life |
| 2) Plant Derivatives for Treatment of Alcohol Abuse | | | Reduction in consumption (animal) |
| 3) Electroacupuncture Effects on Mechanisms Mediating Opiate Withdrawal | PhD (biopsychology) | Animal | Withdrawal symptoms, regional brain activity |
| **Oregon Health and Science University** | | | |
| 1) Natural Antioxidants in the Treatment of Multiple Sclerosis | MD (neurology) MD (neurology) PhD (immunology) PhD (molecular microbiology and immunology) | Animal, leading to human | |

144

| | | | |
|---|---|---|---|
| 2) Preventing Cognitive Decline with Alternative Therapies (gingko) | MD (neurology) | Randomized trial, $n = 128$<br>Double blind<br>Placebo control | Conversion to diagnosis of mild cognitive impairment |
| 3) Effect of Yoga on Attention in Aging and Multiple Sclerosis | MD (neurology) | Randomized trial,<br>$n = 140$ seniors,<br>$n = 69$ MS patients<br>Unblinded<br>Controls = aerobic exercise, wait (no treatment) | Primary: EEG measure of alertness, ability to focus attention<br>Secondary: additional cognitive, flexibility, balance, mood, quality of life, markers of oxidative injury |
| 4) Antioxidant Therapy in an Animal Model of Alzheimer's Disease | PhD (biochemistry and biophysics) | Animal | |
| **Purdue University** | | | |
| 1) Isoflavones and Bone Resorption in Postmenopausal Women | PhD (nutrition)<br>PhD (nuclear physics)<br>PhD (biochemistry)<br>MD (endocrinology)<br>PhD (mathematical statistics) | Randomized trial, $n = 12$<br>Double blind<br>Cross-over interventions | Bone resorption |
| 2) Polyphenols and Neuroprotection | PhD (biophysics)<br>PhD (psychobiology) | Basic science, animal | Proteomics |
| 3) Polyphenols and Cancer | PhD (biochemistry)<br>PhD (nutrition)<br>PhD (pharmaceutical science) | Basic science, animal | NOX activity, mechanisms of action |

*(continued)*

TABLE 6.3 (*continued*)

| Centers, Projects | Researchers' Specializations[a] | Type of Research[b] | Outcome Measures |
|---|---|---|---|
| 4) Polyphenols and Inflammation | PhD (biochemistry) PhD (biochemistry) PhD (physiology and biophysiology) | Basic science | Chemical reactions, immune function, cell proliferation, arterial vessel relaxation, EGH receptor autophosphorylation, estrogen-receptor-dependent reporter gene expression |
| **University of Arizona (Pediatrics)** | | | |
| 1) Echinacea and Osteopathic Manipulation for Ear Infections | MD (pediatrics) MD (pediatrics) DO (pediatrics) PharmD | Randomized, $n = 90$ Single blind Controls = placebo echinacea, osteopathic exam | Parental reports of cold or ear infection |
| 2) Guided Imagery for Recurrent Abdominal Pain | MD (pediatrics) DO (pediatrics) | Randomized, $n = 40$ Single blind Controls = muscle relaxation and breathing | FACES scale (child self-reports), parent reports |
| 3) Chamomile Tea for Recurrent Abdominal Pain | MD (pediatrics) PharmD | Randomized, $n = 20$ Single blind Placebo control | Self-reports |
| 4) Acupuncture and Osteopathic Manipulation for Children with Cerebral Palsy | MD (pediatrics) DO (pediatrics) | Randomized trial, $n = 72$ Unblinded Control = wait | Activities of daily living, motor function, quality of life (assessed by DO, TMC practitioner, physical therapist) |

**University of Arizona** (Phytomedicine)

| Project | Disciplines | Research phase | Focus |
|---|---|---|---|
| 1) Chemistry, Mechanisms of Action and Research Informatics | PhD (phytochemistry) PhD (cell biology/ toxicology) | *In vitro* (natural products chemistry) | Identification of antiinflammatory compounds in ginger, tumeric and boswellia |
| 2) Bioavailability Assessment of Antiinflammatory Botanicals in a Porcine Model | PhD (pharmacokinetics) | Animal studies, leading to human | Assessment of bioavailability in Yucatan minipig |
| 3) Pharmacokinetics and Pharmacodynamics of Antiinflammatory Botanicals in Humans | PharmD (clinical pharmacokinetics and pharmacodynamics) | Phase I trials | Assessment of pharmacokinetics of antiinflammatory compounds in humans |

**UCLA**

| Project | Disciplines | Research phase | Focus |
|---|---|---|---|
| 1) Chinese Red Yeast Rice Mechanisms of Action | MD (endocrinology), PhD (physiology) PhD (genetics) | *In vitro* (animal and human pharmaco-kinetics) | Cholesterol synthesis inhibition, biomarkers of cholesterol synthesis |
| 2) Green Tea Catechins in Antiogenesis, Antioxidation, and Tumor Inhibition | MD (surgery) PhD (endocrinology) | *In vitro* and animal studies, leading to human studies | Tumor growth, tumor blood vessel growth, endothelial cell growth |
| 3) Action and Interaction of Chinese Herbs in Prostrate Cancer Inhibition | MD (medical oncology) PhD (animal nutrition) PhD (botany) | *In vitro* and animal studies, combined with phytochemistry | Cancer cell growth, gene expression profiles, evidence of interactions |

(*continued*)

TABLE 6.3 (*continued*)

| Centers, Projects | Researchers' Specializations[a] | Type of Research[b] | Outcome Measures |
|---|---|---|---|
| **University of Illinois at Chicago** | | | |
| 1) Chemical Standardization of 11 Herbal Supplements Used by Women to Treat Menopausal Symptoms, Premenstrual Syndrome, and Urinary Tract Problems | PhD (pharmacognosy) PhD (pharmacognosy) PhD (pharmacognosy) PhD (natural products chemistry) PhD (biology and botany) | Phytochemistry | Chemical standardization |
| 2) Estrogenic Agents: *In Vitro* and *In Vivo* Evaluation | PhD (organic chemistry) PhD (biochemistry) PhD (biochemistry) | *In vitro*: biochemistry, cell biology, pharmacology *In vivo*: animal studies | Assessment of mechanisms of action (estrogenic and other) |
| 3) In Vitro Studies of Metabolism, Absorption, and Toxicity | PhD (pharmacology) PhD (biochemistry) | Mass spectrometry | Development of high throughput screens for safety and models to assess bioavailability and metabolism of botanicals |
| 4) Clinical Evaluation of Botanical Dietary Supplements | PhD (public administration and policy) MD (obstetrics and gynecology) MPA (health services administration) | RCT, $n = 112$ Double blind Placebo controlled 4 arms: placebo, Prempro®, red clover, black cohosh | Biological (hot flash frequency and intensity, hormone parameters, biochemistry, urinalysis, hematology, lipid profile, DEXA, mammogram, PAP smear, endometrial biopsy, PK analysis); quality of life |

## University of Maryland

| Study | Qualifications | Design | Outcomes |
|---|---|---|---|
| 1) Cost-Effectiveness and Long-Term Outcomes following Acupuncture Treatment for Osteoarthritis of the Knee | MD (rheumatology)<br>PhD (epidemiology)<br>MD (family medicine)<br>PhD (biostatistics) | Longitudinal outcomes study, $n = 570$ | Pain, disability, mood, quality of life, costs |
| 2) Fibromyalgia: A Randomized Controlled Trial of a Mind–Body Intervention | MD (family medicine)<br>MD (rheumatology)<br>PhD (psychology)<br>PhD (biostatistics) | Randomized, $n = 110$ | Pain, mood, quality of life |
| 3) The Effects of Electroacupuncture on Persistent Inflammation and Pain | PhD (physiology), LAc[c]<br>PhD (neurology), LAc[c] | In vitro and animal | Pain, C-fos, protein expression |
| 4) Herbal Therapy in Immune-Mediated Arthritis | MD (rheumatology)<br>MD (rheumatology, immunology), MPH | In vitro | Cytokines GVDH |

## University of Michigan

| Study | Qualifications | Design | Outcomes |
|---|---|---|---|
| 1) A Study of Reiki to Control Pain in Diabetic Patients | MD (endocrinology)<br>BS, reiki master | Randomized trial, $n = 120$<br>Single blind<br>Control = sham reiki | Metabolic measures (blood sugar, lipid); pain (subjective); quality of life |
| 2) A Study of Hawthorn Extract in Chronic | MD (cardiology), MS<br>ND (naturopathy)<br>MPH (epidemiology) | Randomized trial, $n = 120$<br>Double blind<br>Placebo controlled | Ability to exercise (physical tests), quality of life |

(*continued*)

TABLE 6.3 (continued)

| Centers, Projects | Researchers' Specializations[a] | Type of Research[b] | Outcome Measures |
|---|---|---|---|
| 3) Qigong and Psychosocial Effects during Rehabilitation after Cardiac Surgery | MD (family medicine) PhD (psychology), MS acupuncturist PhD (psychology) MD (cardiac surgery) | Randomized trial, $n = 360$ Single blind Controls = no treatment, mimic qigong | Pain (subjective), mental health, quality of life, wound healing, length of hospital stay, biological markers |
| **University of Pennsylvania** | | | |
| 1) Action, Safety, and Clinical Effectiveness of Hyperbaric Oxygen Therapy for Treatment of Head and Neck Tumors | MD (otorhinolargyngology) PhD (nursing science), RN (surgical oncology) PhD (physics) | Randomized trial, $n = 40$ Unblinded Control = standard treatment | Biochemical (tissue oxygenation and angiogenesis); clinical (wound healing, quality of life) |
| 2) Effects of Hyperbaric Oxygen Therapy on Growth of Blood Vessels and Tumors | PhD (microbiology) MD (radiation oncology) PhD (pathology) | Basic science | Assessments of tissue oxygenation, angiogenesis, tumor growth |

| | | | |
|---|---|---|---|
| 3) Effects of Hyperbaric Oxygen Therapy on Cell Adhesion and on Growth of Metastatic Tumor Cells in Lung | MD (general surgery), PhD (physiology) MD (pathology), PhD (cell biology) | Basic science | Evaluation of $O_2$ effects on cell–cell adhesion and tumor cell growth |
| 4) Effects of Elevated Oxygen Pressures on Cellular Levels of Nitric Oxide | MD (emergency medicine), PhD (microbiology) PhD (biomedical engineering) | Basic science | Evaluation of $O_2$ effects of mechanisms for nitric oxide synthase activation |

[a]Unless otherwise indicated, the first person listed is the principal investigator, the others are co-investigators.
[b]In all cases, the persons taking and assessing the outcome measures are blinded; unblinded refers to the patient and practitioner; single blind refers to the patient only; double blind refers to the patient and practitioner.
[c]Licensed Acupuncturist.
[d]Doctor of Chiropractic.

selective. It should be noted that all the centers are engaged in other CAM-related projects funded from a variety of sources, including the NCCAM and other units at the NIH.

Despite the diversity of center specializations, there is a remarkable similarity in the methods of research: all the centers are conducting basic scientific investigations, and all are conducting or planning to conduct moderately large clinical trials. Why this consistency? In a word, pragmatism – on the part of both the NCCAM for encouraging through its funding the kind of research that readily lends itself to scientific methods of investigation, and on the part of the centers for agreeing to follow the standard path to achieving their status as centers and the legitimacy of the treatments they are investigating. However, as the following discussion shows, more novel methods of research are also being undertaken, some of which are pushing the boundaries of convention and laying the groundwork for a new modus operandi in science. My comments throughout are based on personal interviews with center directors and researchers; I do not cite the sources unless I received permission to do so.[10]

### HERBS: JUST LIKE DRUGS?

Overall, people in the United States spend more money on herbs and dietary supplements than any other type of CAM. Concern about safety and efficacy placed botanical research at the top of the NCCAM's priority list. In 1994, Congress passed the Dietary Supplement and Health Education Act, which in essence gave herbs the status of food and not drugs. Supporters of the legislation wanted herbs, as well as vitamin and mineral supplements, to bypass the onerous process of FDA approval, which could delay their availability to consumers for years. In the legislation, Congress placed certain labeling requirements on these products, however, instructing manufacturers not to make misleading claims and to provide a balanced view of available scientific information.

---

[10] Many of the people I interviewed were willing to share with me, not only information about their studies, but also the trials and tribulations they have experienced and their thoughts about the nature of their enterprise. I am grateful for their openness and collegiality.

As with all the projects, each center studying a botanical remedy chose it because there was some preliminary evidence of safety and efficacy for a particular medical condition. Some of the centers are starting from scratch, with basic science studies. Their goal is to identify the mechanisms of action of certain botanicals. For instance, at the University of Illinois at Chicago, researchers are conducting test tube studies of extracts and purified compounds of 11 herbs. They are identifying the active ingredients in the herbs, studying how the compounds are metabolized and formulating standardized preparations. They are then enlisting a manufacturer for both the standardized herbal supplements and placebos in order to conduct clinical trials. Studies at Johns Hopkins University of the use of soy and sour cherries to reduce cancer pain and at Oregon Health and Science University of natural antioxidants to treat multiple sclerosis and Alzheimer's disease are testing the effects of these botanicals on animals with the disorders. These studies will lead to clinical trials. For some researchers, studying herbs is simply an extension of research they were already doing in the lab on other substances, and the research design for the new work did not require significant change.

Basic science studies need not precede clinical trials. Some researchers believe that as long as evidence of saftey is available, clinical trials should establish efficacy before scientists undertake laborious studies to identify mechanisms of action. Still others believe that the two types of research should complement each other. An instance of the latter is occurring at Columbia University, where a clinical trial is examining the effectiveness of black cohosh for the treatment of menopausal hot flashes, as well as whether the herb has any effect on cognitive function and/or bone density. This clinical trial is accompanied by parallel basic science studies to examine whether black cohosh (as well as other herbs) is associated with any estrogenic activity in breast cancer cells and/or any beneficial antioxidant or anticancer activity. The clinical trial is examining safety with respect to the endometrium, and the *in vitro* studies are a first step in the examination of saftey with respect to breast cancer.

Botanical medicines readily lend themselves to RCT methods, making the study of herbs similar to the study of pharmaceuticals. However, although clinical trial research is divided into phases I, II, or III (see Chapter 5, Box 5.1), the labels are inappropriate for botanical research because they apply to investigational drugs not yet available to the public, and herbs are not officially investigational drugs. Some research problems are unique to botanicals. One is standardization of the product. Sometimes, researchers, working with scientists at affiliated labs, specify standardization criteria. If not, researchers select a single source for the botanical – a manufacturer, company, or brand – so that everyone in the clinical trial is receiving the same herb or formula. However, these standards may differ among researchers investigating the same botanical if they use different sources, making cumulative findings difficult.[11] Another problem concerns the form in which the herbs should be taken. Most studies use capsules. Researchers at the University of Arizona, however, believed that chamomile tea would be preferable to capsules because it would be easier to take for the children who were the subject population. When standardization problems in the tea became too cumbersome, they decided to switch to an elixir form of chamomile. However, they had to do more research to develop a placebo elixir whose taste and smell would not reveal its identity.[12]

Problems such as these are not insurmountable. They entail objective and practicable resolutions that are being facilitated by basic research. Also, the NCCAM and the FDA are working together to develop research standards that can be applied to all botanical research as well as specific standards for particular herbs. Researchers are hoping that their studies will elicit a more active role for the FDA. Although none of the center studies has yet reached large phase III clinical trials, studies are beginning to appear in the literature showing that certain herbs are effective for certain disorders, others are ineffective, and still others are dangerous, in and of themselves or in interaction with certain drugs.[13]

---

[11] Even the same herb grown in different locations will have different properties. Also, some samples of the same herb may contain, say, the leaf only, whereas others include parts of the stem.

[12] The methods employed in the Arizona study are novel. Researchers recruited participants through local pediatricians – they believed it was important that the children first receive a medical examination and diagnosis. The elixirs (chamomile and placebo) are delivered through the mail, with instructions to take them 3 times a day. Every day the children's parents phone a toll-free number to report whether their children experienced abdominal pain and how severe it was. This trial is being done in phases, so it will take some time to complete.

[13] The NCCAM, the National Institute of Mental Health and the Office of Dietary Supplements, collaborated on an RCT of St. John's Wort for major depression (Davidson

Is this scientific research remaining true to the systems of knowledge that have for centuries informed the use of botanicals? Some center directors believe that they are revealing what is of value and what is dubious and harmful in botanicals. Others are more circumspect, conveying a certain pragmatism about current research. Basic studies of mechanisms of action have to be done, they agree – it enriches our scientific understanding, helps to improve the product or technique, and paves the path toward legitimacy.[14] Yet, they also believe that someone who understands the holistic context of herbs has to oversee the work of those who do not. The concern is that although herbs can be studied like drugs, they do not function like drugs. For instance, herbs are purportedly slower than pharmaceuticals to take effect; however, they are also purported to have longer-lasting effects. Researchers and those who fund the research have to have a good sense of the particular timeframe for particular herbs. Clinical trials of herbs cannot be as speedy as studies of pharmaceuticals.

A different kind of problem that arises in research on botanicals concerns the issue of reductionism. Studies in mainstream medical journals rarely address it, nor do they seem concerned about the tense if not

et al. 2002). It was double blind and placebo controlled, with 340 participants at 12 sites. There were 2 phases: an 8-week trial and, for those who responded positively to the initial treatment, an additional 18 weeks of therapy. Patients were randomized into 3 groups and given a European preparation of St. John's Wort that was used in earlier trials, or Zoloft, or a placebo. In the first phase, depression scores (measured by the Hamilton Depression Scale) dropped an average of 8.7 points for those taking St. John's Wort, 9.2 points for the placebo group, and 10.5 points for the Zoloft group. Another measure, combining the Hamilton Scale and a Clinical Global Impressions–Improvement Scale, showed that 24% of the St. John's Wort group had full responses to treatment compared with 32% of the placebo and 25% of the Zoloft groups. The authors concluded that neither active treatment proved significantly better than placebo, a finding that occurs in about one-third of the trials on antidepressants. It should be noted that claims for St. John's Wort tend to be confined to minor or mild depression.

14 Most CAM researchers are careful to distinguish studies that seek to identify and discuss the mechanisms of action in various treatments from studies that investigate effectiveness. Basic research into the mechanisms of action should ideally follow research that has suggested or established efficacy (why bother investigating the mechanisms of action if a therapy is not effective?). However, there is a fundamental epistemological dimension to the difference between these two types of research. Research on mechanisms of action constitutes a search for causality; research on efficacy seeks to identify correlations (Rubik 1995, 42). This point becomes particularly important in research discussed below on the biological correlates of mind–body therapies.

contradictory relationship between linear logic and holism.[15] Metaphysics aside, reducing herbs to their active ingredients may miss the material context within which herbs function. Even though herbal components appear to be active or inactive in isolation, these designations are relative and not absolute. Accordingly, some centers are putting the parts back together. They plan to compare the effects of the active ingredients and the whole herbs on specific disorders once the more mainstream research is complete.

Some centers have gone a step further and are studying herbal formulae, work that relies on prior studies of specific herbs. A molecular biologist at Columbia University, for instance, is trying to understand a complex Chinese herbal remedy used to treat menopausal women by examining the whole formula and its component herbs. This researcher is investigating the safety of the herbs, in and of themselves, in interaction, and compared with each other and the whole formula, with respect to breast cancer. Although it is much further down the road, some researchers hope to expand on this kind of work by designing studies that consider the individualization with which practitioners of traditional Chinese medicine construct their formulae, and compare both the methods of the practitioners and the efficacy of their formulae. Such an endeavor bridges the study of herbs to the study of holistic systems of medicine and practice, which is discussed later.

### ACUPUNCTURE: SHAMS AND PLACEBOS

More than one-half of the states in the U.S. license the practice of acupuncture. However, they differ on how they define acupuncture (beyond the use of needles to pierce the skin), how they specify the relationship between acupuncturists and physicians (whether or when referrals or supervision are necessary), and what else they allow acupuncturists to do (suggest herbs, offer nutritional or lifestyle counseling) (Cohen 1998, 43–4). Increasing numbers of insurance companies are offering some coverage for acupuncture treatment, but most require a physician referral. Reflecting consumer interest, research on acupuncture has expanded, and now spans the spectrum of methods from basic science to clinical trials. The majority of the current center projects on

---

[15] Critics claim that studies of single, high-dose nutrients are not only short sighted, but also disregard the known interactive effects of nutrients (Gaby 1999).

acupuncture are basic science. Like basic research on herbs, laboratory studies of acupuncture seek to identify the mechanisms of action
as these pertain to biological correlates; they are attempting to clarify
what exactly happens in the body when a person or animal receives
acupuncture.[16]

One approach at the University of Maryland is to investigate the
effects of electroacupuncture on rats. It is based on earlier work suggesting that electroacupuncture selectively reduces the expression of
spinal protein in rats inflicted with persistent inflammation; behavioral
changes in these rats imply an attenuation of pain. The electroacupuncture study at the Minneapolis center, which focuses on addiction, is
premised on preclinical studies in human subjects that have linked
acupuncture treatment with a lower incidence of physical withdrawal
symptoms in opiate addicts. The study tests whether electroacupuncture can prevent the activation of naxalone – an opioid antagonist –
in regions of the brain that are associated with physical withdrawal
symptoms. It also seeks to determine the effects of electroacupuncture
on other biochemical activities that occur in the brain during opiate
withdrawal. Once the basic study is complete, researchers will compare the effects of electroacupuncture and sham electroacupuncture in
specific brain locations and rate the level of suppression of physical
withdrawal symptoms.[17] They will use magnetic resonance imaging of
the brain to project the blood flows that occur through the release of
endorphins during acupuncture.

Other center research, although premised on basic science, is testing the clinical features of acupuncture.[18] For several years now, researchers at the University of Maryland have been studying the effect of acupuncture on chronic pain – specifically, lower back pain,

---

[16] Piecemeal explanations of the mechanisms of action in acupuncture have appeared
over time. Early research conducted by neurobiologists suggested that pain relief was
due in part to the release of endorphins when needles penetrate the skin. Subsequent
research by investigators from other disciplines has yielded explanations involving
vasodilation and stimulation of the immune system (Eskinazi and Meuhsam 2000,
50). There is as yet no comprehensive theory of why and how acupuncture works.
[17] Sham electroacupuncture is also called mock transcutaneous nerve stimulation; electrodes are applied, but no current is passed.
[18] Studies of efficacy are attuned to issues of safety, even though they do not directly
address these. Although there are risks in acupuncture treatment (Yamashita et al.
1998), there is a general consensus that it is no greater than in medicine in general
and not a constraint on clinical trials of efficacy.

fibromyalgia, and arthritis. A large part of the research has been devoted to developing appropriate controls, which is particularly tricky
with acupuncture. Proof of the efficacy of acupuncture rests on comparing it with something that is not acupuncture but appears to be
true acupuncture to blinded study participants. Most of the published
research during the 1990s relied on what is known as sham acupuncture as the main control. In this procedure, needles are inserted near
the "real" acupuncture point (that is, the sham is off-channel or off-
site).[19] There is no consistency across studies in where exactly the sham
insertion occurs, nor on the depth of insertion. Although the needle-
twisting technique is generally the same as for the true acupuncture in
each study, these too differ across studies. A major problem with sham
acupuncture is that traditional acupuncture theory does not recognize
the possibility of an inactive point at which the insertion of a needle
would create a sham situation. Most practitioners acknowledge that
they simply do not know if there are any neutral places and, if there are,
where they are and how they can be located (Wiseman and Ellis 1985;
Lao 1996).[20] At the same time, studies that date back to the early 1980s
have been demonstrating that sham acupuncture produces an analgesic
effect, making it "a poor form of acupuncture treatment" (Lewith and
Machin 1983, 112; see also NIH 1998; Shlay et al. 1998).[21] However,
as with true acupuncture, the effects of sham acupuncture can also be
negative.

---

[19] Some acupuncturists refuse to do sham acupuncture because it is invasive. Some also
have ethical concerns about participating in clinical trials if treatment is withheld
from the control group. Practitioners of other therapies have similar reserves. The
centers all use trained acupuncturists who are in some way associated with the center.
These acupuncturists are, therefore, fully aware of the need for research and research
protocols; many are researchers themselves.

[20] Researchers (in the West) have investigated acupuncture points and believe that they
contain certain unique anatomical features and high electrical conductivity (Rubik
1995, 43–4). Accordingly, some biomedical researchers and (Western) acupuncture
practitioners believe that sham acupuncture at neutral points is possible, even though
Lewith and Machin (1983) found that its analgesic effect was 40% to 50% compared
with 60% for true acupuncture.

[21] One biochemical explanation for this phenomenon is that some of the neuropeptide
substances released from general stimulation of the skin, muscles, and nerves may
be similar to those released in acupuncture. The therapeutic effects of massage and
spinal manipulation may be similarly explained. However, we need to know more
about how these various therapies work to understand why one of them may be
better than the others for any particular ailment.

Accordingly, during their first round of OAM funding, researchers at the University of Maryland began to work on the development of a truer form of placebo acupuncture, something that would be noninvasive, yet would make patients who had never before received acupuncture believe they were receiving true acupuncture. Thus, they used an empty plastic needle tube that was tapped on the bony area next to each acupuncture point to produce a discernible sensation (Lao et al. 1995).[22] Although the number of patients who completed the study was small (19), the researchers found that patients were generally unaware of their treatment assignment. Also, none of the patients in the control group experienced pain relief and all had to take "rescue pain medication" after oral surgery (426).

Other types of placebo acupuncture that have been developed include a blunt needle that produces a pricking sensation when it touches the skin even though it does not penetrate the skin, simulating the puncturing that occurs in a true acupuncture procedure (Streitberger and Kleinhenz 1998; Park et al. 2001). Researchers at the Oregon School of Oriental Medicine, a member of the Oregon Health and Science University consortium, are conducting a preliminary study of the responses of patients who have never before received acupuncture to 3 different placebos: a blunt-end needle, a needle that comes in a guide tube and is tapped on the skin, and a toothpick in a guide tube.[23] This kind of research is leading to more sophisticated clinical trials whose findings will speak to both the theory and practice of acupuncture, as well as to the significance of the placebo effect.

Another study at the University of Maryland on acupuncture for treatment of osteoarthritis of the knee is now published. Researchers innovated on the standard features of an RCT by using two randomized groups. One received acupuncture treatment for 8 weeks; the second

---

[22] They also inserted electrodes from a mock electrical stimulator to all the needle tubes and told all the patients that because of the high frequency they may or may not feel an electrical current (Lao et al. 1995, 426).

[23] A study that compared real acupuncture with a poke from a toothpick in a guide tube found that one-half of those receiving the toothpick believed that they were "probably" (but none said "definitely") in the real acupuncture group. Of those receiving real acupuncture, a little less than one-third believed that they "probably" and a little more than one-third believed that they "definitely" were in the real acupuncture group. Significantly more subjects in the real acupuncture group reported immediate pain relief (Sherman et al. 2002).

did nothing for 8 weeks and then received acupuncture treatment for 4 weeks (Singh et al. 2001). Patients in both groups experienced strong improvement after 4 weeks of treatment. At the end of the 12-week period, those patients who were more disabled retained the benefits of treatment, whereas those with the least disability and pain rebounded. This kind of study, and there is increasingly more of it in the literature on various types of CAM modalities, is premised on a deeper understanding of the activity of placebo, the potential ethical problems in the use of sham treatments, and the clinical relevance of research that compares a study treatment with what patients normally do – either nothing or receive standard care. The current cost-effectiveness study listed in Table 6.3 is a continuation of a phase III RCT.

For whatever reason, these studies of the use of acupuncture for pain are finding more efficacy than studies using sham needle insertion at off-site points. Two studies of acupuncture for addiction are noteworthy. A large RCT of cocaine addicts found that auricular acupuncture was not more effective than sham needle insertion (using nonspecified points) or relaxation controls in reducing cocaine use (Margolin et al. 2002). A large RCT of alcohol-dependent patients also found that auricular acupuncture did not make a significant contribution to reducing desire for alcohol compared to nonspecified needle insertion or standard treatment (Bullock et al. 2002).

## PHYSICAL MANIPULATION: STILL SEARCHING FOR PLACEBO

Surveys show that Americans use chiropractors more often than any other alternative practitioner group (Eisenberg et al. 1998). Shedding the dubious status of bonesetters, chiropractic became a profession in 1895 and advanced through the 20th century to acquire independent legal status, self-regulation, training in colleges and postgraduate universities (these are accredited by the Council on Chiropractic Education, whose role is certified by the Department of Education), and licensure in all 50 states as well as in several other countries. Chiropractic students spend more hours than medical students in anatomy and physiology, about the same in biochemistry and microbiology, and less in pharmacology and surgery (Meeker and Haldeman 2002). A triumph occurred for the profession in 1983 when the 7th Circuit Court agreed that the AMA and its Committee on Quackery had engaged in a "nationwide conspiracy to eliminate a licensed profession" (Cohen 1998, 21). Since then, insurance companies and MCOs have begun to cover chiropractic, practitioner and physician cross-referrals have grown, and states have begun to grant chiropractors the statutory right and obligation to conduct general examinations of patients and render medical diagnoses. Many chiropractors have straddled the fence about defining themselves as mainstream or CAM practitioners; some have jumped to one side or the other (Meeker and Haldeman 2002).

Researchers have not yet been able to adequately explain the mechanisms of action in chiropractic because too many active agents and nonspecific effects are said to be involved in the treatment and in patients' responses to manipulation. Confounding the variables, most chiropractors do more than spinal adjustment insofar as many do what general practitioners normally do. Although the specific procedures of chiropractic are codified, practitioners individualize their treatment and one practitioner's choices may differ from another's. Also, there is considerable disagreement within the profession on theoretical issues in spinal adjustment techniques and on the scope of the practice (Kaptchuk and Eisenberg 1998). Researchers at the Palmer Center have been conducting basic science studies, using various kinds of technology, such as magnetic resonance imaging, to detect the physiological and biochemical effects of spinal manipulation in both animals and human subjects, including cadavers. Some clinical trials have also begun, but because Palmer is a first-wave center with less funding than those in the second wave, these trials are small-scale pilot studies.

The goal of one pilot, which is now published, was to develop a form of sham chiropractic to pave the way for RCTs that blind patients (Hawk et al. 2002). Although great care was taken in all the design features, the weak results speak to the difficulty of the whole endeavor. To handle the challenge of practitioner variations, the researchers selected as the active intervention a technique for which the best evidence of efficacy existed in the literature. They trained certified chiropractors in its use and tested for consistency across the practitioners, including standardization of the clinical encounter to create similar patient expectations. To develop a sham, they convened a group of experts and instructed them to reach a consensus on a suitable technique. Another group of chiropractors was trained in this sham technique. After the treatments, the patients – women with chronic pelvic pain who had never visited a chiropractor – were asked to assess the clinician–patient interaction and to guess their randomly assigned group. One-half of the responses in both groups were correct. Outcome measures were mixed – greater improvement for the active intervention group on the primary measure of pain, but inconsistent differences using other measures of pain. However, this was a multisite study and the differences in improvement for the experimental group were greatest at the site where the chiropractor had the most experience in using the experimental technique.

A different center study is investigating both acupuncture and osteopathic cranial sacral manipulation.[24] This form of physical manipulation is similar to what chiropractors do in trying to realign bones. However, it is somewhat gentler – an important consideration to researchers at the University of Arizona, whose subjects are children with cerebral palsy. There is little treatment available for these children; the doctors at the university of Arizona knew of preliminary evidence about the effectiveness of acupuncture and osteopathic manipulation and wanted to test these two treatments further. But there is no sham for cranial sacral manipulation and, at any rate, the doctors were not comfortable using sham treatment on the children. They therefore decided to use a wait control. Because they wanted to do something for the 19 children who were randomized to this control group, they recruited student volunteers to read and play games, spending about the same amount of time with them as children in the intervention group were spending in treatment. There was no illusion, however, that this attention was anything more than nontherapeutic play. After the 6-month period of the study, the children in the wait control group and their parents were allowed to choose which active treatment they wanted to receive. Sixty-four children were randomized into the 2 main groups (intervention and control), and the intervention group was further randomized to receive the 2 forms of treatment.[25]

---

[24] Osteopaths (DOs) barely qualify, if at all, as CAM practitioners. They receive more training than chiropractors, and their education is very similar to that of MDs. Although they specialize in neuromuscular-skeletal disorders, they are now licensed to practice all phases of medicine and surgery across the U.S. and are covered by most insurances.

[25] An additional 8 children are receiving both treatments. Their parents were interested in participating in the study but did not want their children randomized. Researchers

The researchers also had to make some important decisions about how they were measuring outcomes. Initially, they had intended to use surface electromagnetic imaging to measure degree of muscle tension in the children. However, in a preliminary pilot study, they found that the children wanted to watch the computer monitors, which meant that they were able to see the measurement lines and the changes that occurred when they did something with their bodies. Because this kind of awareness potentially taints the outcome measure, the technology was abandoned. The choice of an alternative measure came from anecdotal information that parents of children who were receiving the treatments were offering about improvements in certain daily activities. As a result, level of daily functioning became the main outcome variable. It was supplemented by the decision to include a pediatric physical therapist on the team. Based on standard measures of movement, she developed a special inventory applicable to children with cerebral palsy. As with many of the projects, a quality-of-life scale specially adapted for the study population rounded out the measures, which in this case were taken at baseline, midway through, and at the end of the study. Finally, the researchers decided to have 3 different kinds of practitioners conduct the outcome measures. A practitioner of traditional Chinese medicine, 2 osteopaths, and 2 physical therapists, all of whom were blinded, examined all the children, each according to the principles of their practice. These assessments are also being used to develop profiles of children who seem to respond better to one treatment or the other, a task that was undertaken in lieu of actually comparing the 2 forms of treatment.

Another set of researchers at the University of Arizona also wanted to test cranial sacral manipulation as a treatment for recurrent middle ear infection. Although several osteopaths in the community were opposed to the endeavor, voicing concerns about both the concept of a sham control and the issue of withholding treatment, a group was willing to participate. They developed a type of control that all believed would be appropriate for the study of children ages 1 to 5 years without violating information given to parents during recruitment. The control was an osteopathic exam, which is "hands on" but does not include

are monitoring their progress with the same measures they are applying to the other participants.

any form of manipulation. However, it looks like treatment to those who are not familiar with osteopathic treatment. The researchers decided that an important first step would be to test the validity of their control. They conducted a preliminary trial, after which they asked parents in which group they thought their children were placed. The preponderance of incorrect guesses gave the researchers confidence in their control. They then proceeded to compare osteopathic manipulation with echinacea, a common remedy for colds and ear infections, and a product for which placebo controls are standard. The researchers chose one manufacturer and received all the echinacea used in the study from one lot. They allowed the parents to diagnose their child's cold and to administer the herb (or placebo) as a 10-day treatment over the 6-month period of the trial.

The research design involved 4 arms. One group received real echinacea and real osteopathic manipulation, another received real echinacea and an osteopathic exam, a third group received placebo echinacea and real osteopathic manipulation, and the fourth received placebo echninacea and an osteopathic exam. All the children received an osteopathic exam before they were randomized. The researchers reported to parents with children in the control group any osteopathic lesions found either before or during the trial and offered treatment. The data from this study are currently being analyzed and the researchers will soon begin writing up the findings for publication.

## MIND–BODY THERAPIES: RENDERING THE SUBJECTIVE OBJECTIVE

On the surface it would seem that mind–body therapies are the least amenable to RCTs, if not antithetical to science itself. However, basic studies of the biological correlates of several mind–body therapies have captured technologically what happens in the body when a person engages in, for instance, relaxation techniques or biofeedback. Also, a number of RCTs on mind–body therapies have been conducted and published, and there are systematic reviews and meta-analyses of them in the literature.[26] For the most part, these studies are beginning to

---

[26] cf Winstead-Fry and Kijek 1999; Abbot 2000; Astin, Harkness, and Ernst 2000; Hadhazy et al. 2000; Luebbert, Dahme, and Hasenbring 2001). These reviews

demonstrate that scientific methods can structure investigations of efficacy, and that reliable controls – blind participation and the administration of a placebo, sham, or some other appropriate control, including standard treatment and no treatment – are vital to scientific rigor and acceptability. Nevertheless, important and tricky questions arise in this research. Because the procedures in many mind–body therapies are particularly complex and their administration more subjective than what occurs in conventional treatments, the specification of rigorous controls is a balancing act between science and interpretation. How one captures the subjective in objective terms and separates components of a multifaceted therapy without destroying its holistic context, to name a few issues, are judgment calls on the part of investigators. They are therefore subject to debate.

Based on research underway at the centers, we can distinguish two main kinds of mind–body therapies: those that require active involvement by the practitioner, such as reiki, and those that rely more on active involvement by the subject, ranging from physical movement, as in yoga and tai chi, to the metaphysical dimensions of meditation and prayer. Qigong consists of both.

Let us begin with the role of practitioners. The intention of the practitioner is a critical component of many CAM therapies. To be sure, intention enters into all health care in some way. Placebo studies in medical research demonstrate that a clinician's expectation of outcome can be transmitted to patients (Gracely et al. 1985). However, in conventional medicine technology assists a physician's efforts to treat patients, whereas in some CAM therapies intention blends with the treatment. Energy healing is a case in point. It raises particularly bewildering situations for researchers. Confusion and contradiction have developed in some studies that attempt to measure factors in practitioner subjectivity, primarily intention, in this and related CAM therapies. For instance, proponents of therapeutic touch claim that the intent of the practitioner to heal is a *necessary* component of the treatment and that there is a "human energy field" that the practitioner manipulates. A controversial and well-publicized study published in the *Journal of the*

inevitably find various kinds of methodological problems, but amidst the overall inconsistency and inconclusiveness, there are a few gems of methodological rigor and significant evidence of effectiveness.

*American Medical Association* failed to confirm these postulates (Rosa et al. 1998). Designed by a sixth-grade student for a science fair, the study set out to investigate whether practitioners of therapeutic touch can actually perceive the human energy field. The 21 practitioners, with experience ranging from 1 to 27 years, were able to correctly locate the investigator's hand behind a screen in only 44% of the 280 tests, a finding that is "close to what would be expected for random chance" (1005). The authors concluded that their study provides "unrefuted evidence that the claims of TT [therapeutic touch] are groundless and that further professional use is unjustified" (1005). In an editor's note in the same issue, George D. Lundberg confirmed that "[t]his simple, statistically valid study tests the theoretical basis for 'Therapeutic Touch': the 'human energy field.' This study found that such a field does not exist" (1040).[27] Counter to this dismissal, one could say that the study presented a case of what Vickers et al. (1997, 119) called the confusion between no evidence of effect and evidence of no effect: "if a study fails to demonstrate an effect, it does not mean that an effect does not exist, only that it could not be found by the study as carried out."[28]

A few researchers are undertaking the difficult task of specifying the scientific basis of energy healing through identification and measurement of its biophysiological and biochemical effects on patients, as well as identification and measurement of the bioelectromagnetic correlates of the purported human energy field (Wardell and Engebretson 2001; Wilkinson et al. 2002).[29] The difficulty of studying these mechanisms of action is compounded by the fact that there are various types of energy healers, such as practitioners of reiki, healing

[27] He added, "I believe that practitioners should disclose these results to patients, third-party payers should question whether they should pay for this procedure, and patients should save their money and refuse to pay for this procedure until or unless additional honest experimentation demonstrates an actual effect" (1040).

[28] For a critique of the study and its methods, see Eskinazi and Muehsam (1999).

[29] These studies are still at an embryonic stage, especially in the United States. However, various technologies that measure or identify heat are available, such as a super-conducting quantum interference device developed in Japan. Since 1990, it has been used to measure and produce images of magnetic fields emitted by the human body, especially the brain. To detect an energy healer's emission of heat, researchers can also use such standard devices as electroencephalographs, electrocardiograms, electromyograms, new photographic technologies, and measures of voltage change in parts of the skin. The problem with all this, one researcher told me, is that energy healing consists of more than infrared.

touch, therapeutic touch, hands-on healing, and qigong, most of whom are generally certified but in no state are they licensed. What they do is different in terms of both epistemology and technique. Even within one type of energy healing, practitioner differences may occur in the amount and kind of heat emitted because of differences in experience, ability to influence the energy field of a particular subject, assessment of the subject, and such specific features of the technique as extent of touch and body sites targeted. One control for these differences is to use only one practitioner in a clinical trial. Researchers must expect, however, that individualization would still occur, even when different patients have similar health conditions, because individualization is integral to the technique. At the same time, an energy healer may not treat a single patient the same way in consecutive sessions because the patient will have changed and thereby require a different approach. However, if researchers decide to use only one practitioner, they may be faulted because the trial would necessarily be small. A single practitioner can treat only a limited number of patients and having fewer patients endangers the robustness and validity of outcomes. So even this control raises conundrums.

At present, research at the centers is focusing primarily on efficacy, although in some trials mechanisms of action are also being studied. The working assumption is that evidence of efficacy should precede and promote studies of mechanisms (Ai et al. 2001, 95). Two important studies are underway at the University of Michigan.

In one study, researchers opted to conduct a fairly large-scale trial of the effects of reiki on 120 diabetic patients. They also decided to use sham treatment as a placebo-like control, hiring and training actors to pose as reiki practitioners.[30] Patients were first randomized into 2 groups: one receiving real treatment, and the other receiving sham treatment. They were then randomized again into 2 real and

---

[30] Because sham reiki is not invasive, it does not raise the same kinds of ethical concerns as, say, sham acupuncture. The main ethical concern is withholding treatment. In this regard, it is interesting to note that the researchers had hoped to have a third arm of no treatment. However, they had trouble recruiting participants – everyone wanted to have a 50–50 chance of receiving reiki treatment. There are very few remedies available to relieve the pain, especially in the feet, experienced by people with type 2 diabetes. Sometimes researchers offer the treatment to the placebo group after the clinical phase of the study is complete.

2 sham groups so that each of the 4 "practitioners" treated about 30 patients. This design represented a compromise between the need to adhere to the tenets of science and the desire to demonstrate what reiki can and cannot do. The researchers expect to publish the findings soon.

Another ongoing study at the University of Michigan focuses on the dimension of qigong that theorizes a transfer of energy by a trained qigong master.[31] The study has three, layered goals (Ai, 2003). One is to design a conventional efficacy trial. A second is to test the mechanisms of action in qigong, such as the energy alternation that occurs in biological factors (for example, stress hormone and immunological biomarkers). This energy alternation mediates the effect of qigong and, in this case, postoperative wound healing. A third goal is to test the placebo effect. Researchers are randomizing 360 cardiac surgery patients into 3 groups. One group is receiving no treatment, a second mimic qigong, and a third real qigong by a master. Having trained actors provide the mimic treatment was justified by the assumption that only qigong masters can transfer energy. All participants are given brochures that explain the basic elements of qigong related to energy and movement. To further address the placebo effect, the researchers are asking patients after their participation in the trial if they believed they had received the effective (real) treatment. Because the treatment involves a human healer (this is the psychotherapy component of the study as stated in the title), the researchers believe that a placebo effect (hope) is bound to occur in the mimic group. They therefore hypothesized that, in comparison with the no treatment group, the qigong treatment

---

[31] From a Western point of view, qigong can be thought of as a multifaceted form of energy healing (Ai et al. 2001, 94). However, people in China consider it to be primarily an active or inactive form of exercise (personal interview). There are various dimensions of qigong. One is an active dimension in which participants slowly practice exercises as instructed by a qigong master; another is a passive dimension in which participants focus on their breathing while in a still position. Another way of describing qigong is to say that it consists of an external dimension in which a master attempts to heal through the transfer of energy – the master manipulates a patient's qi or transmits energy to a patient – and an internal dimension in which people promote their own self-healing (94). These various dimensions may or may not be combined, depending on whether people consult a qigong master and whom they consult, because determinations differ among masters. Practitioners within the qigong circle in China also recognize that qigong energy can be "dark," that is, misguided by either the person who is incorrectly practicing the exercises or incorrectly breathing or by the person (the master) who is manipulating energy (Ai, 2003).

group will have better outcomes. However, they also hypothesized that the mimic group and those who believed they were in the real qigong group might also have some improvement due to the placebo effect. Struggling to harness subjectivity and the placebo response in healing situations, these researchers suggested, in an earlier publication describing the study's design, that if their study finds qigong to be "effective because of patients' expectations, [they] should not see this as a treatment failure as in a drug trial, but seek an explanation other than the meridian system" (Ai et al. 2001, 96).[32]

The significance of practitioner intent can be probed further by turning to the stance of the subject or recipient of treatment. Some energy healers believe that these two loci of intention are inseparable. Many reiki practitioners, for instance, maintain that their role is only a partial factor in energy healing and that most of the "work" devolves to the recipient. To put it differently, reiki practitioners consider themselves to be facilitators in healing. There is more research on intent as it relates to subjects who are engaging in relaxation techniques; some of it is also applicable to practitioner intent. One study that is particularly noteworthy set 4 experimental situations for all 8 subjects: biofeedback with intended relaxation, biofeedback with no relaxation exercise, random feedback with intended relaxation, and random feedback with no relaxation exercise (Critchley et al. 2001). Positron emission topography data showed that during the "intention to relax" tasks, activity increased in certain (cognitive) regions of the brain and caused a decrease in those regions of the brain that control sympathetic arousal. That is, intention produced relaxation in both feedback situations, but more profoundly when intended relaxation was combined with biofeedback. This study also noted variability within and between subjects in the performance of the tasks. Even when subjects did not achieve relaxation effectively, as well as when they were instructed not to relax, there were similar but lower levels of brain activity.[33]

---

[32] Traditional Chinese medicine is based on a theory of vital energy (qi or chi) that circulates through bodily pathways (the meridian system of channels that connect the entire body) (Ai et al. 2001, 94).

[33] This finding conforms to a claim made in a study comparing the relaxation response and a placebo (Stefano et al. 2001). After demonstrating similar biological correlates in the peripheral and central nervous systems of these two techniques, the authors ask why the placebo effect does not work all the time. They argue that it does at a basal level, with different expressions among individuals (14).

Research on meditation is following along similar lines. There is a large and growing literature on the biology of meditation, and despite the inevitable methodological inconsistencies, there is mounting evidence of health benefits. Researchers at Maharishi University have contributed to this literature (Walton et al. in press). These researchers maintain that transcendental meditation is a highly systematized technique. The courses of instruction for learning transcendental meditation are standardized, as is the training of transcendental meditation teachers, who are certified but not licensed in any state. Teachers are supposed to know how to adjust the lessons for each student and to assess whether students are using too much effort in their meditation.[34] Up to a point, it can be assumed, then, that once people learn to meditate, they are all doing the same thing. Nevertheless, one of the thorniest issues in research on mind–body therapies remains differences among participants in what they are doing and in the intrusion of their minds (subjectivity) in their performance of the experimental task.

Current projects at Maharishi University aim to draw out the clinical relevance of meditation. The issue of controls remains important, but the working assumption is that subjective factors and placebo responses are inevitably involved in these therapies. Both of the research center projects are continuing earlier work on biological correlates, and both are comparing the effects of meditation with health education. Control groups consist of classes that teach exercise, healthy cooking, etc., but not such stress reduction techniques as meditation. The control groups practice what they learn at home and keep a daily diary. Also in both studies, the patients randomized to the meditation groups are new to the practice. The expectation is that, although there might be some minimal improvement in the control groups, there will be considerably more improvement in the meditation groups.

Guided imagery is another technique that is based on patients' ability to control their thoughts; it also requires a trained (and, in most states, a certified) instructor. Frequently, people receive an audiotape to

---

[34] The theory of transcendental meditation holds that meditation is a natural process that makes use of the natural tendency of the mind to settle down and experience its own source, known as "transcendal pure consciousness." Once it is properly learned, it should be effortless. Transcendental meditation is based in Vedic knowledge, which its adherents claim has always been scientific insofar as it is systematic, reliable, comprehensive, and verifiable.

take home for their practice sessions. As with meditation, once a person has learned the technique and has the tape, practice is self-controlled. When investigating therapies that require learning on the part of the subject, researchers must decide how to handle questions about the level of competence and compliance, and about individualization – that is, whether those who seem to be having difficulties with the technique should receive additional assistance. Although these and a host of other questions occur for all participants, their resolution is more complicated when the subjects are children. Researchers at the University of Arizona decided to defer to standardization and expediency.

Their study asks whether guided imagery adds anything to the more conventional techniques with which it is closely related: breathing and progressive muscle relaxation. They randomized 40 children ages 5 to 18 years into 2 groups, all of whom were told that they would be learning "relaxation techniques." One group, the intervention group, received initial, individual, one-hour training in all three techniques. The other group, the control group, received initial, individual, one-hour training in breathing exercises alone. Two therapists, using standardized protocols, did all the initial training and follow-up. All the children were given a tape and instructed to practice at home 2 times per day. Both the children and their parents kept a daily diary of incidences and levels of abdominal pain. The children used the well-validated FACES scale, which contains figure faces with different kinds of smiles and frowns. All the children returned to see the therapist for 3 more individual one-hour sessions. The therapists were careful not to go beyond basic instructions in the weekly follow-ups when the children reported how they were doing. The researchers realized that most parents would discover their child's placement group, insofar as the informed consent disclosures explained all 3 techniques. However, they were confident that the children would remain unaware of their group placement. This study will be completed soon.

One of the more daring center projects is on prayer. As discussed in Chapter 3, studies of the relationship between spirituality and health are growing in number and, despite methodological inconsistencies, so are the positive findings. We saw in Chapter 4 that even some physicians are turning to the healing power of spirituality, for both themselves and their patients. In prior work, researchers at Johns Hopkins University found that, even when they designed studies with control groups that received no spiritual intervention, it was difficult to keep spirituality out of the study (Yanek et al. 2001). Specifically, when activities, such as standard exercises for heart patients, were conducted in a group of churchgoers who knew each other, participants spontaneously included prayer at the start of each session or religious singing to help their movements along. The researchers knew in advance that religion would be an important part of their subjects' lives; their research is premised on the assumption that belief is critical to positive health outcomes. However, they did not think that spirituality would be a factor in a study conducted in a nonspiritual setting (a hotel ballroom) and involving nonspiritual activity (exercise).

The study listed in Table 6.3 is selecting over a period of 4 years 80 breast cancer patients who expressed interest in a recruitment pamphlet on contemplative prayer.[35] Although religious or spiritual factors were not criteria for participation, most of the subjects are Christian. Participants agree to be randomized into 2 groups and know that they will learn contemplative prayer either in the first (the intervention group) or second phase (the 6-month wait-control group) of the trial. A skilled prayer leader teaches contemplative prayer first to the primary intervention group. After a 4-hour training session, participants pray at home twice a day for 6 months. They also meet as a group with the trainer once a week and pray together. While waiting, the control group receives what is called attention placebo. It consists of the same 4 hours of initial training and once-a-week group sessions, but the content of both is health education. The teacher instructs participants on such activities as diet and exercise, on how to do self-exams of the breast, on how to prevent osteoporosis, and so on. Participants receive instructional materials, and are told to practice good health behavior at home and to enter their activities into a log book twice a day. The goal of this design

---

[35] Also known as centering prayer, contemplative prayer is an ancient practice most commonly undertaken by Roman Catholic, Anglo-Catholic, and orthodox believers. It is highly structured and requires considerable discipline. Based on the concept of a dialogue with God, not supplication as occurs in much prayer, practitioners choose a word, usually with two syllables, that is meaningful. They silently repeat the word, breathing in on one syllable and out on the next. It is expected that the repetition blends into nonactivity, inducing a sense of peace and quiet in which there are no thoughts. Although like meditation, practitioners distinguish between contemplative prayer and meditation by the felt connection with a divine being that occurs in contemplative prayer.

is to maximize comparability between the two groups in all factors, except that the emphasis in one is spiritual and, in the other, nonemotional education. After the 6-month wait, members of the control group are offered the opportunity to learn contemplative prayer as promised. The researchers are not conducting outcome measures on them.

The researchers are hypothesizing that contemplative prayer will reduce the stress associated with breast cancer. Based on a biological model of the physiological effects of mental stress, they are measuring such markers of stress as cortisol blood levels. However, they are emphasizing that prayer cannot be reduced to its biological correlates because prayer is not simply a means of stress reduction. More goes on when a person prays (or believes), and the "communion with a divine power" can neither be measured nor fully explained. Nor does supplementing the outcome measures with a quality-of-life component that uses a living-with-cancer scale suffice. But it broaches, they believe, the important subjective dimension of health and healing.

## MOVEMENT THERAPIES: EAST MEETS WEST

Movement therapies are sometimes considered to be mind–body therapies and, in fact, many non-Western movement therapies are contained within larger systems of healing that combine movement with mindfulness practices and diet. Yoga, a component of Ayurvedic medicine, and tai chi and qigong, both embedded in traditional Chinese medicine, are examples. In the United States, these movement therapies are commonly practiced as isolated activities and considered forms of exercise that induce relaxation and build flexibility and strength. Instructors guide students in incorporating mindfulness as they either stretch and breathe into a yoga position, or as they follow a formal progression of postures, movements, and breathing, as in tai chi. The active form of qigong is similar to the slow movement of tai chi; its passive form is essentially mindful breathing. As noted above, qigong can also include a transfer of energy from a master to another individual, or it can consist of an individual summoning his or her own healing powers. Instructors in these 3 movement therapies are certified but not licensed in the United States.

There are a few studies in the medical literature that analyze the biological correlates of yoga and tai chi. There are also a number of similar studies on breathing exercises (which is the subject category for qigong on Medline), but few of these explicitly refer to qigong. Using various types of diagnostic technology and varying degrees of rigor, researchers from around the world have found that yoga, either in general or certain of its specific types, increases alpha waves, decreases serum cortisol levels, improves depression, and enhances subjective well-being (Janakiramaiah et al. 2000; Kamei et al. 2000; Malathi et al. 2000). Studies have found that tai chi increases levels of blood lactate, oxygen, circulation, mental control, flexibility, and muscle strength (Lan et al. 2001; Li, Hong, and Chan 2001; Wang, Lan, and Wong 2001). Similar positive results occur in studies that separate meditation, progressive muscle relaxation, and breathing exercises.[36] One study that compared the latter two found predictable outcomes – improved physical relaxation and disengagement with progressive muscle relaxation and improved awareness with breathing exercises (Matsumoto and Smith 2001). Studies have also found positive results from using these movement therapies for specific health problems: yoga for muskuloskeletal problems (Garfinkel et al. 1998; Garfinkel and Schumacher 2000), tai chi for problems of balance (Zwick et al. 2000; Wu 2002), and breathing exercises for pulmonary and even heart disorders (Bernardi et al. 2002; Calahin et al. 2002). Recommendations are tentative, however, pending more studies with consistent, rigorous methods. Poor or inconsistent methodology is a constant complaint by scholars who review published studies, as well as in letters to the editors of journals publishing these studies.

Although in their infancy, in terms of both numbers and methodological sophistication, RCTs on movement therapies are progressing. Their success as RCTs rests on the reliability of the controls used – a particularly perplexing problem for all mind–body therapies that rely on active participation by the patient or subject. Inventing a form of sham yoga or tai chi in which students are not stretching or slowly moving, however minimally, taxes the imagination. Although it has been done, the use of sham instructors or sham instruction is considered

---

[36] Most of these studies are done with lay participants who are novices to the practice; occasionally, instructors are the subjects. One study of a yoga master suggested that a shift in breathing patterns may have contributed to increased alpha brain activity during meditation as measured by an electroencephalograph (Arambula et al. 2001).

unreliable, more so than with reiki, because approximate movements may have approximate effects. Most investigations are tending, therefore, to bypass the concept of placebo, and to test instead the efficacy of movement therapy compared with other therapies or no therapy. This is an important innovation in RCT research in general, for it assumes a role for the placebo effect (that is, researchers cannot assume a placebo control means no effect) and highlights the importance of no treatment. Researchers at the centers have chosen this route. They are employing expert instructors to develop specialized movement therapies for the populations under study and to guide the participants in their use.

Researchers at Oregon Health and Science University have been working with two populations for whom attention deficits contribute to cognitive and functional decline: people over the age of 65 and people with multiple sclerosis. Reasoning that yoga helps one learn to focus attention on the muscles that are being stretched and on breathing, they decided to compare hatha yoga (specifically, Iyengar) therapy with aerobic exercise programs. The research team included medical specialists who worked with specialists in yoga, exercise, and physical therapy to develop special programs for the two populations. The techniques of teaching and practicing hatha yoga are somewhat standardized, involving at minimum an "orderly" and "progressive" stretch into specific postures or asanas (Garfinkel et al. 1998, 1602). Yoga instructors are commonly certified by the program in which they received training. Having settled the issue of controls, the researchers at Oregon Health and Science still had to confront another methodological problem endemic to any treatment, alternative or conventional, that requires learning on the part of subjects – the question of assessing and monitoring how well subjects learn and perform the therapy. Their response was to remain as true as possible to the theoretical tenets of the therapy while systematizing as much of the research protocol as feasible, and allowing individuals to learn at their own pace and according to their own needs. Each of the two cohorts (seniors ages 65 to 85 years and adults younger than 65 years of age, both with multiple sclerosis) was divided into three groups: one was the treatment group (yoga therapy) and two were control groups (aerobic exercise and a waiting list, that is, a no treatment group). The aerobic exercise for the seniors is a walking class headed by a certified geriatric exercise trainer (who is also a nurse) along with home exercise. For the multiple sclerosis cohort, aerobic exercise is stationary bicycling in a class headed by a physical therapist and home exercise. Each group of subjects (except the no treatment group) participates in a $1\frac{1}{2}$-hour class once a week for 6 months, and each receives instructions on what to do at home and how to record their home practices. After the 6-month wait, subjects in that group can take either yoga or exercise classes. Within these scientific parameters, the researchers allowed the instructor to present yoga not as "a pill to be taken" but as a means to building awareness of the needs of one's body, to develop individualized poses and instructions when necessary, and to encourage patients to create their own proactive yoga practice in class and improvise at home (Kishiyama et al. 2002, 61).[37]

One of the researchers on the tai chi project at Emory University is a neurologist and specialist in movement disorders; the other is a physical therapist who has studied the effects of tai chi on the elderly. The purpose of the study is to investigate the extent to which the kind of slow, continuous, and mindful movements of tai chi can affect the progressive neurological deterioration that occurs in patients with Parkinson's disease. The Neurology Department at Emory specializes in Parkinson's disease. The researchers believed it would be useful to compare tai chi, which involves low caloric expenditure, with a practice that involves more mindfulness and little if any movement (or minimal caloric expenditure), namely, the passive form of qigong, as well as with aerobic exercise, which involves more vigorous movement (moderate caloric expenditure) and little if any mindfulness. Each practice involves an instructor and, although each is fairly standardized, the researchers allowed the instructors to individualize their teaching when necessary because the study population has limited physical capacity and many comorbidities. As with yoga and meditation, the instructor's role is to make sure the patients are performing the movements correctly to the best of their ability. Patients are also given handouts and encouraged to practice at home. The classes are fairly small (6 or 7 patients each) to allow for individual attention. Patients attend classes twice a week

---

[37] Preliminary results on the patients with multiple sclerosis show that while neither yoga nor aerobic exercise appeared to have any impact on cognitive function, there was significant improvement in fatigue for the two intervention groups when compared with the waiting list group.

for 16 weeks and return for follow-up visits 3 and 6 months later. This study is ongoing.

## HOLISTIC SYSTEMS: DO PARTS ADD UP TO WHOLES?

Certain systems of medical practice and healing combine specific elements of the various therapies discussed thus far into a holistic approach. Three that are most relevant to the research at the centers – naturopathy, traditional Chinese medicine, and Ayurvedic medicine – can be thought of as professionalized health care systems insofar as they follow certain formalized practice principles.[38] However, none of the center projects listed in Table 6.3 are investigating these systems as a whole, only parts of them. Because the modalities that are informed by traditional Chinese medicine and Ayurvedic medicine have already been discussed, let us look at naturopathy. First, some background.

Naturopathy traces its roots to the late 19th century when a German practitioner – Benedict Lust, a patient and later a student of Father Sebastian Kneipp – emigrated to the United States and opened a School of Naturopathy in New York City. By the early 1900s, there were more than 20 such schools in the United States. Ebbs and flows occurred throughout the 20th century in accordance with such obstacles as the Flexner Report in 1910 (see note 7 in Chapter 2) and the growth of a medical industrial complex after World War II, and such positive forces as an abiding consumer interest in natural approaches to health care. There are now four naturopathic medical schools in the United States and one in Canada.[39] Twelve states license more than 2,000

---

[38] The first OAM panel charged with defining alternative systems of medical practice suggested these general characteristics of professionalized health care, including conventional Western biomedicine: each has (1) a theory of health and disease; (2) an educational scheme to teach its concepts; (3) a delivery system involving practitioners who usually practice in offices, clinics, or hospitals; (4) a material support system to produce its medicines and therapeutic devices; (5) a legal and economic mandate to regulate its practice; (6) a set of cultural expectations on the role of the medical system; and (7) a means to confer "professional" status on the approved providers (Workshop on Alternative Medicine 1995, 69).

[39] From 1987 to 2000, the U.S. Department of Education recognized the Council for Naturopathic Medical Education as the accrediting institution for these schools. The council is currently waging an effort to reestablish its role. Only the University of Bridgeport College of Naturopathic Medicine failed to meet the accreditation

naturopathic doctors (NDs). The vocabulary the statutes use to describe what these physicians do varies, but the overall understanding is similar (Cohen 1998, 41–2). Although naturopathic physicians are often referred to as general practitioners of complementary medicine (Smith and Logan 2002, 182), and some licensing statutes view them as primary caregivers (Cohen 1998, 42), they can be considered "integrative" practitioners. That is, they know and may practice some of the basics of conventional medicine together with their alternative modalities. The first 2 of the 4 years of naturopathic education closely resemble a premed program with courses in physiology, biochemistry, pharmacology, etc., so naturopaths are cognizant of biomedical approaches to health care. However, only in a few states are they allowed to prescribe pharmaceuticals (Arizona, Oregon, Utah), perform minor surgery (Arizona, Oregon), and facilitate natural childbirth (Arizona, Oregon, Utah, Washington).

In general, naturopaths treat the whole person by identifying the multiple causes of illness; prescribing herbal and pharmaceutical supplements and, sometimes, homeopathic remedies; and suggesting dietary and other lifestyles changes, including, sometimes, spiritual counseling, to both prevent illness and promote health (Workshop on Alternative Medicine 1996, 88–9). Although there is a certain degree of standardization, then, in training and in the storehouse of interventions, and although most naturopaths conduct medical diagnoses, their assessments and treatment protocols are individualized. Differences among naturopaths even extend to contrasting holistic and scientific worldviews (Boon 1998). Shinto et al. (2002) conducted a survey of licensed naturopaths in the United States to discover what treatments were most commonly used to treat patients with multiple sclerosis. Although 70% of those who had treated at least one multiple sclerosis patient cited at least one therapy they considered useful, the total number of therapies used by all the respondents was more than 200.

As a follow-up to the survey, researchers at Oregon Health and Science University are engaged in a novel pilot project designed to systematize a naturopathic approach to the treatment of multiple sclerosis to pave the way for RCT research. The research design allows

requirements of the (inter)national association. It is, however, accredited by the New England Association of Schools and Colleges.

for the evaluation of a complex system of medicine while meeting the scientific criteria of reproducibility. Because it is a pilot, it is not listed in Table 6.3. First, the researchers identified 5 naturopathic experts in multiple sclerosis, elicited their treatments, and circulated the responses among them. Second, they had the experts meet and develop a consensus treatment plan. The product was a core treatment regimen accompanied by a 25-item treatment algorithm. The core treatment regimen included diet, vitamin and mineral supplements, and psychospiritual counseling. The core treatment reflected therapies that the clinical experts deemed beneficial for all patients with multiple sclerosis. The algorithm attempts to capture the patient-individualized approach to naturopathy. Time constraints, while attaining approval from the university's institutional review board for the full model, prevented the inclusion of the treatment algorithm in the trial. The trial is currently underway and is evaluating only the core treatment regimen for people with multiple sclerosis in a pilot randomized clinical trial.

Researchers at the Kaiser Foundation have taken part of the naturopathic repertoire and developed a study that more closely resembles those on herbs. Because there is no standard naturopathic treatment for periodontitis, they prepared 3 models. One is a combination of herbs, and the other two are combinations of vitamins and minerals. This is a phase II trial, so the number of participants is too small to compare the 3 naturopathic treatments to each other. Instead, the 3 treatments together are being compared with a placebo capsule. The recruitment is complete and the project is currently under way. The researchers decided that based on ethical concerns, all 120 participants should receive standard dental treatment first (scaling, root treatment, and oral hygiene). The participants were then randomized into 2 groups. Approximately 30 participants are receiving the placebo capsule. The remaining participants were further randomized into the 3 naturopathic treatment groups. Because the naturopathic treatment is new, patients are being monitored throughout the study for adverse effects. One of the goals of the study is to see if the naturopathic treatments are safe and tolerable, while another is to see if they are an improvement over standard care, or at least a beneficial supplement.

Despite this fragmentation of naturopathy into its parts, we should note that the centers have not abandoned investigation of the holism of these three healing systems (traditional Chinese medicine, Ayurvedic medicine, and naturopathy). In addition to the pilot project at Oregon Health and Science University, a research team from Columbia University is conducting an ethnobotany study in New York City to explore how ethnic practitioners view and treat their patients, including the herbs, dietary lifestyle changes, and other rituals they use and recommend. They are also investigating the range of approaches taken by various practitioners toward the treatment of a single Western diagnosis. Another group at Columbia University is examining the differences among diets that obtain phytonutrients through eating whole foods, compared with dietary supplementation of phytonutrients. A follow-up study will ask if people can make difficult and long-lasting changes in their eating patterns and if those changes are sufficient to have clinically significant effects (for example, change in breast cancer risk factors, cardiovascular risk factors, markers of bone metabolism, etc.).

Also, for more than 15 years researchers at Maharishi University have been studying Vedic medicine as a comprehensive health care system. In conjunction with their sibling universities in other countries, they are building a series of case studies for specific disorders and for problems in aging (Nader et al. 2000; Schneider et al. 2002).

PARTS AND WHOLES

In many of the research projects presented here, we have come across projects that extract parts from wholes. Researchers pursue the active ingredients in herbs, the chemicals released in acupuncture and massage treatments, the biological correlates of meditation, and so on. Are they thereby falling into reductionism? In interviews, several recognized this possibility. Some noted that each part of a CAM therapy can be thought of as important in and of itself; others added that it is the parts that get funded. One said that every CAM researcher rides two horses at the same time. All the researchers are doing the best they can to separate the parts without misrepresenting the therapy and doing a disservice to the study population.

Although the researchers recognize that in the present climate the parts have to be separated, they and others are wondering how and when the parts will be reunited. As noted earlier, the next step in this research might be to study how individualization in, say, herbal remedies varies among practitioners and what difference it makes. Following that, if research proceeds further, the herbal and dietary dimensions of naturopathy, traditional Chinese medicine, and Ayurvedic medicine might be joined with their other components. I would speculate that this last step will be much more difficult for traditional Chinese medicine because its practice is disjointed even in Asia.[40] Practitioners of Ayurvedic medicine, however, are more consistent in combining the parts – diet, exercise, meditation – although what these consist of is individualized. At what point researchers will ask whether the whole is more than the sum of its parts and act upon the question is anybody's guess. It is an especially difficult question because formulating and answering it will entail all the complexities discussed here.

## SO, WHEN ALL IS SAID AND DONE

Will these and related studies suffice to shake off the charge that specific CAM modalities remain unproven? Quantitatively, no – more studies are needed. Qualitatively, it remains to be seen. Although some of the research on CAM, especially those studies with reliable placebo controls, should pass muster, many of the others are pushing the boundaries of RCTs, at least as the RCT is currently understood in medical research. However, to the extent that the methods in this research are deemed to be sophisticated and of high quality, their validity should emerge, especially as the studies are repeated. The main route for this eventuality is publication in peer-reviewed journals.

All the centers aim to have their research published in peer-reviewed journals. It is central to the process of gaining legitimacy. But a roadblock may arise, one that is typical in academics. All disciplines (medicine, nursing, public health, biology, chemistry, sociology, anthropology, etc.) hold certain journals as core in their fields, presenting the mainstreams of their current knowledge. Each specialty within a discipline (neurology, epidemiology, American history, etc.) also has its core journals. Specialists usually aim to publish in the mainstream of

---

[40] In Hong Kong, for example, traditional Chinese medicine practitioners specialize in herbal remedies, but very few are also acupuncturists. Although these 2 practices are combined in Korea, in parts of China a third and sometimes a fourth feature are added – tai chi or qigong and reflexology.

their discipline whenever possible. CAM researchers aspire to publish in mainstream medical journals, and many of these journals do, occasionally, accept articles on CAM, usually fairly large-scale, standard RCT research. An exception is the article on therapeutic touch mentioned earlier. Critics claim that there is publication bias in medicine and that CAM research is held to a higher standard of research and a higher threshold of proof (Cassileth, Jonas, and Cassidy 1995, 293). All that can be said at this point is that it remains to be seen what the response will be in the medical community to the current wave of CAM research.

Some CAM researchers believe that publication in peer-reviewed CAM journals is not only acceptable but necessary (personal interviews). The process of review is as rigorous as elsewhere, the chances of acceptance higher, and, therefore, the time from submission to publication speedier. Also, abstracts of the articles are available through Medline for all who are interested. Furthermore, as studies published in peer-reviewed journals accumulate, the chances are enhanced for systematic reviews and Cochrane Collaboration meta-analyses of the therapies. As discussed in Chapter 5, these analyses are becoming central to evidence-based medicine. The main question in all of this is whether the mainstreaming of CAM will occur more firmly in the literature than in the practice of health care.

What does seem certain is that research on CAM will continue for the foreseeable future, regardless of whether the centers currently in operation are refunded or new ones created, or whether the center program continues. The NCCAM and other centers and institutes at the NIH and elsewhere are committed to funding more studies that "prove" the safety and efficacy of CAM. The NIH in general prefers that claims of "proof" be based on established standards of scientific investigation. However, there is also a general acknowledgment that sometimes a round peg cannot be forced into a square hole. The NCCAM has begun a new program on what it calls "frontier medicine" to develop novel research on therapies that are not well suited to RCT methods.

The issue of safety also raises problems for CAM researchers insofar as standards for measuring safety do not yet exist for most CAM therapies. With regard to herbs, although standards of safety exist (such as side effects and longer-term effects), they have not yet been fully incorporated into research. It is important that tests of safety be built into CAM research – they need not precede the research, as is the norm in medicine. CAM researchers have to study safety because the medical community demands it, even though many of the modalities have been used for years – some for hundreds and even thousands of years. We can expect a greater role in the future for the FDA in overseeing research that entails questions of safety, especially botanical research. The NCCAM and the FDA have begun to collaborate on certain projects by developing research standards. It remains to be seen if they will also stamp the findings of research with their seals of approval and regulate the products that are proven to be safe and effective. Whatever more results from research on CAM, there is little doubt that it is playing a major role in the process of mainstreaming CAM, and in legitimizing certain therapies by demonstrating their safety and efficacy.

# 7

# The Road Ahead: Accommodation or Integration?

The preceding chapters set out to answer certain questions: what is CAM, why are so many people using it, why is this growth occurring now, how is the relationship between CAM and medicine changing, and what consequences will any of this have for health care. In answering these questions, I have outlined at the same time a remarkable change within the last several years in the status of CAM. It has moved from being a vaguely understood collection of marginal and, per some people, disreputable practices to being a mixed bag of practices – some are better understood and becoming valued, others are still fuzzy and unimpressive. There have been a number of drivers behind this change in status: users of CAM, physicians, researchers, insurance companies, and government. All are making distinctions among different alternative therapies and selecting certain therapies for further exploration. Each set of actors is drawing on different but related kinds of knowledge as they engage in these activities. The result is a mainstreaming of certain therapies – those that people are using; that physicians are recommending and, in some cases, practicing; that researchers are investigating and finding to be safe and effective; that insurers are reimbursing; and that government is supporting through NIH funding for research. I turn now to the task of pulling these strands together, highlighting the role of each of these main actors, and weighing their relative contributions to the process of mainstreaming. In offering an overview of where CAM now stands, I introduce a new development in the evolving relationship between CAM and medicine – the appearance of integrative medicine clinics. Although still in their infancy, they offer an indication of how CAM is likely to impact the future of health care.

## CAM: THE WHOLE AND ITS PARTS

Despite the research that is being conducted to clarify mechanisms of action and specify uses, all of which is easing the mainstreaming of certain therapies, CAM remains a disparate set of practices, variously employed by people who seek health and healing and by health care providers who seek more than medicine can offer. To promote understanding of the phenomenon called CAM, researchers tell us to place the different therapies in different categories based on their fields of practice. This formal system, presented in Table 1.1, remains a useful tool for organizing our analytic approach to CAM. It is laying a foundation for mainstreaming by providing a common language and set of references for everyone interested in CAM. However, to understand more deeply some of the distinctions among alternative therapies, we need information that cannot be derived from categories alone.

For instance, we have seen that within any single category of CAM, say, manual healing therapeutics, there are practices, such as massage therapy, that are more widely used, better understood, and gaining more acceptance than others, such as the various biofield therapies (energy healing). These differences in use, apprehension, and acceptability are due only in part to research. Research is bound to influence physicians more than patients, but physicians will read research findings through various lenses. For instance, some physicians who want to encourage their patients to participate in a relaxation program might more readily suggest guided imagery than meditation, even though research is unveiling the biological correlates of meditation. We now know more about the science of why and how meditation works. So why might there be a hesitancy on the part of physicians to include meditation as an option for their patients? Perhaps it is because there are various schools of meditation, and we do not yet know the significance of the differences among them. Nor do we know why some patients choose transcendental meditation, while others prefer Benson's method for eliciting a relaxation response through self-directed mantras. Perhaps it is because certain kinds of meditation, such as transcendental meditation, are, at least on the surface, more spiritual than others, such as the relaxation response, or they embody a philosophy that goes beyond health care per se. Recall, however, that many of Benson's patients choose a prayer as their mantra, but the choice is theirs alone and no further context for their choice of mantra is needed, unlike what happens in transcendental meditation. Many physicians are still unsure about the spiritual dimensions of their jobs, so they may prefer to recommend methods of relaxation that avoid the topic. These considerations refine our understanding of CAM, but they are not the sorts of ideas that can easily be incorporated in definitions and categories. Nor will their significance be easily captured by scientific research.

## HEALTH AND HEALING SEEKERS

Examining how people who use CAM make distinctions among seemingly similar therapies also expands our approach to understanding CAM. Surveys tell us that CAM is used by millions of people from all walks of life, with different backgrounds, different economic and social circumstances, different values and beliefs, and different health and illness conditions. Each individual has his or her own set of reasons for using CAM, and each evaluates any one therapy from his or her own unique perspective. For most people, CAM is a partner in health care. Some people who are ill have incorporated CAM into their treatment regimen. Some people who used CAM when they were ill continue to use it to maintain their health. Some people have begun to use CAM even though they are not ill, perhaps to enhance their well-being, perhaps to broaden their understanding of their bodies, their health, and their selves. These approaches to CAM embody many motives and many kinds of knowledge. Individuals gain information about alternative therapies from diverse sources. Because only a few physicians are recommending or referring patients to practitioners, we can surmise that people are making their own decisions, perhaps searching for scientific information in libraries or on the Internet, perhaps coming across anecdotes, perhaps reaching deep inside themselves to discover their preferences. People may be limited in their choices because of their financial situation or where they live. In part, choices are rational. This is why many patients are using CAM alongside medicine because both contribute to health and healing. In part, choices draw on the diverse foundations of human action, including nonrational factors (values) and irrational factors (emotions). Any given individual can be quite rational in selecting a particular therapy for his or her particular needs while also recognizing his or her willingness to suspend rationality in order to fully experience that therapy.

Different kinds of knowledge, based on different sources of information and different experiences, guide people to use different kinds of CAM. One person may try both acupuncture and visualization for low back pain, another may go to a chiropractor, another to a massage therapist and a reiki master. The capacity of people to construct for themselves the immediate relevance of different pieces of information, different messages, and different norms and values helps to explain why patients have not rejected medicine, despite disenchantment with certain features of medicine. Many recognize the limits of medicine, however, so they supplement medicine with CAM. Health and healing seekers integrate for themselves the array of options that are at hand and that they can find.

There is no doubt that growing use of CAM is advancing the process of mainstreaming. Although mainstreaming based on use grants legitimacy to CAM, this legitimacy is confined in scope. Any particular therapy, while legitimate for those who use it, is not necessarily legitimate for others, even those with the same illness, background, social values, and so on. Mainstreaming based on the legitimacy of CAM to individuals who use it is tentative and unsystematic. To be sure, growing use initiated and hastened mainstreaming, and consumers remain major stakeholders in this process. However, critical dimensions of mainstreaming are now occurring in other arenas. Because of growing use, physicians have become interested in CAM and government is funding research on the alternative therapies that people are using the most and for which there is some evidence, even anecdotal, of efficacy. Ultimately, legitimacy in health care and, hence, the mainstreaming of CAM, rests on the actions of the medical community. Accordingly, the bulk of this book has explored mainstreaming from the perspective of medicine and the relationship between CAM and medicine at an institutional level of analysis.

## PHYSICIANS AND RESEARCHERS

As late as 1990, the AMA still used the word *quackery* to judge at least some alternative therapies. Derogative terms continue to appear on occasion in mainstream medical journals. In general, however, the medical profession is no longer as hostile to CAM as it once was. This is not to say that the profession has embraced CAM, although some of its members seem to have done so. For the most part, physicians are gradually accepting the possibility that CAM can contribute to health care. Among the professional reasons for growing interest in CAM is patient use. However, there are disturbing features in this growth because some patients do not inform their physicians of their use of CAM and people as a whole are visiting CAM practitioners more than they visit primary care providers. Yet, some patients have clearly benefited from CAM. As clinicians, physicians put considerable weight on experience, even when it defies conventional wisdom. However, the most important factor behind the change in physician attitudes is research that is proving certain therapies to have specific benefits for specific disorders. As we have seen, however, there are a number of caveats in the extent to which we can expect this research to influence the attitudes of physicians.

I have suggested that first and foremost the medical profession will only consider research based on the model of an RCT. Most of the research, past and present, on herbs and acupuncture adheres closely if not always fully to the standard model of an RCT. I suspect that as these studies accumulate, the medical profession will accept their findings – as long as the studies also demonstrate safety and circumscribe the claims for efficacy. This latter task entails a major hurdle for botanical research because it requires researchers to specify the substance, the formula, the dosage, and the source, as well as the disorder and the type of patient for which they are claiming efficacy. It is a hurdle similar to those faced in investigations of new drugs. It is not insurmountable, but it will require close liaisons between researchers and producers of herbs, from the farmer to the manufacturer. The NCCAM and the FDA are working together to formulate current good manufacturing practices to ensure that dietary supplements are not adulterated and are accurately labeled to reflect the active and other ingredients in the product (http://www.fda.gov).

It may be more difficult to make similar specifications for the other therapies. Their uses are many and diverse, and funding for research on several uses for any one therapy may tighten – especially because most alternative therapies do not involve products that can bring profits, as is the case with herbs. However, it may not be as necessary as it is with herbs to test for all the possible uses of certain other therapies, insofar as their modalities are less invasive. Certain mind–body therapies are in a unique position here, especially those that use the mind more than the body. They have a highly generalized applicability because their central role pertains to relaxation, which is a factor in all illness and well-being. Also, the patient is very much in control of certain of these therapies (even hypnosis is a technique that patients learn and then practice on their own). Researchers are hoping that once they establish the safety and efficacy of certain mind–body therapies for certain disorders, the medical community will grant legitimacy to the healing potential of these therapies in general.

Research on other therapies is in a more precarious position because there are questions about the safety of some of them. Even yoga, which is classified as a mind–body therapy, faces an uncertain future. A number of oncologists, for instance, oppose yoga for their patients. They may, however, be swayed by positive findings about tai chi because it is less strenuous, or by findings that clearly specify the practice of yoga for specific kinds of cancer patients. Another example is that some physicians consider acupuncture to be invasive insofar as the needles stimulate the skin, which is an organ, and nerves. Also, questions about the safety of acupuncture, chiropractic, and massage therapy remain because practitioners vary in skill. We do not yet know how much RCT research will be needed on such issues before these therapies are deemed legitimate and more fully mainstreamed.

As these examples indicate, RCT research in and of itself may not be the single determining factor in physician acceptance of a therapy. Physicians use a variety of criteria to evaluate therapies, both medical and CAM. Consider, for instance, RCT research on certain biofield therapeutics, such as reiki. Even though these studies adhere as fully as possible to the RCT format, some of them are, arguably, more successful than others. At present, there is no basis for anticipating how their efforts will be judged. This uncertainty about how physicians read RCT studies is not unique to evaluations of CAM. The medical profession has recognized that facts do not always speak for themselves. For instance, confronted with new data about the effects of hormone replacement therapy, some physicians are advising women to continue their treatments, others are warning them to desist, and still others are providing women with as much information (or sources of information) as they can and delegating the decision to women themselves.

Chapter 6 surveyed a number of research projects that do not fully conform to the standard RCT model. In some cases, it has not been possible to randomize patients, or to blind certain or all participants except the person who is evaluating the data, or to use a placebo control, or to use any control. Similar divergences from the standard model also occur in medical research and for similar reasons. However, in medical research, not adhering to the standard usually occurs because of the dire condition of patients, not because of peculiarities in the treatment. We can only speculate as to how physicians will respond to the creative use of RCT methods in CAM research. My own guess is that they will be attentive to studies with convincing explanations for not randomizing, or for not blinding anyone but the data analyst, or for not using a placebo control and choosing the particular control that was used. Studies that can be and are replicated stand a better chance of acceptance.

We might obtain some answers to some of these questions as more researchers begin to submit articles for publication. Whether studies currently underway in a number of research settings across the U.S. will be published, let alone published in mainstream medical or CAM journals, rests on the interpretation of peer reviewers.[1] Where research is published also affects the process of mainstreaming. Researchers often decide first who they want their audience to be. An article on tai chi for heart patients aimed at CAM researchers and practitioners will be written differently than one intended for cardiologists. Sometimes, authors hope to publish in a mainstream medical journal and, when their articles are rejected, they may turn to other venues. Reviewers generally indicate whether their rejection was due to the research method, the research topic, the way the article was written, or other reasons. Based on their reading of reviewers' comments, authors decide on their next steps.

In some cases, there will be disagreement among the reviewers, which is common throughout academia. RCT research that makes

---

[1] For the most part, peers are from the same discipline or field as the author. Most journals have editorial boards whose members read submissions. Editors in chief decide who on the board should review manuscripts and which outside reviewers to ask.

flexible and creative use of the standard model is more likely to engender disagreement. For any number of reasons, some reviewers will not be satisfied with explanations for divergence, whereas others will feel that the transgression was minor and the results outweigh the methodological innovations. When reviewers disagree, editors decide the fate of the submission based on their judgments of the reviews and the article itself. Without belaboring the point further, peer evaluation is both an art and a science; it rests on both subjective and objective criteria; and it involves personal, collective, and institutional points of reference. Where CAM researchers submit their work tells us who they consider (or want) their peers to be. How these peers evaluate that research tells us something about where the relationship between CAM and medicine is heading.

Other kinds of research, based on case and observational studies as well as small clinical trials, are less important to the health care community, but these studies will not necessarily be dismissed. Case studies, observational studies, and small trials of medical products and medical disorders regularly appear in medical journals. These studies are based on and inform everyday clinical experience, and they help physicians build a multifarious "stock of knowledge." All physicians conduct case studies and collect observations, whether formally or not, as part of their daily work. Discovering that other physicians have made similar observations and assessing how they have treated certain cases is an important part of clinical practice. Journals publish case and observational studies after peer reviewers have judged them to have merit beyond their specific setting. Sometimes case and observational studies suffice to provide physicians with the information they need. Not all case and observational studies warrant further investigation, nor can all be brought to the clinical trial phase. These circumstances occur in both medical and CAM research. However, we can expect that CAM research based on case and observational studies will be judged by a higher standard than medical research. When CAM researchers decide to end their investigations without proceeding to small clinical trials, it will be incumbent upon them to fully explain their decisions – especially if they have found a positive effect and believe a particular therapy has value. These explanations will have to convince physicians that the particular methodological difficulties entailed are insurmountable. Simply asserting that the therapies are not like drugs and cannot be tested like drugs is not enough. Researchers will also have to meticulously detail their proof of safety and of potential benefit to make the case that further investigation is not necessary and that the particular therapy warrants legitimacy.

In sum, change in attitude toward CAM on the part of the medical profession is primarily influenced by research. We can imagine that physicians approach this research above all from the perspective of formal knowledge, grounded in the methodological standard they commonly use to judge all new treatments. As I suggested, however, physicians – as readers, reviewers, researchers, and clinicians – also draw on informal knowledge to understand information about health care. They must read the expressions of patients, interpret the significance of new ideas, and be aware of their own biases in the recommendations they make. To be sure, their ideologies and self-interests influence the everyday working lives of physicians and their approach to CAM and CAM research. There are any number of reasons, professional and personal, why physicians hold certain attitudes toward CAM and why they judge and interpret CAM research as they do.

Overall, it seems that physicians are accommodating themselves and their profession to CAM. They are allowing CAM to expand the idea of health care and their practice of medicine, some willingly and openheartedly, others more reservedly. In a growing number of ways, CAM and conventional medicine are becoming partners in the shared goal of health and healing. We cannot say that medicine has changed profoundly as a result of this partnership. But some of its members believe it is being enriched as a profession and as a form of treatment by this expanded scope. Some physicians have also accepted CAM as an indirect route toward improvement in their interpersonal relations with patients. Patients stand to benefit from all these changes. As research continues to distinguish those therapies that are safe and effective from those that are not and as the impact of CAM on medicine becomes clearer, I would expect that fewer physicians would see CAM as a threat to their profession and that they would interpret the challenges posed by CAM as constructive to health care. We can expect growth in the ranks of those who are accommodating CAM and allowing it to influence and even enter their practice of medicine. Whether physicians will actually recommend CAM, refer patients to CAM practitioners, or simply be better informed in their discussions with patients depends largely on the role of actors outside the medical profession – insurers, the hospitals and clinics that deliver health care and the administrators that make decisions about delivery systems, and government.

### INSURANCE COMPANIES AND DELIVERY SYSTEMS

Changing physician attitudes must also be seen in light of developments in the corporatization of health care. As discussed in Chapter 4, physicians sense a loss of autonomy, a strain in their relations with patients, and a general disenchantment with medicine, in large part because of the demands of MCOs,[2] insurers, administrators, and other corporate actors. In this way, the demeanor of physicians resonates with the complaints of patients. Many patients are attracted to CAM because it offers a quality of care and caring that they are not finding in conventional medical settings. It is possible that physicians who are becoming more interested in CAM are seeking similar respites. Therefore, along with various patients' interests in CAM and physicians' interests in science, the corporatization of health care is another factor shaping the mainstreaming of alternative medicine and its impact on American health care.

Interestingly, despite the fact that the inadequacies in corporate health care are driving patients and physicians to turn to CAM, corporate actors are not adverse to the possibility of a new partnership with CAM. Take the case of MCOs. Market rationality dictates MCOs' perceptions of the benefits and costs of including coverage of CAM in their health care plans, and it seems that consumer demand is the major market force. A survey found that at the top of MCOs' decisions about CAM are "retain existing enrollees," "demand from consumers," and "attract new enrollees" (Pelletier and Astin 2002, 42). Lower in importance is "demonstrated clinical efficacy." The same ranking informs MCOs' decisions on continuing to expand coverage for alternative medicine. This should not be read as saying that research is not important to MCOs. Its role is secondary, however, in that it helps MCOs legitimize their approach to CAM. At the moment, MCOs do not appear to be generous in meeting consumer demand for

---

[2] MCOs integrate insurance for and delivery of health care. In this discussion, I also refer to insurance companies and health delivery systems that are not MCOs.

CAM. Only about 10% of the money spent by consumers on CAM is reimburseable (Marber 2000). Understandably, insurance companies are testing the extent of consumer demand and determining how low they can go to maintain consumer satisfaction and increase their market advantage.

There is another side to MCO support for and interest in CAM. Insofar as MCOs have their roots, if not their heart and soul, in health maintenance, there is a potential affinity between MCOs and CAM at the level of preventive health care. Incorporating the goal of prevention into a system of health care enables MCOs to address, to some extent, patients' needs, physicians' frustrations, and their own financial solvency. From the perspective of patients and physicians in general, prevention is or should be the purpose of health care. When patients are ill, they want a cure, to be sure. They also want to know how they can avoid the unpleasant situation of being ill. However, the contemporary practice of medicine is oriented toward cure, and patients tend to visit physicians only when they are ill and seeking a cure. Burdened as they are in curing illness, physicians welcome preventive health care. Encouraging patients to engage in prevention is unlikely to put physicians out of business because there is enough illness demanding their attention; furthermore, it educates patients about their role as partners in health care. MCOs tried and failed to make prevention an integral part of medical practice – it proved to be too expensive, insofar as it was accompanied by costly diagnostic technology, and physicians were too preoccupied with curing illness. CAM may offer an opportunity to try again.

To the extent that CAM as a form of preventive health care can reduce patients' use of health care resources, MCOs benefit. At the same time, to the extent that CAM is an adjunct to medicine, it might enable physicians to cure while using fewer resources. However, we do not know at this time whether the potential of CAM to save on costs can and will be realized. This uncertainty may also be holding MCOs back from offering more generous CAM benefits at present. It is widely assumed that CAM could curtail ever-mounting expenditures in conventional health care, whether as a form of preventive care or in direct comparison to conventional treatments. However, very few studies have confirmed this view and taken into account the multiple and diverse organizational layers and institutional interests in cost–benefit analyses. Interestingly, one national survey found that one-half of the MCOs in their sample believed that CAM adds to total health care costs and only about 20% believed that it reduces costs (Landmark Healthcare, Inc. 1999).

That insurance companies offer some coverage for CAM is an important factor in the process of mainstreaming. If and when they expand their coverage, insurance companies might contribute to an increase in the use of CAM. This too may be holding them back from offering more.[3] At present, we can conclude that most MCOs and other insurance companies are accommodating themselves to CAM, but they are not, for the most part, embracing it. In this sense, the role of insurance in mainstreaming CAM may not be critical, even though it is important.

A few MCOs are doing more than simply reimbursing expenditures for CAM. They are developing wellness centers on their premises. For a discount, patients can receive massage or shiatsu, take yoga or meditation classes, and, if the primary care physician has given a referral, receive acupuncture. MCOs have hired these practitioners and are financially supporting the overhead costs of their services. They are developing a more integrative relationship with CAM by making it a more visible and regularized component of their health care system. Other health delivery systems are engaging in a similar but more expansive practice. To elaborate this development, I turn to the example of what is called integrative medicine clinics.[4] Their experience casts a different perspective on the role of health care providers in mainstreaming CAM and the new role of CAM in health care.

## INTEGRATIVE MEDICINE CLINICS

Across the United States, a sampling of hospitals, medical centers, and health care plans, including MCOs, are offering patients a range of

---

[3] There are inconsistent findings on the relationship between insurance coverage and use of CAM. One national survey found that people who have insurance coverage for CAM are more likely to use it than those without insurance coverage (Wolsko et al. 2002). However, another survey, focused on Washington state, found that only 1% of patients with CAM coverage used it, resulting in lower per member costs than expected (Stewart, Weeks, and Bent 2001).

[4] The NCCAM currently defines integrative medicine as health care that "combines mainstream medical therapies and CAM therapies for which there is some high-quality scientific evidence of safety and effectiveness" (http://nccam.nih.gov/health/whatiscam/index.htm#3).

CAM services in integrative medicine clinics.[5] There are no reliable figures on the number of these clinics across the country, but we do know that the number is growing.[6] They are called integrative clinics because they *systematically* join conventional medicine and CAM. This feature distinguishes integrative clinics from wellness centers. Medical care is a priority in integrative medicine. Therefore, most integrative clinics are directed by MDs; in those few directed by NDs, DOs, or PhDs, MDs are invariably on the staff. Directors of integrative clinics believe it is important that illnesses requiring medical care be ruled out before patients receive CAM (personal interviews). They also try to keep primary care physicians fully informed about the care their patients are receiving at the clinics. Although CAM practitioners or others at a clinic commonly initiate contact with physicians outside the clinic, once the providers have established communication, they tend to regularly consult each other on patient care and to coordinate care when necessary. Within the clinics, physicians and CAM practitioners may work as a team. Some clinics schedule regular group sessions in which all staff members discuss the care of certain patients. Many clinics also have technologically based information-sharing systems to facilitate coordination of care. This close working relationship between CAM practitioners and physicians, regardless of whether the physicians are at the clinics, is what makes integrative clinics unique.

Within any one integrative clinic, the number and variety of CAM services is limited and determined by such factors as consumer demand, availability of practitioners, research evidence, and funding. The most frequently available therapies are massage, acupuncture, mind–body

[5] This section is part of a larger project, "Legal and Social Barriers to Alternative Medicine," funded by NLM grant # IG13LM07475-01.

[6] A survey of 5,810 hospitals found that 15% offered some type of CAM, most frequently pastoral care, massage therapy, relaxation treatment, guided imagery, and therapeutic nutrition (American Hospital Association 2002). However, these services are not necessarily offered through integrative clinics. Because so many hospitals are using CAM and establishing integrative clinics, the Joint Commission on Accreditation of Healthcare Organizations has entered the field. It recently included CAM therapies in one of its "examples of implementation." (These offer hospitals various examples of good practices in a number of areas, such as patient care, that meet accreditation requirements.) Designed specifically for pain management, this example lists certain CAM therapies that "may be used individually, in combinations . . . or in combination with medication" (Weeks 2002, 33).

(relaxation), and movement. Some integrative clinics, especially those that are hospital based, cater to patients with particular disorders, such as cancer, heart disease, and those undergoing surgery. These tend to have a broad range of more focused services and to be more integrative in their methods of delivery than integrative clinics catering primarily to outpatients. Some of the hospital-based clinics have both inpatient and outpatient facilities.

At present, insurance coverage plays a minimal role in the financial solvency of integrative medicine clinics. Patients generally pay for the CAM services out of pocket. Even when an MD who is also an acupuncturist provides acupuncture, that service is typically paid directly by patients. When needed, clinic staff help those patients who do have insurance coverage to deal with claims for reimbursement. By and large, clinic directors do not believe their immediate future involves insurance reimbursement. The main reason is low rates – in some cases, one-half to two-thirds of what practitioners charge. Structurally, integrative medicine clinics are inherently unable to absorb these differences in the same way that physicians and hospitals can, that is, by averaging out costs. Compared with the dozens of patients physicians see in a normal day, CAM practitioners see only a few. Although a typical visit with a physician lasts 10 to 15 minutes, a CAM practitioner takes 45 to 90 minutes with each patient and some practitioners (massage therapists, reiki masters) take 15- to 30-minute breaks in between patients to rebalance their energy. This labor intensity is not reflected in payment. Acupuncturists and massage therapists commonly earn $80 to $100 per patient, depending on their geographic location. Directors of integrative clinics admit, then, that their ventures are not money-making enterprises. Nor are many clinic directors actively seeking growth because increased volume requires a concomitant expansion in facility capacity, which requires more funds.

How, then, do integrative clinics survive? The more stable and successful clinics have raised millions of dollars in private donations, and their continued survival rests on their ability to continue to raise funds. A number of integrative clinics began because a wealthy donor benefited in some way from CAM or became interested in it, usually for personal reasons. Other clinics were the brainchild of physicians who believed that CAM could benefit patient care and who had the ability to raise funds and realize a vision. Hospitals support integrative clinics for their contributions to health and healing. In addition, patients who want these services make their views known and hospital administrators are in the business not only of keeping patients happy, but also of attracting prospective patients who are made aware of the happiness of previous patients.

The future of integrative clinics is conflated with the fate of CAM. If patients continue to use and demand CAM, if research proves the safety and efficacy of CAM, if physicians accept CAM, if the benefits of CAM extend to cost savings, and if insurers and health care plans offer CAM coverage, integrative clinics will prosper and grow. The many ifs in this scenario involve one more actor – government – whose role cuts across all the variables and who can determine whether one variable will work at cross-purposes with another, or whether they will work together to make the whole greater than the sum of its parts.

### GOVERNMENT

This study has referred to the contributions of several government officials and agencies in advancing the process that now constitutes the mainstreaming of alternative medicine. Congress and the NIH have been especially important in this role and have worked in unison to achieve an impact. The Appropriations Committee chaired by Senator Tom Harkin ignited the engine of change by mandating and funding a new division at the NIH devoted to CAM research. This fact begs a question: were it not for Senator Harkin, would the mainstreaming of CAM have begun? It is a type of question that engrosses many historians and historical sociologists and that is settled only through analysis and interpretation. Frequently, it seems that events would not have occurred were it not for the appearance of "great men" or singular acts. Frequently, however, that certain individuals gained visibility, that their ideas or their charisma had an impact, that certain acts took place, or that consequences occurred are all themselves deeply embedded in social contexts – of ideas and opportunities, the availability of material goods, the presence of favorable winds, and much more. Senator Harkin was in a powerful position, but he was not alone in his support for CAM. Although the time was right, continued funding for CAM research, and of such magnitude, would not have occurred were it not for the results engineered by astute officials at the OAM who steered the funds in a different direction than Senator Harkin wanted.

Other elected representatives in Congress and other officials at the NIH are now in policy-making positions. Congress continues to increase the budget of the NCCAM, and CAM research is no longer confined to the NCCAM. Overall, NIH funding for CAM research rose to $247.6 million in 2002. New government officials are also now contributing to the trajectory of CAM. For instance, in March 2000, President Clinton established a White House Commission on Complementary and Alternative Medicine Policy. Its charge was to take the task of policy making to a more comprehensive level by coordinating developments in research with the concerns of health care providers, insurers and delivery systems, organizations and institutions that train and educate CAM practitioners, and the public at large. Its lengthy final report, issued in March 2002, details the work of the commission, its findings, its deliberations and debates, and its recommendations. The road map offered by the commission continues the process that I have called the mainstreaming of CAM. It recommends increasing funding for scientific research on safety and efficacy of alternative therapies as a basis for informed and intelligent decision making by CAM users, physicians, and health care insurers and delivery systems; improving the education, training, certification, licensing, and regulation of CAM practitioners and products; and improving the dissemination of accurate and authoritative information about CAM (http://www.whccamp.hhs.gov). The report also outlines the role that a number of government and private sector actors could take in advancing knowledge about CAM and supporting integration into the health care system of those therapies that prove to be safe and effective. As health care in the United States falters under the weight of its past mistakes and present stagnation, CAM may offer a healthy shot in the arm.

The interface between government and business will also be important as results materialize from CAM research, especially research on herbs. The NCCAM and the FDA are beginning to coordinate their efforts to study those CAM therapies that involve products and devices. At issue here is the current status of herbs as dietary supplements, which exempts them from FDA regulation. Because of this status, companies are not interested in conducting research on herbs and other alternative therapies insofar as they cannot patent the products. The NCCAM and other federal agencies offer grants to the private sector. However, at present the incentive for the private sector to conduct research is insufficient, leaving government to cover the lion's share of research costs. If and when the FDA assumes a greater role in regulating certain alternative therapies, there may be a concomitant demand for patent privileges by researchers, including those in the private sector. The White House Commission recommended that Congress and the Executive Branch consider such options as low-interest loans, tax incentives, market exclusivity, and the resolution of intellectual property issues to induce the private sector to play a greater role in CAM research and the production of CAM products and devices.

FINAL THOUGHTS

This study has had less to say about CAM practitioners than about other actors who are shaping the process of mainstreaming, for in many ways the role of CAM practitioners and their future are contingent on how the medical community responds to studies on safety, efficacy, and mechanisms of action. If these studies find that certain therapies are effective and if they explain how these therapies work in terms that physicians can understand, we can expect that CAM practitioners will benefit. Furthermore, If studies explain how certain alternative therapies differ in theory and practice from conventional medicine in ways that physicians can not only understand but also appreciate, we can expect a degree of mutual respect for the differences. Some CAM practitioners – as individuals, not as representatives of their field – anticipate these happy scenarios and welcome mainstreaming for the legitimacy it promises. These practitioners are particularly interested in developments in research and integrative medicine because these directly impact their livelihoods. Many hope that positive research findings will increase their clientele and that the expansion of integrative clinics will increase their opportunities.[7]

However, other CAM practitioners question the motives for mainstreaming and are concerned about its outcomes. They wonder if

---

[7] Many practitioners who work in integrative clinics prefer this kind of setting because it allows for more regular hours and a more certain income.

mainstreaming entails a medicalization that will jeopardize the autonomy of CAM practitioners and curtail their scope of practice. They suspect that integration will bring a cooptation that signals the loss of what is unique in CAM. They worry that the ability of each practitioner to draw on intuition will be questioned until proven, that their failures will be judged first as individual failures and eventually as failures in CAM, and that, indeed, their capacity to engage their intuition will be thwarted. They fear a deterioration, if not a fundamental transformation, of the values, beliefs, and norms that have characterized CAM thus far.

Although hard to predict at this stage, I would venture to say that CAM practitioners, including those who currently work in integrative clinics, need not see themselves as becoming medicalized as mainstreaming proceeds – unless they as individuals want to consider themselves and their practice in medical terms. They can expect to continue working as they always have been, only with more certainty about their role in health care. Coordinating their work with physicians will not necessarily change the practice of CAM. At the same time, in light of the current structure of integrative clinics, there is no reason to expect that respect for what CAM contributes to health care will necessarily create equality in status between CAM and conventional medicine.

If alternative medicine is becoming mainstreamed, it is because the therapies have been shown to have some benefit. Integration that involves accommodation means that differences coexist, albeit along with some measure of inequality. Try as they may, researchers will not be able to fully explain through scientific concepts and scientific methods of investigation the reasons for all the benefits of CAM. Some therapies, in other words, will have to be appreciated for what they are, taken on their own terms. Science is not changing CAM – its practice or its mechanisms of action or its theories. Science is only changing how these are understood and whether the therapies will be used and perhaps recommended. Science and the understanding it provides is one of the vehicles for legitimacy. However, the process of mainstreaming has several dimensions. Ultimately, that CAM continues to be used, recommended, reimbursed, and researched is the test of its unique contribution to health care. We can also expect that physicians and medicine as an institution will be affected by the incorporation of CAM into health care. I have suggested that to the extent that physicians appreciate those qualities in CAM that are integral to health care but have been lost in the contemporary practice of medicine, a more generalized humanization of medicine can occur.

It has been analytically useful to make a number of distinctions in this study – between kinds of knowledge, between scientific and nonscientific communities, between methods of providing health care, and so on. In the end, however, it has been necessary to demonstrate how boundaries are both present and porous. The kind of social change that has been described here is perhaps best understood as evolutionary rather than revolutionary. Yet, there will come a time when we will be able to say that all the little changes have added up to a substantial mass and health care has become qualitatively different than it was.

# Bibliography

Abbot, Neil C. 2000. "Healing as a therapy for human disease: A systematic review." *Journal of Alternative and Complementary Medicine* 6: 159–69.

Achterberg, Jeanne. 1996. "What is medicine?" *Alternative Therapies in Health and Medicine* 2 (3): 58–61.

Adler, Shelley R. and Jennifer R. Fosket. 1999. "Disclosing complementary and alternative medicine use in the medical encounter: A qualitative study in women with breast cancer." *Journal of Family Practice* 48 (6): 453–8.

Ai, Amy L., et al. 2001. "Designing clinical trials on energy healing: Ancient art encounters medical science." *Alternative Therapies in Health and Medicine* 7 (4): 93–9.

Ai, Amy L. 2003. "Assessing mental health in clinical study on qigong: Between scientific investigation and holistic perspectives." *Seminar in Integrative Medicine* 1 (2): 112–21.

Anandarajah, Gowri, and Ellen Hight. 2001. "Spirituality and medical practice: Using the HOPE questions as a practical tool for spiritual assessment." *American Family Physician* 63 (1): 1–13.

Angell, Marcia, and Jerome P. Kassirer. 1998. "Alternative medicine: The risks of untested and unregulated remedies." *New England Journal of Medicine* 339 (12): 839–41.

Arambula, Pete, Erik Peper, Mitsumasa Kawakami, and Katherine Hughes Gibney. 2001. "The physiological correlates of Kundalini yoga meditation: A study of a yoga master." *Applied Psychophysiology and Biofeedback* 26 (2): 147–53.

Astin, John A. 1998. "Why patients use alternative medicine: Results of a national study." *Journal of the American Medical Association* 279 (19): 1548–53.

Astin, John A., et al. 1998. "A review of the incorporation of complementary and alternative medicine by mainstream physicians." *Archives of Internal Medicine* 158 (21): 2303–10.

Astin, John A., Elain Harkness, and Edzard Ernst. 2000. "The efficacy of 'distant healing': A systematic review of randomized trials." *Annals of Internal Medicine* 132: 903–10.

Barnes, Linda L., et al. 2000. "Spirituality, religion, and pediatrics: Intersecting worlds of healing." *Pediatrics* 106 (4): 899–908.

Bausell, R. Baker, Wen-Lin Lee, and Brian M. Berman. 2001. "Demographic and health-related correlates of visits to complementary and alternative medical providers." *Medical Care* 39 (2): 190–6.

Becker, Howard Saul, Everett C. Hughes, Anselm L. Strauss, and Blanche Geer. 1961. *Boys in White: Student Culture in Medical School.* Chicago: University of Chicago Press.

Beecher, Henry K. 1955. "The powerful placebo." *Journal of the American Medical Association* December 24: 1602–6.

Belenky, Mary Field, Blythe McVicker Clinchy, Nancy Rule Goldberger, and Jill Mattuck Tarule. 1986. *Women's Ways of Knowing: The Development of Self, Voice, and Mind.* New York: Basic Books.

Bell, Daniel. 1973. *The Coming of Post-Industrial Society: A Venture in Social Forecasting.* New York: Basic Books.

Bell, I. R., et al. 2001. *Validation of a Global Well-Being Rating Scale for Integrative Medicine Outcomes Research* (updated/revised). Poster presented at the International Scientific Conference on Complementary, Alternative and Integrative Medicine Research, San Francisco, CA, May 17–19.

Benson, Kjell, and Arthur J. Hartz. 2000. "A comparison of observational studies and randomized, controlled trials." *New England Journal of Medicine* 342 (25): 1878–86.

Benson, Herbert. 1975. *The Relaxation Response.* New York: Morrow.

Berger, Allan S. 2002. "Arrogance among physicians." *Academic Medicine* 77 (2): 145–7.

Berger, Vance W., and Derek V. Exner. 1999. "Detecting selection bias in randomized clinical trials." *Controlled Clinical Trials* 20 (4): 319–27.

Berman, Brian M., et al. 1998. "Primary care physicians and complementary-alternative medicine: Training, attitudes, and practice patterns." *Journal of the American Board of Family Practice* 11 (4): 272–81.

Berman, Brian M., et al. 1999. "Compliance with requests for complementary-alternative medicine referrals: A survey of primary care physicians." *Integrative Medicine* 2 (1): 11–17.

Bernardi, Luciano, et al. 2001. "Effect of rosary prayer and yoga mantras on autonomic cardiovascular rhythms: Comparative study." *British Medical Journal* 323 (7327): 1446–9.

Bernardi, Luciano, et al. 2002. "Slow breathing increases arterial baroreflex sensitivity in patients with chronic heart failure." *Circulation* 105 (2): 143–5.

Beyerstein, Barry L. 2001. "Alternative medicine and common errors of reasoning." *Academic Medicine* 76 (3): 230–7.

Bhattacharya, Bhaswati. 2000. "M.D. programs in the United States with complementary and alternative medicine education opportunities: An ongoing listing." *Journal of Alternative and Complementary Medicine* 6 (1): 77–90.

Birke, Lynda. 2000. *Feminism and the Biological Body*. New Brunswick, NJ: Rutgers University Press.

Blumberg, Daniel I., et al. 1995. "The physician and unconventional medicine." *Alternative Therapies in Health and Medicine* 1 (3): 31–5.

Boon, Heather. 1998. "Canadian naturopathic practitioners: Holistic and scientific world views." *Social Science Medicine* 46 (9): 1213–25.

Boon, Heather, et al. 1999. "Breast cancer survivors' perceptions of complementary/alternative medicine (CAM): Making the decision to use or not to use." *Qualitative Health Research* 9 (5): 639–53.

Borkan, Jeffrey, et al. 1994. "Referrals for alternate therapies." *Journal of Family Practice* 39 (6): 545–50.

Boyle, Philip J., and Daniel Callahan. 1995. *What Price Mental Health? The Ethics and Politics of Setting Priorities*. Washington, DC: Georgetown University Press.

Branch, William T., Jr. 2000. "The ethics of caring and medical education." Academic Medicine 75 (2): 127–32.

Branch, William T., Jr. et al. 2001. "Teaching the human dimensions of care in clinical settings." *Journal of the American Medical Association* 286 (9): 1067–74.

Brody, Baruch A. 1997. "When are placebo-controlled trials no longer appropriate?" *Controlled Clinical Trials* 18: 602–12.

Brown, David. 1992. "A new look at alternative therapies." *Washington Post, Health* June 23: 8.

Brown, Lawrence D. 1983. *Politics and Health Care, Organization: HMOs as Federal Policy*. Washington, DC: The Brookings Institution.

Bullock, Milton L., et al. 2002. "A large randomized placebo controlled study of auricular acupuncture for alcohol dependence." *Journal of Substance Abuse Treatment* 22 (2): 71–7.

Burger, Walter. 2001. "The relation between medical education and the medical profession's world view." *Medicine, Health Care, and Philosophy* 4: 79–84.

Cahalin, Lawrence P., et al. 2002. "Efficacy of diaphragmatic breathing in persons with chronic obstructive pulmonary disease: A review of the literature." *Journal of Cardiopulmonary Rehabilitation* 22 (1): 7–21.

Caspi, Opher, Cori Millen, and Lee Sechrest. 2000. "Integrity and research: Introducing the concept of dual blindness. How blind are double-blind clinical trials in alternative medicine?" *Journal of Alternative and Complementary Medicine* 6 (6): 493–8.

Cassileth, Barrie, Wayne Jonas, Claire M. Cassidy, et al. 1995. "Research methodologies." Workshop on Alternative Medicine, *Alternative Medicine: Expanding Medical Horizons* (pp. 289–98). Washington, DC: U.S. Government Printing Office.

Christensen, Damaris. 2001. "Medicinal mimicry: Sometimes, placebos work – But how?" *Science News* 159: 74–8.

Cicourel, Aaron V. 1986. "The reproduction of objective knowledge: Common sense reasoning in medical decision making." In Gernot Bohme and Nico Stehr (eds.), *The Knowledge Society* (pp. 87–122). Boston: D. Reidel Publisher.

Clouser, K. Danner, David J. Hufford, and C. J. Morrison. 1995. "What's in a word?" *Alternative Therapies in Health and Medicine* 1 (3): 78–9.

Cohen, Michael H. 1998. *Complementary and Alternative Medicine: Legal Boundaries and Regulatory Perspectives.* Baltimore and London: The Johns Hopkins University Press.

*Complementary and Alternative Medicine at the NIH.* 1995. December. II: 5, 6.

Concato, John, Nirav Shah, and Ralph I. Horwitz. 2000. "Randomized, controlled trials, observational studies, and the hierarchy of research designs." *New England Journal of Medicine* 342 (25): 1887–92.

Congressional Office of Technology Assessment. 1978. *Assessing the efficacy and safety of medical technologies.* Washington, DC: U.S. Government Printing Office.

Cooper, Richard A., et al. 2002. "Economic and demographic trends signal an impending physician shortage." *Health Affairs* 21 (1): 140–54.

Corbin Winslow, Lisa, and Howard Shapiro. 2002. "Physicians want education about complementary and alternative medicine to enhance communication with their patients." *Archives of Internal Medicine* 162 (10): 1176–81.

Corless, Inge B., et al. 2002. "Self-care for fatigue in patients with HIV." *Oncology Nursing Forum* 29 (5): E60–9.

Cozzens, Susan E., and Thomas F. Gieryn (eds.). 1990. *Theories of Science in Society.* Bloomington: Indiana University Press.

Critchley, H. D., et al. 2001. "Brain activity during biofeedback relaxation: A functional neuroimaging investigation." *Brain* 124 (Part 5): 1003–12.

Cushman, Linda F., et al. 1999. "Use of complementary and alternative medicine among African-American and Hispanic women in New York City: A pilot study." *Journal of the American Medical Women's Association* 54 (4): 193–5.

Davidoff, Frank. 1998. "Weighing the alternatives: Lessons from the paradoxes of alternative medicine." *Annals of Internal Medicine* 129 (12): 1068–70.

Davidson, Jonathan R. T., et al. 2002. "Effect of Hypericum perforatum (St. John's Wort) in major depressive disorder." *Journal of the American Medical Association* 287 (14): 1807–14.

Dehaven, Mark J. 2001. "Comments on spiritual assessment and medicine." *American Family Physician* 64 (3): 373–4.

Dinnerstein, Albert J., Milton Lowenthal, and Bernard Blitz. 1966. *Perspectives in Biology and Medicine* Autumn: 103–17.

Drivdahl, Christine E., and William F. Miser. 1998. "Comment: The use of alternative health care by a family practice population." *Journal of the American Board of Family Practice* 11 (3): 244–6.

Druss, Benjamin, and Robert A. Rosenheck. 1999. "Association between use of unconventional therapies and conventional medical services." *Journal of the American Medical Association* 282 (7): 651–6.

Dull, Valerie T., and Laurie A. Skokan. 1995. "A cognitive model of religion's influence on health." *Journal of Social Issues* 51 (2): 49–64.

Dunfield, J. Fraser. 1996. "Consumer perceptions of health care quality and the utilization of non-conventional therapy." *Social Science and Medicine* 43 (2): 149–61.

Durkheim, Emile. 1947 [1912]. *The Elementary Forms of Religious Life*. New York: Free Press.

1964 [1895]. *The Rules of Sociological Method*. New York: Free Press.

Eisenberg, David M., et al. 1993. "Unconventional medicine in the United States: Prevalence, costs, and patterns of use." *New England Journal of Medicine* 328 (4): 246–52.

Eisenberg, David, et al. 1995. "Research infrastructure: Institutions and investigators." *Alternative Medicine: Expanding Medical Horizons* (pp. 275–82). Washington, DC: U.S. Government Printing Office.

Eisenberg, David M., 1997. "Advising patients who seek alternative medical therapies." *Annals of Internal Medicine* 127 (1): 61–9.

Eisenberg, David M., et al. 1998. "Trends in alternative medicine use in the United States, 1990–1997: Results of a follow-up national survey." *Journal of the American Medical Association* 280 (18): 1569–75.

Eisenberg, David M., et al. 2001. "Perceptions about complementary therapies relative to conventional therapies among adults who use both: Results from a national survey." *Annals of Internal Medicine* 135 (5): 344–51.

Elder, Nancy E., Amy Gillchrist, and Rene Minz. 1997. "Use of alternative health care by family practice patients." *Archives of Family Medicine* (6): 181–4.

Ellis, Christopher G., and Jeffrey S. Levin. 1998. "The Religion–Health connection: Evidence, theory, and future directions." *Health Education and Behavior* 25 (6): 700–20.

Ellis, Andrew, and Nigel Wiseman. 1985. *Fundamentals of Chinese Medicine*. Brookline, MA: Paradigm Publications.

Ellis, Mark R., Daniel C. Vinson, and Bernard Ewigmann. 1999. "Addressing spiritual concerns of patients: Family physicians' attitudes and practices." *Journal of Family Practice* 48 (2): 105–9.

Ellison, Christopher G. 1998. "Introduction to symposium: Religion, health, and well-being." *Journal for the Scientific Study of Religion* 37 (4): 692–4.

Ellison, Christopher G., and Jeffrey S. Levin. 1998. "The Religion–Health Connection: Evidence, Theory, and Future directions." *Health Education and Behavior* 25 (6): 700–4.

Ergil, Kevin V. 1999. "Zhong yi acupuncture and low-back pain: Traditional Chinese medical acupuncture differential diagnoses and treatments for chronic lumbar pain: Editorial comment on Birch and Sherman." *Journal of Alternative and Complementary Medicine* 5 (5): 427–8.

Ernst, E. 2001. "Exeter's frantic work on systematic reviews." *Cochrane Collaboration Complementary Medicine Field Newsletter* Spring (8): 1, 4.

Ernst, E., and K. L. Resch. 1995. "Concept of true and perceived placebo effects." *British Medical Journal* 311: 551–3.

Ernst, Edzard, Karl-Ludwig Resch, and Adrian R. White. 1995. "Complementary medicine. What physicians think of it: A meta-analysis." *Archives of Internal Medicine* 155 (22): 2405–8.

Eskinazi, Daniel. 1998a. "Methodologic considerations for research in traditional (alternative) medicine." *Oral Surgery, Oral Medicine, Oral Pathology* 86 (6): 678–81.

Eskinazi, Daniel P. 1998b. "Factors that shape alternative medicine." *Journal of the American Medical Association* 280 (18): 1621–3.

Eskinazi, Daniel, and David Muehsam. 2000. "Is the scientific publishing of complementary and alternative medicine objective?" *Journal of Alternative and Complementary Medicine* 5 (6): 587–94.

Evans, Martyn. 2001. "The 'medical body' as philosophy's arena." *Theoretical Medicine* 22: 17–32.

Evidence-Based Medicine Working Group. 1992. "Evidence-based medicine: A new approach to teaching the practice of medicine." *Journal of the American Medical Association* 268 (17): 2420–5.

Ezzo, Jeanette, Brian Berman, Andrew Vickers, and Klaus Linde. 1998. "Complementary medicine and the Cochrane Collaboration." *Journal of the American Medical Association* 280 (18): 1628–30.

Fairfield, Kathleen M., et al. 1998. "Patterns of Use, Expenditures, and Perceived Efficacy of Complementary and Alternative Therapies in HIV-infected Patients." *Archives of Internal Medicine* 158 (20): 2257–64.

Federspil, Giovanni, and Roberto Vettor. 2000. "Can scientific medicine incorporate alternative medicine?" *Journal of Alternative and Complementary Medicine* 6 (3): 241–4.

Feinstein, Alvan R., and Ralph I. Horwitz. 1997. "Problems in the 'evidence' of 'evidence-based medicine.'" *American Journal of Medicine* 103: 529–35.

Feldman, Debra S., Dennis H. Novack, and Edward Gracely. 1998. "Effects of managed care on physician–patient relationships, quality of care, and the ethical practice of medicine: A physician survey." *Archives of Internal Medicine* 158 (15): 1626–3.

Fox, Renee C. 1977. "The medicalization and demedicalization of American society." *Daedalus* 106 (1): 9–22.

Freidson, Eliot. 1970. *Profession of Medicine: A Study of the Sociology of Applied Knowledge.* New York: Harper & Row.

Friedman, Lester D. 2002. "The precarious position of the medical humanities in the medical school curriculum." *Academic Medicine* 77 (4): 320–2.

Fuller, Robert C. 1989. *Alternative Medicine and American Religious Life.* Oxford: Oxford University Press.

Furnham, Adrian, and R. Beard. 1995. "Health, just world beliefs and coping style preferences in patients of complementary and orthodox medicine." *Social Science and Medicine* 40 (10): 1425–32.

Furnham, Adrian, Charles Vincent, and Rachel Wood. 1995. "The health beliefs and behaviors of three groups of complementary medicine and a general practice group of patients." *Journal of Alternative and Complementary Medicine* 1 (4): 347–59.

Furnham, Adrian, and Julie Forey. 1994. "The attitudes, behaviors and beliefs of patients of conventional vs. complementary (alternative) medicine." *Journal of Clinical Psychology* 50 (3): 458–69.

Gaby, A. R. 1999. "Orthomolecular medicine and mega-vitamin therapy." In Jonas, Wayne B. and Jeffrey S. Levin (eds.), *Essentials of Complementary and Alternative Medicine* (pp. 459–71). Philadelphia: Lippincott, Williams & Wilkins.

Gallo, Joseph J., et al. 2002. "Do family physicians and internists differ in knowledge, attitudes, and self-reported approaches for depression?" *International Journal of Psychiatry in Medicine* 32 (1): 1–20.

Garfinkel, Marian, and H. Ralph Schumacher, Jr. 2000. "Yoga." *Rheumatic Diseases Clinics of North America* 26 (1): 125–32.

Garfinkel, Marian S., et al. 1998. "Yoga-based intervention for carpal tunnel syndrome: A randomized trial." *Journal of the American Medical Association* 280 (18): 1601–3.

Gatchel, Robert J., and Ann Matt Maddrey. 1998. "Clinical outcome research in complementary and alternative medicine: An overview of experimental design and analysis." *Alternative Therapies in Health and Medicine* 4 (5): 36–42.

George, Linda K., David B. Larsons, Harold G. Koening, and Michael E. McCullough. 2000. "Spirituality and health: What we know, what we need to know." *Journal of Social and Clinical Psychology* 1 (19): 102–16.

Geertz, Clifford. 1983. *Local Knowledge: Further Essays in Interpretive Anthropology.* New York: Basic Books.

Gevitz, Norman. 1995. "Alternative medicine and the orthodox canon." *Mount Sinai Journal of Medicine* 62: 127–31.

Gevitz, Norman (ed.). 1988. *Other Healers: Unorthodox Medicine in America.* Baltimore: Johns Hopkins University Press.

Gieryn, Thomas F. 1983. "Boundary-work and the demarcation of science from non-science: Strains and interests in professional ideologies of scientists." *American Sociological Review* 48 (6): 781–95.

Gilligan, Carol. 1982. *In a Different Voice: Psychological Theory and Women's Development.* Cambridge, MA: Harvard University Press.

Goffman, Erving. 1959. *The Presentation of Self in Everyday Life.* Garden City, NY: Doubleday.

    1961. *Asylums: Essays on the Social Situation of Mental Patients and Other Inmates.* Garden City, NY: Anchor Books.

Gracely, R. H., R. Dubner, W. R. Deeter, and P. J. Wolksee. 1985. "Clinicians' expectations influence placebo analgesia." *The Lancet* 1: 43.

Graham-Pole, John. 2001. "'Physician, heal thyself': How teaching holistic medicine differs from teaching CAM." *Academic Medicine* 76 (6): 662–4.

Gray, John Armstrong Muir. 1997. *Evidence-Based Healthcare, How To Make Health Policy and Management Decisions.* London: Churchill Livingstone.

Greene, Jay. 2000a. "Patients, doctors talking more about alternative care." *Amednews.com* May 1: 1–2.

Greene, Jay. 2000b. "FSMB developing guidelines for complementary care." *Amednews.com* May 8: 1–3.

Greene, Jay. 2000c. "CME sleuths: Some continuing medical education classes under scrutiny." *Amednews.com* August 14: 1–5.

Greene, Jay. 2001. "Dissatisfied docs may soon be singing 'California, here I go.'" *Amednews.com* Aug 6: 1–3.

Greiner, K. Allen, Jane L. Murray, and Ken J. Kallail. 2000. "Medical student interest in alternative medicine." *The Journal of Alternative and Complementary Medicine* 6 (3): 231–4.

Haber, Richard J., and Lorelei A. Lingard. 2001. "Learning oral presentation skills." *Journal of General Internal Medicine* 16 (5): 308–14.

Hadhazy, Victoria A., Jeanette Ezzo, Paul Creamer, and Brian M. Berman. 2000. "Mind–body therapies for the treatment of fibromyalgia. A systematic review." *Journal of Rheumatology* 27: 2911–8.

Health Forum/American Hospital Association (AHA). 2002. *Health Forum/AHA 2000–2001 Complementary and Alternative Medicine Survey.* Chicago: American Hospital Association (www.hospitalconnect.com).

Hawk, Cheryl, et al. 2002. "Issues in planning a placebo-controlled trial of manual methods: Results of a pilot study." *Journal of Alternative and Complementary Medicine* 8 (1): 21–32.

Herman, Joseph. 1995. "The demise of the randomized controlled trial." *Journal of Clinical Epidemiology* 48 (7): 985–8.

Hill, A. Bradford. 1963. "Medical ethics and controlled trials." *British Medical Journal* 1: 1043–9.

Hojat, Mohammadreza, et al. 2000. "Physicians' perceptions of the changing health care system: Comparisons by gender and specialities." *Journal of Community Health* 25 (6): 455–71.

Horton, Richard. 2001. "The clinical trial: Deceitful, disputable, unbelievable, unhelpful, and shameful – What next?" *Controlled Clinical Trials* 22: 593–604.

Hrobjartsson, Asbjorn, and Peter C. Gotzsche. 2001. "Is the placebo powerless? – An analysis of clinical trials comparing placebo with no treatment." *New England Journal of Medicine* 344 (21): 1594–1602.

Idler, Ellen L. 1995. "Religion, health, and nonphysical senses of self." *Social Forces* December: 683–704.

Jacobsen, Paul B., et al. 2002. "Efficacy and costs of two forms of stress management training for cancer patients undergoing chemotherapy." *Journal of Clinical Oncology* 20 (12): 2851–62.

Janakiramaiah, N., et al. 2000. "Antidepressant efficacy of Sudarshan Kriya Yoga (SKY) in melancholia: A randomized comparison with electroconvulsive therapy (ECT) and imipramine." *Journal of Affective Disorders* 57 (1–3): 255–9.

Johnson, Alan G. 1994. "Surgery as a placebo." *Lancet* 344: 1140–2.

Jonas, Wayne B. 1997. "Clinical trials for chronic disease: Randomized, controlled clinical trials are essential." *Journal of the National Institute of Health Research* 9: 33–9.

Kamei, Tsutomu, et al. 2000. "Decrease in serum cortisol during yoga exercise is correlated with alpha brain activation." *Perceptual and Motor Skills* 90 (3 Part 1): 1027–32.

Kao, Gary D., and Pamela Devine. 2000. "Use of complementary health practices by prostate carcinoma patients undergoing radiation therapy." *Cancer* 88 (3): 615–19.

Kappauf, Herbert, et al. 2000. "Use of and attitudes held towards unconventional medicine by patients in a department of internal medicine/oncology and haematology." *Support Care Cancer* 8 (4): 314–22.

Kaptchuk, Ted J., Peter Goldman, David S. Stone, and William B. Stason. 2000. "Do medical devices have enhanced placebo effects?" *Journal of Clinical Epidemiology* 53 (8): 786–92.

Kaptchuk, Ted J. 1998. "Powerful placebo: The dark side of the randomized controlled trial." *Lancet* 351: 1722–5.

Kaptchuk, Ted J., and David M. Eisenberg. 1998. "The persuasive appeal of alternative medicine." *Annals of Internal Medicine* 129 (12): 1061–5.

Kaptchuk, Ted J., and David M. Eisenberg 2001. "Varieties of healing. 2: A taxonomy of unconventional healing practices." *Annals of Internal Medicine* 135: 196–204.

Kassirer, Jerome P. 1992. "Clinical problem-solving – a new feature in the *Journal*." *New England Journal of Medicine* 326 (1): 60–1.

Kelner, Merrijoy, and Beverly Wellman. 1997. "Health care and consumer choice: Medical and alternative therapies." *Social Science and Medicine* 45 (2): 203–12.

Kemler, Marius A., and Henrica C. W. de Vet. 2000. "Does randomization introduce bias in unblinded trials?" *Epidemiology* 11 (2): 228.

Kessler, Ronald C., et al. 2001. "Long-term trends in the use of complementary and alternative medical therapies in the United States." *Annals of Internal Medicine* 135 (4): 262–8.

King, D. E., and B. Bushwick. 1994. "Beliefs and attitudes of hospital in-patients about faith healing and prayer." *Journal of Family Practice* 39 (4): 349–52.

Kirsch, Irving, and Michael J. Rosadino. 1993. "Do double–blind studies with informed consent yield externally valid results?" *Psychoparmacology* 110: 437–42.

Kishiyama, Shirley, et al. 2002. "Yoga as an experimental intervention for cognition in multiple sclerosis." *International Journal of Yoga Therapy* 12: 57–62.

Kissell, Judith Lee. 2001. "Embodiment: An introduction." *Theoretical Medicine* 22: 1–4.

Kligler, Benjamin, et al. 2000. "Suggested curriculum guidelines on complementary and alternative medicine." *Family Medicine* 32 (1): 30–3.

Knorr Cetina, Karin. 1981. *The Manufacture of Knowledge: An Essay on the Constructivist and Contextual Nature of Science.* Oxford: Pergamon Press.

Knorr Cetina, Karin. 1999. *Epistemic Cultures: How the Sciences Make Knowledge.* Cambridge, MA: Harvard University Press.

Koenig, Harold G. 2000. "Religion, spirituality, and medicine: application to clinical practice." *Journal of the American Medical Association* 284 (13): 1708.

Kuper, Adam. 1999. *Culture: The anthropologists' account.* Cambridge, MA: Harvard University Press.

Lamont, Michele, and Marcel Fournier (eds.). 1992. *Cultivating differences: Symbolic boundaries and the making of inequality.* Chicago: University of Chicago Press.

Lan, Ching, Ssu-Yuang Chen, Jin-Shin Lai, and May-Kuen Wong. 2001. "Heart rate responses and oxygen consumption during tai chi chuan practice." *American Journal of Chinese Medicine* 29 (3–4): 403–10.

Landmark Healthcare, Inc. 1998. *The Landmark Report I on Public Perceptions of Alternative Care: 1998 Nationwide Study of Alternative Care.* Sacramento, CA: Landmark Healthcare, Inc.

Landmark Healthcare, Inc. 1999. *The Landmark Report II on HMOs and Alternative Care: 1999. Nationwide Study of Alternative Care.* Sacramento, CA: Landmark Healthcare, Inc.

Lang, Forest, Kevin Everett, Ramsey McGowen, and Bruce Bennard. 2000. "Faculty development in communication skills instruction: Insights from a longitudinal program with 'real-time feedback.'" *Academic Medicine* 75 (12): 1222–8.

Lao, Lixing. 1996. "Acupuncture techniques and devices." *Journal of Alternative and Complementary Medicine* 2 (1): 23–5.

Lao, Lixing, et al. 1995. "Efficacy of Chinese acupuncture on postoperative oral surgery pain." *Oral Surgery, Oral Medicine, Oral Pathology* 79 (4): 423–8.

Larimore, Walter L. 2001. "Providing basic spiritual care for patients: Should it be the exclusive domain of pastoral professionals?" *American Family Physician* 63 (1): 36, 38–40.

Larson, David B., James P. Swyers, and Michael E. McCullough. 1997. *Scientific Research on Spirituality and Health: A Consensus Report*. Rockville, MD: National Institute for Healthcare Research.

Lasagna, Louis. 1955. "Placebos." *Scientific American* 193: 68–71.

Latour, Bruno. 1987. *Science in Action: How to Follow Scientists and Engineers through Society*. Cambridge, MA: Harvard University Press.

Lawrence, Raymond J. 2002. "The witches' brew of spirituality and medicine." *Annals of Behavioral Medicine* 24 (1): 74–6.

Leber, Paul D., and Charles S. Davis. 1998. "Threats to the validity of clinical trials employing enrichment strategies for sample selection." *Controlled Clinical Trials* 19 (2): 178–87.

Levin, Jeffrey S., et al. 1997. "Quantitative methods in research on complementary and alternative medicine: A methodological manifesto." *Medical Care* 35 (11): 1079–94.

Lewith, George, and D. Machin. 1983. "On the evaluation of the clinical effects of acupuncture." *Pain* 16: 111–27.

Li, J. X., Y. Hong, and K. M. Chan. 2001. "Tai chi: Physiological characteristics and beneficial effects on health." *British Journal of Sports Medicine* 35 (3): 148–56.

Lin, Chen-Tan, Gwyn E. Barley, and Maribel Cifuentes. 2001. "Personalized remedial intensive training of one medical student in communication and interview skills." *Teaching and Learning in Medicine* 13 (4): 232–9.

Linde, Klaus. 2000. "How to evaluate the effectiveness of complementary therapies." *Journal of Alternative and Complementary Medicine* 6 (3): 253–6.

Luebbert, Karin, Bernhard Dahme, and Monika Hasenbring. 2001. "The effectiveness of relaxation training in reducing treatment-related symptoms and improving emotional adjustment in acute non-surgical cancer treatment: A meta-analytical review." *Psycho-Oncology* 10 (6): 490–502.

MacDonald, Jeffery L. 1995. "Inventing traditions for the new age: A case study of the earth energy tradition." *Anthropology of Consciousness* 6 (4): 31–45.

Macklin, Ruth. 1999. "The ethical problems with sham surgery in clinical research." *New England Journal of Medicine* 341 (13): 992–6.

Mainous, Arch G., III, James M. Gill, James S. Zoller, and Maggie G. Wolman. 2000. "Fragmentation of patient care between chiropractors and family physicians." *Archives of Family Medicine* 9 (5): 446–50.

Malathi, A., et al. 2000. "Effect of yogic practices on subjective well being." *Indian Journal of Physiology and Psychopharmacology* 44 (2): 202–6.

Mannheim, Karl. 1936. *Ideology and Utopia.* New York: Harcourt Brace & World.

Marber, Scott. 2000. "Putting the squeeze on traditional medicine." *Managed Healthcare* 10 (2): 35–6.

Marcus, Donald M. 2001. "How should alternative medicine be taught to medical students and physicians?" *Academic Medicine* 76 (3): 224–9.

Margolin, Arthur, S. Kelly Avants, and Herbert D. Kleber. 1998. "Investigating alternative medicine therapies in randomized controlled trials." *Journal of the American Medical Association* 280 (18): 1626–8.

Margolin, Arthur, et al. 2002. "Acupuncture for the treatment of cocaine addiction: A randomized controlled trial." *Journal of the American Medical Association* 287 (1): 55–63.

Martin, Emily. 1996. "The egg and the sperm: How science has constructed a romance based on stereotypical male–female roles," In Evelyn Fox Keller and Helen E. Longino (eds.), *Feminism and Science* (pp. 103–17). New York: Oxford University Press.

Maskarinec, Gertraud, Dianne M. Shumay, Hisako Kakai, and Carolyn C. Gotay. 2000. "Ethnic differences in complementary and alternative medicine use among cancer patients." *Journal of Alternative and Complementary Medicine* 6 (6): 531–8.

Masters, Judith C. 1995. "Evolutionary theory: Reinventing our origin Myths," In Lynda Birke and Ruth Hubbards (eds.), *Reinventing Biology* (pp. 173–187). Bloomington, IN: Indiana University Press.

Matsumoto, Mia, and Jonathan C. Smith. 2001. "Progressive muscle relaxation, breathing exercises, and ABC relaxation therapy." *Journal of Clinical Psychology* 57 (12): 1551–7.

McCarthy, E. Doyle. 1996. *Knowledge as Culture: The New Sociology of Knowledge.* London: Routledge.

McGregor, Katherine J., and Edmund R. Peay. 1996. "The choice of alternative therapy for health care: Testing some propositions." *Social Science and Medicine.* 43 (9): 1317–27.

McKeown, Robert E., et al. 2002. "Shared decision making: Views of first-year residents and clinic patients." *Academic Medicine* 77 (5): 438–45.

McQuay, Henry, Dawn Carroll, and Andrew Moore. 1995. "Variation in the placebo effect in randomized controlled trials of analgesics: All is as blind as it seems." *Pain* 64: 331–5.

Mead, George Herbert. 1934. *Mind, Self, and Society.* Chicago: University of Chicago Press.

Mechanic, David. 1998. "The functions and limitations of trust in the provision of medical care." *Journal of Health Politics, Policy and Law.* August: 661–86.

Medical School Objectives Writing Group. 1999. "Learning objectives for medical student education – Guidelines for medical schools: Report I of the Medical School Objectives Project." *Academic Medicine* 74 (1): 13–18.

Meeker, William C., and Scott Haldeman. 2002. "Chiropractic: A profession at the crossroads of mainstream and alternative medicine." *Annals of Internal Medicine* 136 (3): 216–27.

Mishler, Elliot George. 1984. *The Discourse of Medicine: Dialectics in Medical Interviews*. Norwood, NJ: Ablex Publishing Corporation.

Moher, David, Kenneth F. Schulz, and Douglas G. Altman. 2001. "The CONSORT statement: Revised recommendations for improving the quality of report of parallel-group randomized trials." *Journal of the American Medical Association* 285 (15): 1987–91.

Moore, Nancy G. 1996. "Spirituality in medicine." *Alternative Therapies* 2 (6): 24–6, 103–5.

Mulrow, Cynthia D., and Kathleen Lohr. 2001. "Proof and policy from medical research evidence." *Journal of Health Politics, Policy, and Law* 26 (2): 250–66.

Nadar, Tony, et al. 2000. "Improvements in chronic diseases with a comprehensive natural medicine approach: A review and case series." *Behavioral Medicine* 26 (1): 34–46.

National Center for Complementary and Alternative Medicine (NCCAM). 2000, September 25. *Expanding Horizons of Health Care: Five-Year Strategic Plan 2001–2005* (http://nccam.nih.gov).

National Center for Complementary and Alternative Medicine (NCCAM) 2001, January 23. *About NCCAM* (http://nccam.nih.gov).

National Institutes of Health. 1998. "Acupuncture: NIH consensus conference." *Journal of the American Medical Association* 280 (17): 1518–24.

Nelson, Heidi D., Annette M. Matthews, Glen R. Patrizio, and Thomas G. Cooney. 1998. "Managed care, attitudes, and career choices of internal medicine residents." *Journal of General Internal Medicine* 13: 39–42.

Norred, Carol L., Stacy Zamudio, and Susan K. Palmer. 2000. "Use of complementary and alternative medicine by surgical patients." *AANA Journal* 68 (1): 13–18.

O'Connor, Bonnie Blair. 1995. *Healing Traditions: Alternative Medicine and the Health Professions*. Philadelphia: University of Pennsylvania Press.

O'Connor, Bonnie B., et al. 1997. "Defining and describing complementary and alternative medicine." *Alternative Therapies in Health and Medicine* 3 (2): 49–57.

Olfson, Mark, Steven C. Marcus, Benjamin Druss, and Harold Alan Pincus. 2002. "National trends in the use of outpatient psychotherapy." *American Journal of Psychiatry* 159 (11): 1914–20.

Oneschuk, Doreen, J. Hanson, and E. Bruera. 2000. "Complementary therapy use: A survey of community- and hospital-based patients with advanced cancer." *Palliative Medicine* 14 (5): 432–4.

Oubré, Alondra. 1995. "Social context of complementary medicine in Western society: Part I." *Journal of Alternative and Complementary Medicine* 1 (1): 41–56.

Oz, Mehmet C., Gerard C. Whitworth, and Eric H. Liu. 1998. "Complementary medicine in the surgical wards." *Journal of the American Medical Association* 279 (9): 710–11.

Pablos-Méndez, Ariel, R. Graham Barr, and Steven Shea. 1998. "Run-in periods in randomized trials: Implications for the application of results in clinical practice." *Journal of the American Medical Association* 279 (3): 222–5.

Palinkas, Lawrence A., and Martin L. Kabongo. 2000. "The use of complementary and alternative medicine by primary care patients. A SURF*NET study." *Journal of Family Practitioners* 49 (12): 1121–30.

Paramore, L. Clark. 1997. "Use of alternative therapies: Estimates from the 1994 Robert Wood Johnson Foundation national access to care survey." *Journal of Pain and Symptom Management* 13 (2): 83–9.

Pargament, Kenneth Ira. 1997. *Theory, Rresearch, Practice: The Psychology of Religion and Coping.* New York: Guilford.

Park, J., A. R. White, C. Stevanson, and E. Ernst. 2001. "Who are we blinding? A systematic review of blinded clinical trials." Poster presented at the International Scientific Conference on Complementary, Alternative and Integrative Medicine Research, San Francisco, CA, May 17–19.

Park, J., et al. 2001. "Credibility of a newly developed sham needle unit for controlled trials." Poster Presented at the International Scientific Conference on Complementary, Alternative and Integrative Medicine Research, San Francisco, CA, May 17–19.

Pelletier, Kenneth R., and John A. Astin. 2002. "Integration and reimbursement of complementary and alternative medicine by managed care and insurance providers." *Alternative Therapies in Health and Medicine* 8 (1): 38–48.

Pillemer, Stanley R. 1999. "Experiments, evidence, and explanations." *Journal of Alternative and Complementary Medicine* 5 (4): 323–5.

Pocock, Stuart J., and Diana, R. Elbourne. 2000. "Randomized trials or observational tribulations?" *New England Journal of Medicine* 342 (25): 1907–9.

Porter, Roy. 1988. "Before the fringe: 'Quakery' and the eighteenth-century medical market." In Roger Cooter (ed.), *Studies in the History of Alternative Medicine* (pp. 1–27). New York: St. Martin's Press.

Ray, Paul H., and Sherry Ruth Anderson. 2000. *The Cultural Creatives.* New York: Harmony Books.

Reilly, David. 2000. "The unblind leading the blind: The achilles heel of too many trials." *Journal of Alternative and Complementary Medicine* 6 (6): 479–80.

Relman, Arnold S. 1979. "Holistic medicine." *New England Journal of Medicine* 300 (6): 312–13.

Richardson, P. H. 1994. "Placebo effects in pain management." *Pain Reviews* (1): 15–32.

Richardson, Mary Ann, et al. 2000. "Complementary/alternative medicine use in a comprehensive cancer center and the implications for oncology." *Journal of Clinical Oncology* 18 (13): 2505–14.

Rochon, Paula A., et al. 1999. "Are randomized control trial outcomes influenced by the inclusion of a placebo group?: A systematic review of nonsteroidal anti-inflammatory drug trials for arthritis treatment." *Journal of Clinical Epidemiology* 52 (2): 113–22.

Rodwin, Marc A. 2001. "The politics of evidence-based medicine." *Journal of Health Politics, Policy and Law* 26 (2): 439–46.

Rosa, Linda, Emily Rosa, Larry Sarner, and Stephen Barrett. 1998. "A close look at therapeutic touch." *Journal of the American Medical Association* 279 (13): 1005–10.

Rowell, Donna M., and David J. Kroll. 1998. "Complementary and alternative medicine education in United States pharmacy schools." *American Journal of Pharmaceutical Education* 62 (4): 412–9.

Rothman, Kenneth J. and Karin B. Michels. 1994. "The continuing unethical use of placebo controls." *The New England Journal of Medicine* 331 (6): 394–8.

Rubik, Beverly A. 1995. "Can Western science provide a foundation for acupuncture?" *Alternative Therapies in Health and Medicine* 1 (4): 41–7.

Ruggie, Mary. 1996. *Realignments in the Welfare State: Health Policy in the United States, Britain, and Canada.* New York: Columbia University Press.

Ruzek, Sheryl Burt, Virginia L. Olesen, and Adele E. Clarke (eds.). 1997. *Women's Health: Complexities and Differences.* Columbus: Ohio State University Press.

Sackett, David L., and Deborah J. Cook. 1993. "Can we learn anything from small trials?" In Kenneth S. Warren and Frederick Mosteller (eds.), *Doing More Good Than Harm: The Evaluation of Health Care Interventions* (pp. 25–32). New York: BiC/PCP.

Sackett, David L., et al. 1996. "Evidence based medicine: What it is and what it isn't." *British Medical Journal* 312 (7023): 71–2.

Sampson, Wallace. 2001. "The need for educational reform in teaching about Alternative therapies." *Academic Medicine* 76 (3): 248–50.

Schneider, Robert H., et al. 2002. "Disease prevention and health promotion in the aging with a traditional system of natural medicine: Maharishi Vedic medicine." *Journal of Aging and Health* 14 (1): 57–78.

Schulz, Kenneth F. 1996. "Randomised trials, human nature, and reporting guidelines." *Lancet* 348: 596–8.

Sepucha, Karen R., Jeffrey K. Belkora, Stephanie Mutchnick, and Laura J. Esserman. 2002. "Consultation planning to help breast cancer patients prepare for medical consultations: Effect on communication and satisfaction for patients and physicians." *Journal of Clinical Oncology* 20 (11): 2695–700.

Shapin, Steven. 1995. "Here and everywhere: Sociology of scientific knowledge." *Annual Review of Sociology* 21: 289–321.

Shapiro, Johanna. 2002. "How do physicians teach empathy in the primary care setting?" *Academic Medicine* 77 (4): 323–8.

Sherman, Karen J., Charissa J. Hogeboom, Daniel C. Cherkin, and Richard A. Deyo. 2002. "Description and validation of a noninvasive placebo acupuncture procedure." *Journal of Alternative and Complementary Medicine* 8 (1): 11–19.

Shinto, Lynne, et al. 2002. "Survey of licensed naturopathic physicians in the United States who treat people with multiple sclerosis." Poster Presented at the International Scientific Conference on Complementary, Alternative and Integrative Medicine Research, Boston, MA, April 12–14.

Shoor, Stanford, and Kate R. Lorig. 2002. "Self-care and the doctor–patient relationship." *Medical Care* 40 (4) Supplement II: 40–4.

Shlay, Judith C., et al. 1998. "Acupuncture and amitriptyline for pain due to HIV–related peripheral neuropathy." *The Journal of the American Medical Association* 280 (18): 1590–5.

Sikand, Anju, and Marilyn Laken. 1998. "Pediatricians' experience with and attitudes toward complementary/alternative medicine." *Archives of Pediatric and Adolescent Medicine* 152 (11): 1059–64.

Simon, Robin W. 2002. "Revisiting the relationship among gender, marital status, and mental health." *American Journal of Sociology* 107 (4): 1065–96.

Singh, Betsy B., et al. 2001 "Clinical decisions in the use of acupuncture as an adjunctive therapy for osteoarthritis of the knee." *Alternative Therapies in Health and Medicine* 7 (4): 58–65.

Sliwa, J. A., G. Makoul, and H. Betts. 2002. "Rehabilitation-specific communication skills training: Improving the physician–patient relationship." *American Journal of Physical Medicine and Rehabilitation* 81 (2): 126–32.

Sloan, Richard P., et al. 2000. "Should physicians prescribe religious activities?" *New England Journal of Medicine* 342 (25): 1913–16.

Sloan, R. P., E. Bagiella, and T. Powell. 1999. "Religion, spirituality, and medicine." *Lancet* 353: 664–7.

Smith, Michael J., and Alan C. Logan. 2002. "Naturopathy." *Medical Clinics of North America* 86 (1): 173–84.

Smith, Richard. 1991. "Where is the wisdom...?" *British Medical Journal* 303 (6806): 798–9.

Sobel, David S. 2000. "Mind matters, money matters: The cost-effectiveness of mind/body medicine." *Journal of the American Medical Association* 284 (13): 1705.

Sparber, Andrew, et al. 2000. "Use of complementary medicine by adult patients participating in HIV/AIDS clinical trials." *Journal of Alternative and Complementary Medicine* 6 (5): 415–22.

The Standards of Reporting Trials Group. 1994. "A proposal for structured reporting of randomized controlled trials." *Journal of the American Medical Association* 272 (24): 1926–31.

Stefano, George B., Gregory L. Fricchione, Brian T. Slingsby, and Herbert Benson. 2001. "The placebo effect and relaxation response: Neural processes and their coupling to constitutive nitric oxide." *Brain Research: Brain Research Reviews* 35 (1): 1–19.

Starr, Paul. 1982. *The Social Transformation of American Medicine.* New York: Basic Books.

Stein, C. Michael, and Theodore Pincus. 1999. "Placebo-controlled studies in rheumatoid arthritis: Ethical issues." *Lancet* 353: 400–3.

Stehr, Nicor, and Richard V. Ericson. 1992. "The culture and power of knowledge in modern society." In Nicor Stehr and Richard V. Ericson (eds.), *The Culture and Power of Knowledge: Inquiries into Contemporary Societies* (pp. 3–20). Berlin: Walter de Gruyter.

Stewart, Darrell, John Weeks, and Stephen Bent. 2001. "Utilization, patient satisfaction, and cost implications of acupuncture, massage, and naturopathic medicine offered as covered health benefits." *Alternative Therapies in Health and Medicine* 7 (4): 66–70.

Stokstad, Erik. 2000. "Stephen Straus's impossible job." *Science* 288: 1568–70.

Stolberg, Sheryl Gay. 1999. "Sham surgery returns as a research tool." *New York Times* April 29: wk3.

Strawbridge, William J., et al. 1998. "Religiosity buffers effects of some stressors on depression but exacerbates others." *Journals of Gerontology, Series B: Social Sciences* 53B (3): S118–26.

Streitberger, K., and J. Kleinhenz. 1998. "Introducing a placebo needle into acupuncture research." *Lancet* 352: 364–5.

Strom-Gottfried, Kim. 1998. "Is 'ethical managed care' an oxymoron?" *Families in Society* 79 (3): 297–307.

Sturm, Roland, and Jürgen Unützer. 2000–2001. "State legislation and the use of complementary and alternative medicine." *Inquiry* 37: 423–9.

Swidler, Ann. 1979. *Organization Without Authority: Dilemmas of Social Control in Free Schools.* Cambridge, MA: Harvard University Press.

Swidler, Ann, and Jorge Arditi. 1994. "The new sociology of knowledge." *Annual Review of Sociology* 20: 305–29.

Temple, Robert, and Susan E. Ellenberg. 2000. "Placebo-controlled trials and active-control trials in the evaluation of new treatments." *Annals of Internal Medicine* 133 (6): 455–63.

Thom, David H. 2000. "Training physicians to increase patient trust." *Journal of Evaluation in Clinical Practice* 6 (3): 245–53.

Truog, Robert D., Walter Robinson, Adrienne Randolph, and Alan Morris. 1999. "Is informed consent always necessary for randomized, controlled trials?" *New England Journal of Medicine* 340 (10): 804–7.

Trutnovsky, G., C. Law, J. M. Simpson, and A. Mindel. 2001. "Use of complementary therapies in a sexual health clinic setting." *International Journal of STD and AIDS* 12 (5): 307–9.

*U.S. Code of Federal Regulations. Title 21, Volume 5.* 2001, April 1. Washington, DC: U.S. Government Printing Office.

VandeCreek, Larry, Elizabeth Rogers, and Joanne Lester. 1999. "Use of alternative therapies among breast cancer outpatients compared with the general population." *Alternative Therapies* 5 (1): 71–6.

Vanderford, Marsha L., Terry Stein, Robert Sheeler, and Susan Skochelak. 2001. "Communication challenges for experienced clinicians: topics for an advanced communication curriculum." *Health Communication* 13 (3): 261–84.

Vickers, Andrew, et al. 1997. "How should we research unconventional therapies?: A panel report from the conference on complementary and alternative medicine research methodology, National Institutes of Health." *International Journal of Technology Assessment in Health Care* 13 (1): 111–21.

Von Gruenigen, Vivan E., et al. 2001. "A comparison of complementary and alternative medicine use by gynecology and gynecologic oncology patients." *International Journal of Gynecological Cancer* 11 (3): 205–9.

Waldfogel, Shimon. 1997. "Spirituality in medicine." *Primary Care: Clinics in Office Practice* 24 (4): 963–76.

Walton, Kenneth G., et al. In press. "Psychosocial stress and cardiovascular disease 2: Effective of transcendental meditation technique in treatment and prevention." *Behavioral Medicine.*

Wang, Jong-Shyan, Ching Lan, and May-Kuen Wong. 2001. "Tai chi chuan training to enhance microcirculatory function in healthy elderly men." *Archives of Physical Medicine Rehabilitation* 82 (9): 1176–80.

Wardell, Diane Wind, and Joan Engebretson. 2001. "Biological correlates of reiki touch healing." *Journal of Advanced Nursing* 33 (4): 439–45.

Weber, Max. 1958 [1904]. *The Protestant Ethic and the Spirit of Capitalism.* New York: Charles Scribner's Sons.

Weeks, John. 2002. "JCAHO includes CAM therapy; CAM proponents see the decision as a big step forward for integrative medicine." *Health Forum Journal* 45 (2): 33.

Weiss, Stefan C. 2000. "Humanities in medical education: Revisiting the doctor–patient relationship." *Medicine and Law* 19: 559–67.

Wetzel, Miriam S., David M. Eisenberg, and Ted J. Kaptchuk. 1998. "Courses involving complementary and alternative medicine at U.S. medical schools." *Journal of the American Medical Association* 280 (9): 784–7.

White House Commission on Complementary and Alternative Medicine Policy (WHCCAMP). 2002, March. *Final Report*. Washington, DC: U.S. Government Printing Office.

WHOQOL Group. 1995. "The World Health Organization Quality of Life Assessment (WHOQOL): Position paper from The World Health Organization." *Social Science and Medicine* 41 (10): 1403–9.

Wilkinson, Dawn S., et al. 2002. "The clinical effectiveness of healing touch." *The Journal of Alternative and Complementary Medicine* 8 (1): 33–47.

Wilson, Keenan, et al. 2000. "Prayer in medicine." *Journal of the Mississippi State Medical Association* 41 (12): 817–22.

Wilson, Sven E. 2002. "The health capital of families: An investigation of the inter-spousal correlation in health status." *Social Science and Medicine* 55 (7): 1157–72.

Winstead-Fry, Patricia, and Jean Kijek. 1999. "An integrative review and meta-analysis of therapeutic touch research." *Alternative Therapies in Health and Medicine* 5 (6): 58–66.

Wiseman, Nigel W., and Andrew Ellis. 1985. *Fundamentals of Chinese Medicine*. Brookline, MA: Paradigm Publications.

Wolinsky, Fredric D. 1980. "Alternative healers and popular medicine." *The Sociology of Health* (pp. 291–302). Boston, MA: Little, Brown and Co.

Wolsko, Peter, et al. 2000. "Alternative/complementary medicine: Wider usage than generally appreciated." *Journal of Alternative and Complementary Medicine* 6 (4): 321–6.

Wolsko, Peter M., et al. 2002. "Insurance coverage, medical conditions, and visits to alternative medicine providers: Results of a national survey." *Archives of Internal Medicine* 162 (3): 281–7.

Workshop on Alternative Medicine. 1995. *Alternative Medicine: Expanding Medical Horizons. A Report to the National Institute of Health on Alternative Systems and Practices in the United States*. Washington, DC: U.S. Government Printing Office.

World Medical Association. 1997. "World Medical Association Declaration of Helsinki: Recommendations guiding physicians in biomedical research involving human subjects." *Journal of the American Medical Association* 277 (11): 925–6.

Wu, Ge. 2002. "Evaluation of the effectiveness of tai chi for improving balance and preventing falls in the older population – A review." *Journal of the American Geriatric Society* 50 (4): 746–54.

Yamashita, Hitoshi, Hiroshi Tsukayama, Yasuo Tanno, and Kazushi Nishijo. 1998. "Adverse events related to acupuncture." *Journal of the American Medical Association* 280 (18): 1563–4.

Young, James Harvey. 1992. *American Health Quackery.* Princeton, NJ: Princeton University Press.

Young, James Harvey. 1998. "The development of the Office of Alternative Medicine in the National Institutes of Health, 1991–1996." *Bulletin of the History of Medicine* 72: 279–98.

Zola, Irving Kenneth. 1972. "Medicine as an institution of social control." *Sociological Review* 20 (4): 487–504.

Zuckerman, Harriet. 1988. "The sociology of science." In Neil J. Smelser (ed.), *Handbook of Sociology* (pp. 511–74). Newbury Park, CA: Sage.

Zwick, Dalia, Alon Rochelle, Amee Choksi, and Joe Domowicz. 2000. "Evaluation and treatment of balance in the elderly: A review of the efficacy of the Berg balance test and tai chi quan." *NeuroRehabilitation* 15 (1): 49–56.

# Index